GROWTH OPPORTUNITY ANALYSIS

GROWTH OPPORTUNITY ANALYSIS

Associate Professor of Marketing
and International Business
University of Notre Dame

WARNER MEMORIAL LIBRARY
EASTERN COLLEGE
ST. DAVIDS, PA. 19087

Reston Publishing Company, Inc.
Reston, Virginia
A Prentice-Hall Company

Library of Congress Cataloging in Publication Data

Weber, John.
    Growth opportunity analysis.

    Includes index.
    1. Marketing. 2. New products. I. Title.
HF5415.125.W4   658.8   76-841
ISBN 0-87909-308-0
ISBN 0-87909-307-2 pbk.

© 1976 by
Reston Publishing Company, Inc.
A Prentice-Hall Company
Reston, Virginia 22090

10 9 8 7 6 5 4 3 2 1

Printed in the United States of America

To
Hannelore

Contents

Preface

The boomtime periods of growth enjoyed by U.S. corporations during the 1950s and 1960s are not likely to return. Firms desiring to realize consistent and continuous sales volume growth in the years ahead will need new perspectives and tools to actively and systematically plan that growth. This book presents such perspectives and tools.

The firm's growth and performance perspectives constitute the focal point for its growth planning decisions and are also the main topic discussed in the first part of the book. Given certain growth and performance objectives, the firm then must come up with strategies to achieve those objectives. In Parts Two and Three, a new tool—*market structure profile analysis*—is offered to help the firm analyze the whole range of relevant growth opportunities and to select and design an appropriate mix of growth strategies.

In *market structure profile analysis,* profiles are generated for a firm's individually defined product lines. These profiles in turn provide visual and quantitative perspectives for considering and evaluating the interrelationships among and between fifteen specific growth opportunities relating to each product line. The treatment centers on *consumer* goods and services, but the tool is equally as relevant and applicable for *industrial* goods and services.

Most of the logic and concepts involved in developing and using market structure profiles have been developed earlier—by other practitioners and scholars. The uniqueness of this book centers about the integration of these older concepts into a new operational framework of analysis. Hopefully, firms can use this new tool to improve the productivity and efficiency of their growth oriented strategies.

John A. Weber

Acknowledgements

My greatest debt in the conception of this book is to my students who indirectly challenged me to develop the framework and then quite directly aided me in expanding and debugging it. The thoughts of Robert S. Weinberg were influential and stimulating in providing an initial direction and mode of inquiry. Numerous marketing scholars (acknowledged in the footnotes to the text) both directly and indirectly contributed various bits and pieces of the internal logic of the overall framework.

Practitioners from Market Facts, Miles Laboratories, Kraftco Corporation, Quaker Oats, Bell and Howell, and Brunswick aided with insightful criticisms and suggestions. A student assistant, Greg Upah, was most helpful and patient in challenging the system throughout its development and in his editorial suggestions. Thanks, too, to Linda Fletcher who prepared the manuscript.

Finally, to my wife, Lore, a special note of gratitude for her direct help in editing and proofreading and for the moral support she provided while I was developing and completing this book.

GROWTH OPPORTUNITY ANALYSIS

PART ONE

Growth and Performance Perspectives of the Firm

Perhaps no corporate strategy determinants are more important than the firm's own attitudes and objectives concerning the desired direction(s) and speed of its future growth path. Part One examines the motivation and need for the individual firm methodically and continuously to plan sales growth and maintain acceptable performance levels.

In considering the growth and performance perspectives of the firm as important corporate strategy determinants, this part discusses such questions as the following: Why does the growth potential of individual product lines peak out? What new product lines should a firm add if its growth aspirations exceed the growth potential of its current product lines? Why do not firms choose for themselves more aggressive growth and performance objectives? Why is inadequate planning itself a major reason why so many firms regularly fail to meet their growth and profit performance objectives? How can a firm realistically project its growth and profit paths into the future, thus anticipating future growth gaps and profit gaps and being warned to act in the present to close off potential gaps in the future?

1

Directions for Future Growth

Firms are well aware of their existing product lines and individual products. Appropriate directions for future growth in terms of adding new products and product lines are not nearly so obvious. Why is it so important for firms to be thinking about adding new products (and possibly deleting old products)? What are the firm's primary determinants in selecting new products and new product lines? These are some of the questions considered in this chapter.

THE IMPORTANCE OF NEW PRODUCTS

Merely observing changes in the relative importance of different product lines for specific firms suggests that new products do indeed account for significant proportions of the growth achieved by individual firms. For example, Table 1-1 shows changes over time in the relative importance (as percentages of total firm sales) of different product lines for three separate firms: Interco, Revlon, and Liggett/Meyers. For Interco, footwear has become less important, while apparel (e.g., Big Yank, GTO, Mr. Golf, and Bold Breed clothing) and retail merchandising (e.g., Kent's,

Table 1-1
EXAMPLES OF CHANGES IN THE RELATIVE IMPORTANCE OF DIFFERENT PRODUCT LINES FOR INDIVIDUAL FIRMS

Interco, Inc.

Product Lines (% of Total Firm Sales in Each)

Year	Footwear	Apparel	Retail Merchandising
1966	70%	8%	22%
1968	55	19	26
1970	49	20	31
1972	44	22	34
1974	38	25	37

Revlon, Inc.

	Beauty Products	Health Care Products
1966	84%	16%
1968	81	19
1970	74	26
1972	73	27
1974	70	30

Liggett & Meyers, Inc.

	Tobacco Products	Alcoholic Beverages	Pet Food	Other
1966	64%	28%	7%	1%
1968	56	24	15	5
1970	47	22	24	7
1972	41	22	26	11
1974	35	22	29	14

Thornton's, Central Hardware, and Eagle Family Discount stores) have become relatively more important. For Revlon, beauty products (e.g., skin and hair products, deodorants, soaps, talcs, lipsticks, suntan oil, etc.) have become less important, while health care products (ethical drugs such as sedatives and antidepressants and proprietary drugs such as Amitone antacid and Liquiprin analgesic) have become relatively more important. For Liggett and Meyers, tobacco products (e.g., L & M's, Chesterfields, Lark, and Eve cigarettes) and alcoholic beverages (e.g., J & B scotch, Wild Turkey bourbon, and Bombay gin) have become less important, while pet food (e.g., Alpo and Vets) and other products have become relatively more importanᵣ.

Such changes in the relative importance of different product lines for individual firms are not at all unusual and reflect to some degree the importance which new products play in helping firms achieve regular growth of overall firm sales. For example, a study of 11 major United States industries during the 1960's showed that firms participating in the study planned to achieve, on the average, 75 percent of their sales growth over the next five years by means of introducing new products. The range ran from a 45 percent planned contribution of new products for food and paper industries to a 100 percent planned contribution for machinery and rubber products.[2]

WHY DROP OLD PRODUCTS?

Firms drop products with some regularity. Goodyear's industrial product division makes more than 30,000 different products: "About 20 percent of any product line is really obsolete," says a Goodyear manager. "When we phase out such an item, we fill that floor space with a product with a future and a better profit margin." [3] American Standard, a manufacturer of bathroom showerheads and fixtures, recently dropped over 2000 marginal products.[4]

Individual products may yield satisfactory profits for a time and then sometimes slowly and sometimes very quickly, become unprofitable or, at best, marginally profitable. What causes such adverse changes is of concern to and must be watched very carefully by the firms.

Passage through a product life cycle is one explanation of why the profitability of an individual product declines over time. Figure 1-1 shows the shape of the sales life cycle for a product. Note how the profitability of the product falls as market maturity is reached, bringing with it heavy competitive pressures. According to this line of thought, in order to maintain profits over time, the firm's most appropriate strategy is regularly to drop older, more unprofitable products and add new potentially more profitable products. This may mean simply extending or differentiating the firm's existing product line(s), or it may mean introducing a product (and product line) totally new for the firm.

In recent years, many products have been dropped not so much because of a peaking out or decline of sales but more because of supply shortages and increasing costs. In this era, many firms have pruned back product lines because of these pressures. For example, Castle & Cooke, Inc. (Dole pineapple) recently reduced the number of fruit cuts and can sizes from 27 consumer retail items to eleven—eliminating all but 20-oz and 8-oz can sizes, which previously accounted for 75 percent of their pineapple sales.[5] In these times a noticeable trend has taken place

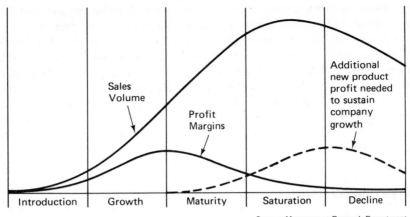

Source: Management Research Department
Booz·Allen & Hamilton Inc.

FIGURE 1-1.   Basic life cycle of products.

toward making available to the customer somewhat less variety—dropping many bottom-of-the-line, low-profit-margin products while holding onto higher-profit-margin items.[6]

Such cutbacks in products that sometimes have not yet hit their sales peaks (in terms of the product life cycle concept) do not necessarily result in a direct reduction of sales (and certainly do not have an adverse effect on profits). For example, in the Dole pineapple case mentioned above, Castle & Cooke claims to have experienced no decline in sales—and to have actually experienced a 10 to 15 percent sales boost in some markets——attributing this to making the buying decision easier for the customer.[7]

The firm should have a system enabling it quickly to detect products that are no longer pulling their weight in terms of contributing to the firm's overall sales and profit growth. In order to handle this need, many firms have developed and are now using product audit systems that help the firm to maintain a continual surveillance over the sales and profit performance of the firm's individual products—signaling if and when the appropriate time comes to consider dropping each product.[8]

WHAT NEW PRODUCTS AND PRODUCT LINES TO ADD

Old products being dropped are not always replaced by new products. As considered above, some firms in the early and mid-1970's cut back on the variety of product offerings within individual product lines as a reaction to supply shortages, increasing costs and increasing pressures on profit margins.

Given the very real phenomenon of the product life cycle and the eventual decline of profits as individual products move through that cycle, however, firms desiring continual growth of sales and profits must add new products and new product lines on a fairly regular basis. The key question at this point becomes: What new products and/or product lines should be added?

Virtually every major firm has made a mistake at one time or another by adding a product that then failed in the marketplace to live up to the firm's plans and expectations. For example, what happened to the products listed in Table 1-2? Many new products fail when they

Table 1-2
EXAMPLES OF NEW PRODUCTS WHICH
FAILED TO MEET THEIR GOALS

Campbell's Red Kettle soups
Lever Bros. Vim tablet detergent
Best Foods Knorr soups
Colgate's Cue toothpaste
GF's Post cereals with freeze-dried fruit
Bristol-Myers Aerosol Ipana toothpaste
Rheingold's Gablinger's beer
Hunt's flavored ketchups
Bristol-Myers Resolve analgesic
Scott Paper's Babyscott diapers
Sylvania's Colorslide TV viewer
Gillette's Nine Flags men's cologne
Hunt-Wesson Supreme spaghetti sauce
Warner-Lambert Reef mouthwash

are fully commercialized. One study estimates the failure rate at 33 percent.[9] Other studies suggest that the rate is much higher.[10] Some of these mistakes are very costly—for example, RCA's computer business ($250 million write-off), DuPont's Corfam ($100 million), and Ford's Edsel ($100 million).[11] For a wide variety of reasons the life cycles for these products just never got far enough off the ground and therefore cost the respective firms a great deal of money.[12]

In order to help companies avoid such mistakes, some rather elaborate new product systems are available for quickly screening out new product ideas with the least likelihood of commercial success before the firm is forced to bear significant new product development costs. Figures 1-2 and 1-3 summarize the typical steps involved in such systems.[13]

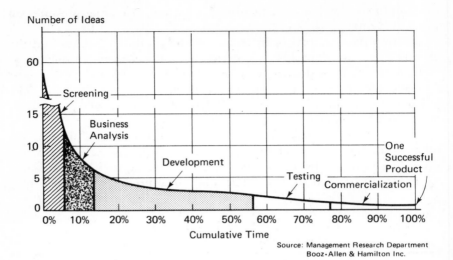

FIGURE 1-2.   Mortality of new product ideas (by stage of evolution—51 companies).

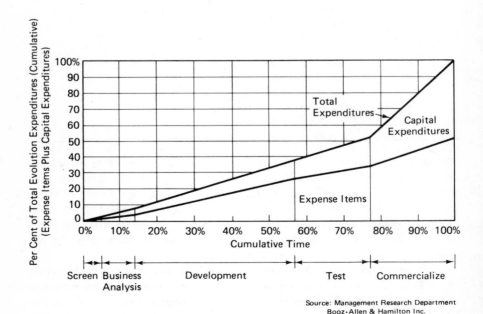

FIGURE 1-3.   Cumulative expenditures and time (by stage of evolution—all-industry average).

Two factors are critical for determining the most appropriate product horizons for a firm: (1) the firm's entrepreneurial philosophy, and (2) the firm's synergistic advantages.

(1) THE ROLE OF ENTREPRENEURSHIP IN ADDING NEW PRODUCTS

Neither all businessmen nor all business firms can accurately be described as having entrepreneurial characteristics. Entrepreneurship connotes an active search for innovation, be it in terms of product design or in terms of the very methodologies involved in doing business. Entrepreneurship also implies a willingness to assume the risks that are usually inherent in following through on those innovative ideas. Not all business firms and certainly not all businessmen actively seek out such innovative products, views, and methodologies. Fewer yet are willing to take the risks involved in attempting to implement such innovations, especially in a time when costs are rising rapidly with the resulting increased financial risk.

It is that very quality of entrepreneurship which most differentiates dynamic, high-growth companies from more staid and static companies. Without an active search for innovative ideas, without a willingness to take a leadership role in implementing new ideas (be they products or internal business methods), an individual firm will take a follower's role and a follower's mentality, "following" not only in terms of the "me-too" late introduction of new products and methods, but usually following in terms of growth rates of sales and profits as well.

Nonentrepreneurial firms tend to follow the leader. Such firms spend most of their time scrambling for shares of limited markets rather than uncovering and fulfilling new customer demands. Most really successful high-growth companies in the United States closely monitor customer demand and use their technological genius to invent new products fulfilling significant customer demands. Look at such industries as photography, computers, semiconductors, aerospace, office machines, etc. The leaders in these industries are entrepreneurial firms. The leaders in these industries clearly outshine their followers in terms of growth rates of sales and profits achieved.

This is not to say that every entrepreneur and every entrepreneurial firm is successful in every venture. A difference exists between being indiscriminately entrepreneurial and being selectively entrepreneurial. In terms of the question at hand (the role of entrepreneurship in adding new products), an entrepreneur acting indiscriminately in generating and following through on new product ideas is going to make numerous, costly mistakes—mistakes that may consistently prevent his firm from attaining significant growth rates of sales and profits. A firm that lets its "synergistic advantages" serve as a guide in its screening and selection of new entrepreneurial ventures, however, can considerably reduce the chances of making such expensive mistakes.

(2) SYNERGISTIC GUIDELINES

A good synergistic match between a firm and a new product idea gives the firm a differential advantage over competitors in introducing such a product.

Good "synergy" may exist between a firm and a new product idea for many reasons, because synergy can take multiple forms. *Production synergy* exists to the extent that the firm can produce the new product with its existing equipment and engineering knowledge and can tap its existing raw material sources. *Management synergy* is present if current management personnel and planning systems are capable of readily handling the types of administrative problems likely to be encountered relating to the new product.

Good *marketing synergy* implies that the firm's present distribution facilities, channels, and outlets can be readily adapted to handle the new product, that the existing sales force can be easily trained to sell the new product, and that the advertising and sales promotion programs can be easily adjusted to effectively market the new product. The name that a firm has built up for itself over time in the minds of the consuming public operates as perhaps the most valuable of all the elements of marketing synergy.

Good *financial synergy* is as important as any synergistic component.[14] Are adequate funds for adding the new product available within the constraints the firm sets on its own financial ratios for maintaining a healthy financial position? Is the investment consistent with the firm's current liquidity position and needs? Questions concerning the likely return on investment criteria and/or other likely profit ratios are best considered later on—in preliminary business analysis—for product ideas that have made it through the initial synergistic screening process.

Taking advantage of a firm's synergistic advantages and using them as guides in the initial screening of new product opportunities help to minimize risks involved in adding new products and/or new lines. Table 1-3 presents the kind of synergistic checklist that a firm might use in originally screening new product ideas.

DEFINITION OF A FIRM'S BUSINESS(ES)
AS A SYNERGISTIC ADVANTAGE

One important synergistic advantage that is too frequently overlooked is the real nature of a firm's business.

Table 1-3
SYNERGISTIC CHECKLIST FOR SCREENING
NEW PRODUCT IDEAS

Production Synergy—Can the product be produced with our:
—Existing equipment?
—Existing production capacities?
—Existing technological knowhow?
—Existing raw material sources? (Further, are enough raw materials available to us from these sources to support additional productions?)

Management Synergy—Can the administrative problems likely to be encountered in producing the new product be readily handled by using another:
—Existing organizational setup?
—Existing management personnel and knowhow?
—Existing planning and control system?
—Existing supervisory and labor personnel and knowhow?

Marketing Synergy—Can the new product be sold by using our:
—Existing distribution facilities (warehouses, transportation, etc.), channels, and outlets?
—Existing sales force personnel and knowhow?
—Existing advertising and sales promotion personnel, agencies, and general internal knowledge?
—Existing brand name(s) as an implicit selling point?

Financial Synergy—Is the new product addition likely to be consistent with the realities of our:
—Current funding ability (within our indebtedness ratio constraints)?
—Liquidity position and needs?

A generic definition of a firm's business in terms of the nature of the customer needs the firm is satisfying can help lead a firm on to innovative new product horizons.[15] Many firms lose markets because they place too much emphasis upon defining products in terms of "products" rather than in terms of "needs being fulfilled." What is Scotch Tape, for example? According to the line of thinking above, 3M (the manufacturer of Scotch Brand Tape) should not have been (and probably was not) caught unprepared by the wide-scale introduction and adoption of glue sticks (e.g., Pritt and Dennison's brand sticks), during the early 1970's.

One important element of synergy exists, therefore, which many firms overlook, because they take it too much for granted. This element of synergy consists of the body of "loyal customers" for the firm's existing need-fulfilling products. This body of customers should be viewed as a synergistic advantage for the firm's potential new products. The firm is in the best position to study the relevant needs of these customers and thus to come up with innovative products to adjust to changing needs and/or to replace and improve upon the old products.

This is most likely to happen if the firm recognizes its business as attempting to satisfy particular ranges of customer needs, rather than as producing and selling particular narrowly defined products. It is not surprising, therefore, to find that firms which have adopted this view have defined their product lines very broadly. IBM, for example, now refers to its office products as "word processing" equipment. Xerox refers to itself as being in the "communications" business.

WHAT ABOUT NONSYNERGISTIC ENTREPRENEURIAL IDEAS?

Synergy, it has been suggested, is a key differentiating variable between following an indiscriminate entrepreneurial path leading to mediocrity and a selective entrepreneurial path leading to success.

What can a company do with innovative new product ideas (or inventions) for which the firm has poor synergy? The firm can attempt to overcome its related synergistic shortcomings through internal modifications over time. This is costly and, more importantly, very time consuming. By the time the firm has the required production, management, marketing, and financial capabilities, the market may already be saturated by competitors.

Alternatively, the firm can attempt to obtain "instant synergy" by acquiring another firm that already has the desired synergy package or by simply buying a particular capacity such as the product itself from another manufacturer and then selling it under one's own brand name, through one's own distribution channels, etc. Such purchases are usually expensive, however, with the costs frequently outweighing the advantages to be gained. For example, Singer ("Sewing Machine Company") purchased Friden during the 1960's in an attempt to gain quick entry into electronic calculator and cash register markets. Despite growing sales and profits resulting from the acquisition, Singer has been faced with growing pressures on her return on investment because of the substantial investment required for the acquisition. If Singer had possessed better synergy in relation to these electronics products and markets, the acquisition would not have been necessary, and return on investment pressures would probably not have resulted.[16]

In view of the time and cost disadvantages of other alternatives, it is not surprising to see firms in many instances merely dropping ideas for products for which they do not have good synergistic advantages or, in other instances, licensing or selling such ideas to firms with better synergy relating to the particular idea. For example, why might a chemical company that invents a uniquely different and effective detergent wisely opt to sell or license the exclusive right to market that product to another company such as Procter and Gamble, Lever Bros., or Colgate rather than attempting to market that product itself? Synergy, or lack of synergy in this case, is the answer.

SYNERGY IN SUM

In sum, a firm that is well aware of the benefits with regard to time, cost, and overall effectiveness to be gained through taking advantage of its synergy will orient its new product development efforts toward areas which can effectively utilize existing manufacturing facilities and technology, which can effectively utilize existing administrative manpower and mechanisms, and which can effectively utilize existing distribution and promotion channels and capabilities. Such a firm wisely uses synergy as one important criterion in selecting from among various entrepreneurial opportunities.

Market potential is also a critical variable to be considered in selecting new product entries. The concept of synergy, however, is not intended to cover market analysis, since synergy focuses upon the internal differential advantages of the firm rather than upon considerations external to the firm—such as the market itself. Part II of the text, which examines market structure profiles, focuses upon such market analysis as it relates to evaluating new product ideas and evaluating alternative corporate growth strategies in general.

SUMMARY

The first part of the chapter considers the importance of new products, the need to drop old products, and the methods a firm can effectively and regularly use to find and add new products to aid the firm in its quest for continual sales growth.

As a firm's products move through their life cycles, their profitability declines, eventually creating a need to drop those products and at the same time add new products to maintain and increase the firm's overall sales and profits. The chapter included a discussion concerning how the firm should go about adding new products—i.e., what products and product lines should be added. New product development screening procedures were considered. Two major factors were mentioned as being critical in the design of a firm's future product horizons: (1) the firm's entrepreneurial philosophy and (2) the firm's synergistic advantages.

Although the text cautioned against indiscriminate entrepreneurship, the chapter encouraged selective entrepreneurship based upon the firm's existing synergistic advantages. Management, production, marketing, and financial synergy were considered, as well as one form of synergy often overlooked by business managers—the generic definition of a firm's business. This form of synergy is important for stimulating the firm to look at its product line offerings as attempting to satisfy the broad needs of its target market rather than specific isolated needs.

REVIEW QUESTIONS

1. Why is it important to monitor the sales and profit performance of a firm's individual products?

2. What is meant by a firm's being "selectively entrepreneurial"?

3. How does a firm's entrepreneurial philosophy affect its determination of future product horizons?

4. Why is the "definition of a firm's business" important—especially with regard to the selection of new product additions? For such purposes, would you suggest a broad definition of a firm's business or a narrow one? What business(es) is American Airlines in? MacDonald's? Chase Manhattan Bank? General Mills?

5. Explain the synergistic advantages of each of two firms, Kodak and U.S. Steel, with respect to marketing a new line of television sets.

NOTES

1. For an annual list of significant new products developed and introduced by firms listed on the New York Stock Exchange, see *The New Product Directory of N.Y.S.E. Listed Companies,* published annually by Market Development Corporation (Concord, Mass.). In the 1975 edition, this index included nearly 5000 new product descriptions categorized by company and industry.

2. Booz, Allen, & Hamilton, Inc., New York, N.Y. 1968. *Management of New Products.*

3. "Culling the Losers," *Wall Street Journal* (October 15, 1971), p. 1.

4. Ibid.

5. "Toward Higher Margins and Less Variety," *Business Week* (September 14, 1974), p. 98.

6. Ibid. Also see: "Demand, Controls Spur Many Concerns to Drop Bottom-of-Line Goods," *Wall Street Journal* (August 28, 1973), p. 1.

7. "Toward Higher Margins and Less Variety," *Business Week* (September 14, 1974), p. 98.

8. See "Putting Products Through an Audit Wringer," *Business Week* (February 1, 1974), pp. 60–66. For a model of such an audit system, see J. T. O'Meara, "Selecting Profitable Products," *Harvard Business Review* (January 1961), pp. 9ff.

9. Booz, Allen, & Hamilton, Inc., op. cit.

10. See O'Meara, op. cit.; T. L Angelus, "Why Do Most New Products Fail?" *Ad Age* (March 24, 1969), pp. 85–86; and B. Schorr, "Many New Products Frizzle," *Wall Street Journal* (April 5, 1961).

11. See "New Products: The Push Is on Marketing," *Business Week* (March 4, 1972), pp. 72–77, and "The $250-Million Disaster That Hit RCA," *Business Week* (September 25, 1971), pp. 34–36.

12. See references in footnote 11 for discussion of these reasons.

13. Most texts on introductory marketing describe these development steps in some detail. The interested reader is referred to:

E. J. McCarthy, *Basic Marketing*, 5th ed. (Chicago: Richard D. Irwin, 1975).

W. J. Stanton, *Fundamentals of Marketing*, 4th ed. (New York: McGraw-Hill Book Company, 1975).

P. Kotler, *Marketing Management* (Englewood Cliffs, N.J.: Prentice-Hall, Inc., 1975).

14. Financial constraints have become particularly important in recent years for many firms. In the future, financial constraints will become even more important. For a discussion, see "The Capital Crisis: the $4.5 Trillion America Needs to Grow," *Business Week* (September 22, 1975), pp. 42ff. (Special Section).

15. In a classic marketing article, Theodore Levitt refers to such narrowsightedness of firms as "Marketing Myopia." See *Harvard Business Review* (September 1975), pp. 26ff.

16. For a discussion of Singer's experiences in this regard, see *Wall Street Journal* (February 15, 1975), p. 1, and (December 30, 1975), p. 1.

2

Revenue Objectives and Plans

A firm must generate profits in order to ensure its long-term viability. Without profits, investors have better alternative uses for their funds. Nor is a constant level of profits adequate. Participating investors want to see the value of their investment grow, and they expect their return on investment to keep pace. Regular profit growth is, therefore, a most important goal of the firm.

A firm's profits in a given year are determined by two main factors: the firm's total revenue and the firm's total costs. Profits equal total revenue (i.e., price times unit volume) minus total costs.[1] This is the *basic profit equation*. The firm can bring about profit growth by increasing revenue and/or by reducing costs.

This chapter first considers how a firm can draw up realistic revenue growth objectives. Following this is a brief overview of three of the methods the firm can use to bring about regular revenue growth—through acquisitions, through adding new products and/or new product lines, and/or through expanding the unit volume sale of the firm's existing products (at current prices). Each of these three growth vehicles focuses upon the real key to achieving long-run growth of revenue and profits—i.e., bringing about an increase in unit sales volume for the firm.

Revenue growth alone, however, is not enough to guarantee profit growth. To ensure long-run profit growth, the firm must use careful price setting and must maintain continual control over its costs. Chapter 3 reviews the setting of performance (i.e., profit) objectives and the role that careful control over prices and costs plays in the drive to meet such objectives.

SETTING REVENUE OBJECTIVES

A firm that carefully pulls apart and analyzes its past revenue growth can foresee well ahead of time when action is necessary in the short term to prevent a decline in growth over the long term. Even more careful analysis and planning are necessary to improve growth rates in the future.

A plan of action regarding the growth of the firm begins by setting growth objectives. For the purposes of this text and as justified above, such growth objectives are set in terms of sales revenue.

In setting growth objectives, an analysis of the firm's growth over the recent past (six to eight years) can yield meaningful perspectives for setting growth objectives for the future. In looking at and evaluating past growth, the *absolute volume* of sales revenue achieved by the firm over the years being studied is *not as important as* are the *growth rates* of sales realized over each of those years. As Exhibit 2-1 shows, a plot of such growth rates adds considerably more insight than does the simple plot of sales revenues.

The first question to ask in the analysis of recent growth is *Does the firm currently have a growth gap?* It is in answering this question that the firm is forced to consider its growth aspirations and set its growth objectives for the future. If the firm in Exhibit 2-1 is satisfied with the 10 percent growth rate realized in the most recent year (1977), then no growth gap exists in the present year. Certainly, such a firm is not very aggressive if it is satisfied with a growth rate that is significantly lower than the average growth rates it has achieved in recent years. Such an attitude of being more or less satisfied with whatever happens is likely to lead a firm to serious growth problems in the future years.

A firm with a somewhat more critical view of its own growth may feel that its growth in the most recent year should have at least been up to par with its average growth achieved over recent years. Such a firm may take an annual average growth rate over the recent past (up to but not including the last year) and use this as a yardstick for evaluating present growth and setting future objectives. A *simple average of the annual growth rates* achieved by the firm in Exhibit 2-1 for the years 1971 through 1976 was 12.3 percent, which becomes the firm's growth

Exhibit 2-1
PLOT OF SALES REVENUE GROWTH RATES
VERSUS SIMPLE PLOT OF SALES REVENUE

Years	Sales	Annual Growth of Sales
1970	$100 million	
1971	110 million	10%
1972	130 million	18%
1973	140 million	8%
1974	150 million	7%
1975	170 million	13%
1976	200 million	18%
1977	220 million	10%

(a)   Data

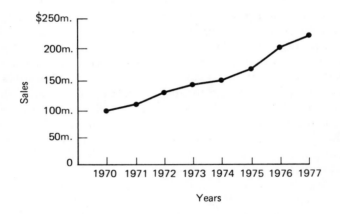

(b)   Plot of Sales Revenue

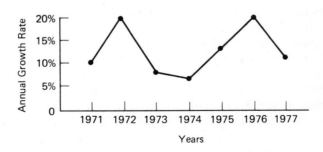

(c)   Plot of Sales Revenue Growth Rates

objective for the future. Exhibit 2-2(b) shows the projection of such a yardstick and a growth gap of 2.3 percent for this firm in the most recent year, 1977—a growth gap with which the firm will have to deal over the next few years.

In the event that the firm had failed to grow in any or all recent years, such an average annual growth rate approach would yield a very low standard against which to compare the most recent year's growth and would offer a very unaggressive objective for future growth. In such an instance, a firm would be ill-advised to use such a benchmark for evaluating its present growth path and setting its future growth objectives.

As an alternative to using the average annual growth rate achieved

Exhibit 2-2
DOES THE FIRM HAVE A GROWTH GAP TODAY?

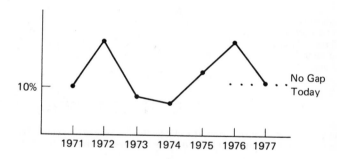

(a) No Gap for a Firm That is Satisfied with Whatever Happens

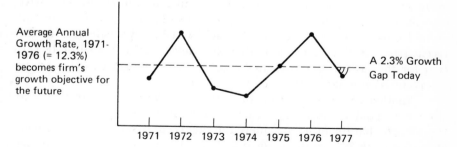

(b) A Small Gap for a Firm Desiring to Keep Its Growth Rate
Up to Its Own Average Growth Achieved in Recent Years

Exhibit 2-2 *(Continued)*

Best Growth Rate(s) achieved over the recent past (= c. 18%) becomes firm's growth objective for the future.

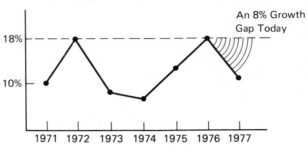

(c)   An Aggressive Firm Compares Growth Achieved This Year with Growth Achieved in Its Best Year(s) in the Recent Past

Golden Mean is between best growth achieved recently and average growth in recent years.

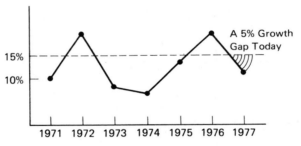

(d)   The Golden Mean: Firm Chooses an Objective Somewhere Between Its Average Recent Growth and Its Best Growth Rate Achieved in the Recent Past

over the recent past (six to eight years) when the average yielded is really quite unaggressive and/or when a firm wants to follow an aggressive growth path in the future, a firm might set its *objective equal to the best annual growth rate* that the firm has achieved in any single year in the recent past. Exhibit 2-2(c) shows that this yields a growth goal of 18 percent for the firm in question and suggests that the firm experienced an 8 percent growth gap in the most recent year.

Another alternative means of setting a growth path objective is to aim at a "golden mean" growth rate somewhere *between the average growth rate* that the firm has achieved in the recent past *and the best single annual growth rate* realized during that same period. In the example above, the firm would set as its sales growth objective an annual growth target of somewhere between 12.3 percent per year and 18 percent per year—for example, a 15 percent annual growth rate objective. Exhibit

2-2(d) depicts such a target and displays a 5 percent growth gap for the most recent year.

WHY NOT UNLIMITED REVENUE GROWTH?

Before we close the discussion on setting revenue growth objectives for the firm, a relevant question can be raised: Why would any firm not desire to realize virtually unlimited growth of revenue every year? This is a legitimate question. A number of forces act as constraints working against such a philosophical objective.

First of all, to a certain extent the separation of management and ownership that is fairly typical in the United States corporate system can serve to dampen growth and performance aspirations of individual firms. The growth and performance that management achieves this year, investors/owners expect management to meet or surpass next year. In a sense, the faster one runs, the faster one is expected to run. Such pressures imply that a manager's future is to a considerable degree determined by his ability to meet last year's growth and performance. A less aggressive, mediocre performance in the present year, therefore, may be advantageous for a manager in terms of his long-run security with a firm. Superior growth and performance in the present year, on the other hand, is more difficult to match next year and may, therefore, eventually jeopardize the manager's position and security in the longer run.

Second, and more importantly, as the revenue of a firm grows, certain adjustments within the firm itself must take place to support such growth and to ensure that profits increase along with sales. New production facilities must be brought on line (or new service facilities, for firms in service industries). New manpower must be secured, trained, and integrated into the overall organizational structure of the firm. The organizational structure itself must be regularly adjusted to facilitate the consolidation of previous sales gains and to lay a sound base for achieving future sales growth.

In the past, some firms have totally or significantly decentralized operations in an attempt to overcome organizational constraints to growth. Westinghouse, for example, followed such a policy during the late 1960's and early 1970's. In that instance, the desired growth did result in sales rising from $2 billion in the mid-1960's to $6 billion by the mid-1970's. The decentralization, however, meant too little control over individual product line subsidiaries. With the economy booming in the 1960's, this presented little problem, but with the downturn of the economy in the early 1970's, Westinghouse found that a number of her product line subsidiaries had financially overextended themselves, leaving a very unstable foundation for future growth. Overall, the firm found itself with short-term debt almost equal to its long-term debt and with a far from healthy 1.67 to 1 current asset to current liability ratio. By the mid-1970's, Westinghouse found it necessary to pull in the reins, centralize controls, and temporarily slow down growth in order to consolidate past gains and lay better foundations for future growth of sales and profits.[2]

In a very real sense, a fast growing firm regularly experiences growing pains—pains which call for making continual internal adjustments. These adjustments take some time to plan and implement. Continuing to move ahead in terms of sales growth without taking the time for such internal modification can threaten the sales base from which the firm is building and leave a very shaky, uncertain foundation for future growth of sales and profits. Firms growing too quickly in the short run to set a good financial base for future growth and too quickly to ensure parallel profit growth cannot expect to maintain such a pace over the long run.

How quickly and how well can a firm design and implement the internal changes necessary to consolidate past sales gain? The time this takes will ultimately define the realistic upper limit facing an individual firm in setting its objective for future annual sales growth. For this reason, it is not surprising that firms which have traditionally achieved high sales revenue growth rates will find it easier in the future to grow quickly than will firms which have traditionally realized relatively slow growth rates. A high sales growth rate capability *must permeate a firm* before the firm can realistically aspire to lofty growth rates on a continuous basis in the future.

PROJECTING THE FIRM'S FUTURE REVENUE GROWTH PATH

Once a growth objective has been set, the comparison of a growth rate achieved last year versus such an objective is quite straightforward. For example, Exhibit 2-2 shows a firm realizing anywhere from a 0 percent growth gap to an 8.0 percent growth gap in the present year, depending upon the firm's aspirations.

It is much more difficult to project a firm's growth path into the future for the purpose of comparing the firm's growth path objective with the growth path that the firm is likely to follow if it stays with its present products and present growth strategies.

Projecting a firm's likely growth path is much different from setting a firm's objectives for future growth. A manager is guilty of wishful thinking if he simply equates his projection with these objectives for future growth.

Is the firm likely to experience a gap in the future (over the next four to six years) between its projected sales growth and its sales growth aspirations and objectives? The firm must consider this before the fact if it expects to meet its sales growth objectives year after year.

BREAKING DOWN THE FIRM'S SALES BY INDUSTRY GROUP

Considering the firm's own growth in relation to the growth of the industries in which the firm is involved offers one useful basis for projecting the likely growth path of the firm's sales in its present product lines. In order to use this basis, a firm must know quite a bit about the past sales and the future sales projections for the various industries covering his present product lines. Trade association sources, syndicated commercial sources, and government sources provide the firm with those past sales figures and required future sales projections for the relevant industries.

The firm begins by breaking down its overall sales (for the past six to eight years) by industry groups. Often individual firms, particularly very diversified firms, have their product lines defined much too broadly for such purposes. In such instances, the firm should break down its broadly defined product lines into smaller industry groups. For example, a firm describing one of its lines as "consumer durables" and desiring to use this industry-related method of projection would break its consumer durable sales into television sets, refrigerators, radios, and whatever other products fall into its consumer durable product group. If, in a very simple case, a firm sells products falling into only two industry groups (i.e., only two product lines), the firm would break down sales for each of the past six to eight years [as in Exhibit 2-3(a)], would find the annual growth of past sales for each product line [as in Exhibit 2-3(b)], and would plot the annual growth rates of past sales for each product line [as in Exhibit 2-3(c)].

How have the firm's sales in each product line grown in the past in comparison with the growth of sales for that entire industry in the past? Have firm sales generally grown faster or slower than the industry? If the firm's own sales growth has had a consistent relationship with industry sales in the past, then one can make a projection of firm sales for the future by utilizing projections for future industry sales.

Exhibit 2-3
BREAKING DOWN THE FIRM'S PAST SALES
BY INDUSTRY GROUP (I.E., BY PRODUCT LINE)

Year	Product Line A	Product Line B
1970	$60 million	$40 million
1971	$64	$46
1972	$72	$58
1973	$70	$70
1974	$70	$80
1975	$71	$99
1976	$76	$124
1977	$77	$143

(a)   Sales For Each Product Line

Year	Product Line A	Product Line B
1970 – 71	7%	15%
1971 – 72	13%	26%
1972 – 73	– 3%	21%
1973 – 74	0%	14%
1974 – 75	1%	24%
1975 – 76	7%	24%
1976 – 77	1%	15%

(b)   Annual Growth Rates of Sales for Each Product Line

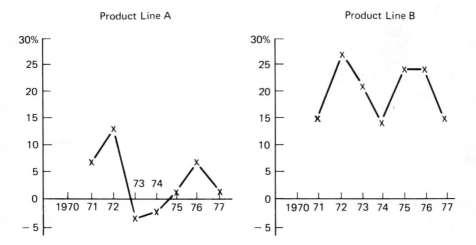

(c)   Plotting the Growth Rates of Past Sales for Each Product Line

PAST SALES GROWTH OF THE FIRM COMPARED WITH SALES GROWTH FOR THE ENTIRE INDUSTRY

Beginning with a look at the past, Exhibit 2-4(a) plots the growth rates for total industry sales for each industry covering the firm's product lines (i.e., Industry A and Industry B). Exhibit 2-4(b) then compares the annual industry sales growth rates in the past with the annual growth rates realized by our firm in each product line. Interpreting Exhibit 2-4, we see that in product line A the industry growth rate seems to have flattened out. Meanwhile, our firm's annual growth rate of sales for product line A has regularly been below that of the industry. For the seven years considered, the average annual sales growth for the industry has been 5.6 percent compared with an average of only 3.7 percent for the firm's sales in product line A. The growth rate for this firm's sales for product line A has, therefore, generally lagged behind the industry growth rate by approximately two percent. For the latest year, 1977, the firm's product line A sales grew at a rate of 3 percent less than the rate achieved by the industry as a whole.

In product line B, the industry experienced a continually increasing growth rate until the most recent year, 1977. Despite such impressive growth by the industry as a whole, the firm has consistently grown faster than the industry except for the latest year, when total industry sales grew 18 percent while product B sales for our firm grew at a 15 percent rate. All in all, for the seven years considered, the industry B sales grew at an annual rate of 15 percent, while product line B sales for the firm grew at an average rate of almost 20 percent per year. This firm's sales for product line B have grown, therefore, at an average annual rate approximately five percent faster than the industry. It is important to note, however, that this differential has been declining through the years from a peak differential of 13 percent in 1972 (when firm sales for product line B grew 26 percent versus a 13 percent growth rate for the entire industry) to a 3 percent sales growth gap for the firm in this product line for the most recent year.

PROJECTING FUTURE SALES GROWTH OF THE FIRM BASED UPON INDUSTRY PROJECTIONS

Interpreting Exhibit 2-4 and looking to the future while assuming no changes in the firm's growth strategies for these two product lines, we see that the firm's annual sales growth rate for product line A will

Exhibit 2-4
COMPARING PAST INDUSTRY SALES GROWTH
WITH PAST SALES GROWTH FOR EACH
OF THE FIRM'S PRODUCT LINES

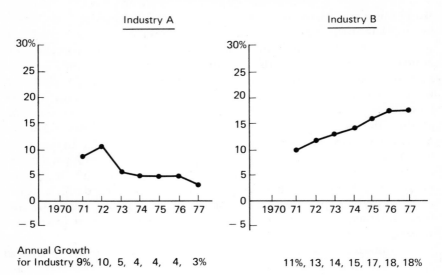

Annual Growth
for Industry 9%, 10, 5, 4, 4, 4, 3%   11%, 13, 14, 15, 17, 18, 18%

(a) Past Sales Growth Rates for Industries A and B

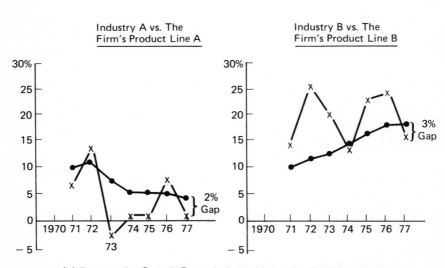

(b) Comparative Growth Rates: Industry Versus the Firm's Product Line

probably continue to lag behind the growth achieved by industry A as a whole by an average of approximately two percent per year. Meanwhile, assuming the firm stays with its present growth strategies, the firm's annual sales growth for product line B will probably continue to equal or slightly surpass that achieved annually by the entire industry B. For purposes of the projection, the assumption is made that for product line B, the firm's sales growth rate will surpass by two percent that achieved by industry B each year.

It should be noted that when a firm's sales growth rate for a product line is slower than that of the industry, the firm is losing market share. This can go on continually year after year for some time after the firm has once established itself in an industry. When a firm's growth rate is faster than that of the industry, the firm is gaining market share each year. This obviously cannot go on indefinitely since there is only 100 percent market share to capture. As a firm's sales approach a substantial market share, under most competitive conditions, the differential between its own rate of growth of sales for the relevant product line and the industry sales growth rate will narrow—as has been assumed for product line B sales of the firm above.

As suggested earlier in the chapter, industry sales projections are readily available from trade associations, commercial sources, and government sources. For example, the *United States Industrial Outlook,* published annually by the United States government and available at most libraries, is one useful source for making industry sales projections four to six years into the future. In order to achieve some consistency in industry definition, it is advisable to use the same source for the projections as was used in analyzing past industry sales figures. Carrying on with the example used above in the analysis of past sales, Exhibit 2-5 presents the projections for future industry sales for Industry A and Industry B (available in one of the sources mentioned above, such as the *United States Industrial Outlook*).

A sales projection for the firm is now possible, given these industries' projections and given the relationship over the recent past between the firm's annual sales growth rates for its two product lines, A and B, and the annual sales growth rates achieved by the relevant industries, A and B, over the same time period.

Exhibit 2-5(b) compares two alternative means of projecting the sales growth rates of each product line. The simpler of the two is to assume that the product line sales for the firm will grow at the same rates as projected for total industry sales. Looking at the firm's historical growth rates in comparison to the relevant industry's growth rates [Exhibit 2-4(b)] comprises a second and usually a more realistic basis for projecting the future annual sales growth rates for the firm's product lines.

Exhibit 2-5

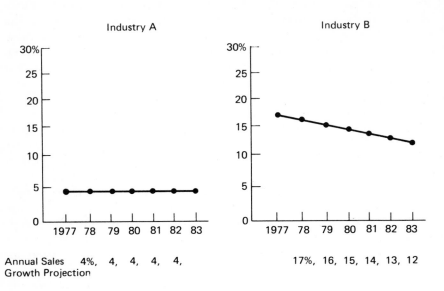

Industry A

Annual Sales   4%,   4,   4,   4,   4,
Growth Projection

Industry B

17%, 16, 15, 14, 13, 12

*(From a source such as *United States Industrial Outlook*)

(a)   Sales Growth Rate Projections for Industries A and B*

Product Line A

Two Methods of Projection

Product Line B

Two Methods of Projection

Year	1. Growth at Same Rate as Industry	2. Continuation of Historical Relationship* (Lag Behind Industry Rate by approximately 2%)		1. Growth at Same Rate as Industry	2. Continuation of Historical Relationship* (Growth approximately 2% Faster Than Industry Rate)
1978	4%	2%	1978	17%	19%
1979	4%	2%	1979	16%	18%
1980	4%	2%	1980	15%	17%
1981	4%	2%	1981	14%	16%
1982	4%	2%	1982	13%	15%
1983	4%	2%	1983	12%	14%

*Recommended Method

(b) Sales Growth Rate Projections for the Firm's Product Lines A and B

Following through on the projected growth rates for each product line as determined by method 2 (continuation of historical relationship between firm's sales growth rate and industry's growth rate) and displayed in Exhibit 2-5(b), the firm's projected sales for product line A and product line B are presented in Table 2-1(a). Sales for product

Table 2-1

(a) *Sales Projections for Each of the Firm's Product Lines*

	Product Line A Projected Sales Growth Rate			Product Line B Projected Sales Growth Rate	
Year	*(1)*	*Sales*	*Year*	*(1)*	*Sales*
1977		$77 million (actual sales now)	1977		$143 million (actual sales now)
1978	2%	$78.5 m.	1978	19%	$170 m.
1979	2%	$80.1 m.	1979	18%	$201 m.
1980	2%	$81.7 m.	1980	17%	$235 m.
1981	2%	$83.4 m.	1981	16%	$273 m.
1982	2%	$85.0 m.	1982	15%	$313 m.
1983	2%	$86.7 m.	1983	14%	$357 m.

(b) *Sales Projection for Total Firm Sales*

Year	*Total Projected Sales*	*Projected Growth Rate for Total Firm Sales*
1977	$220 million (actual sales now)	
1978	$249 m.	13.2%
1979	$281 m.	12.9%
1980	$317 m.	12.8%
1981	$356 m.	12.3%
1982	$398 m.	11.8%
1983	$444 m.	11.6%

line A climb from $77 million in 1977 to $86.7 million in 1983. Meanwhile, product line B sales for the firm leap ahead from $143 million (1977) to $357 million (1983). Adding the sales figures together for the two product lines for each year [in Table 2-1(b)] shows projected total firm sales over the next six years.

Plotting these projections for total firm sales will indicate for a firm whether and when it will experience a sales growth gap over the planning horizon (six years, in this case). If it is assumed that the firm's growth objective is a 15 percent sales increase per year as de-termined by the "golden mean" projection method shown in Exhibit 2-2(d), the firm's 5 percent sales growth gap of 1977 closes somewhat in 1978 but then gradually and continually opens again over the planning period until the gap equals 3.4 percent in 1983. Figure 2-1 displays the evolution of this sales growth gap over time.

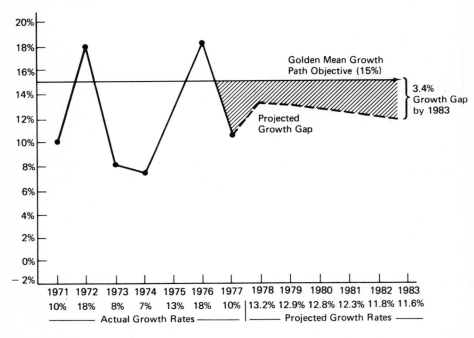

FIGURE 2-1.   Plot of firm's projected revenue growth path versus firm's revenue growth objective.

USING THE SALES PROJECTION AS A GROWTH BASE

The industry-oriented method of projection used above is intended to guide the firm in recognizing and fully taking into consideration the existence of industry life cycles and the direct influences that passage through industry life cycles has upon sales growth rates for the in-dividual firm—influences that are positive in the growth phase and negative in the maturity, saturation, and decline stages.

The ultimate purpose of growth gap analysis is to help ensure that the firm will meet its growth objective over the planning period and that any growth gap projected under existing growth strategies will be closed. The firm considered above will achieve the growth rates listed in Table 2-1(b) by simply carrying on with its existing product lines and existing growth strategies. This sales projection should be regarded by the firm as *a growth base*. The firm cannot afford to resign itself to that base. Rather, the firm must now plan appropriate strategies to add to that base enough growth to meet its annual sales growth rate objective (15 percent in the case above) over the planning period. Industry life cycles for this firm's product lines are peaking out. What are the firm's alternative means of improving its growth in the future?

SOURCES OF FUTURE
REVENUE GROWTH

Since total revenue equals price times volume, increases in total revenue can come from price changes and/or increases in unit volume sold. Careful price setting on an operating-period-by-operating-period basis is necessary for a firm to achieve profits over the long run. The next chapter reviews the role that such price changes can play as a source of revenue growth and profit growth.

Although careful price setting is necessary, the real key to continuous revenue growth (and profit growth) is for the firm regularly to experience increases in unit volume sold—primarily by means other than price changes (usually price decreases). Parts Two and Three of the text provide new tools and perspectives for planning such unit sales volume increases. The following is an overview of three major sources of these volume increases: acquisitions, adding new products internally, and expanding the volume sales of existing products (through means other than price changes).

ACQUISITIONS AS A SOURCE OF REVENUE GROWTH AND PROFIT GROWTH

During the 1960's and again in recent years many firms depended upon acquisitions of existing companies as a major vehicle for growth of total revenue. Such acquisitions provide a firm with new synergistic advantages, as discussed in Chapter 1. Considered as such, acquisitions can lay the foundation for future growth and can also make immediate contributions to the firm's gross revenue.

Acquisitions, however, can involve sizable new investments and, therefore, frequently tend to depress investment-related performance ratios such as "return on investment." The case of Singer's acquisition of Friden, as considered in Chapter 1, provides a good example of this phenomenon. Facing such problems, not a few firms in the late 1960's and early 1970's realized that they had depended too heavily upon acquisitions as a revenue growth route and consequently pulled back from that strategy. Acquisitions remain, however, as a very legitimate means of increasing total firm sales.

ADDING NEW PRODUCTS AND NEW PRODUCT LINES AS SOURCES OF REVENUE GROWTH AND PROFIT GROWTH

The importance of adding new products as a major growth vehicle for the firm was emphasized earlier in the book. This growth strategy can overlap with acquisitions—since a firm with poor synergy relating to a particular new product or service that it desires to market may opt for acquiring another firm(s) as a means of obtaining capabilities needed to sell that product successfully.

A firm with good synergy relating to a particular new product can produce and sell such a product without significant new investments in technology, equipment, personnel, and/or general knowhow. If a ripe market for such products is assumed (market potential is considered in Part Two), this can offer a very attractive sales growth strategy alternative.

EXPANDING THE VOLUME OF SALES (IN UNITS SOLD) OF THE FIRM'S ESTABLISHED PRODUCTS AS A SOURCE OF REVENUE GROWTH AND PROFIT GROWTH

As also indicated earlier, a firm that depends solely upon the expansion of sales volume of its present products for its sales growth is not likely to achieve significant annual sales growth rates over the long run. Expanding the sales volume of the firm's established products should, nevertheless, be assigned a primary role in helping the firm to achieve continual growth of sales revenue.

Market structure profile analysis (in Parts Two and Three) includes a consideration of a wide variety of the alternative means that are available to the firm for stimulating the unit sales volume growth of the firm's already established products.

SUMMARY

Regular profit growth is a most important goal of the firm. The firm can realize profit growth year after year by continually increasing its total revenue and/or reducing its costs. This chapter considered how a firm can draw up realistic objectives and plans for realizing continuous growth of total revenue.

Setting revenue growth objectives and planning ahead of time to attain those objectives is necessary in order to prevent a decline in sales growth over the long term. The text presented three methods of setting such objectives, and, therefore, three possible bases to use for examining any past, present, or future revenue growth gaps that the firm might face.

The method suggested as best developed a "golden mean" growth rate target, which is an average between the firm's best annual sales growth rate achieved over the recent past and its average annual growth rate over the recent past. This rate can be compared with past sales figures to determine past and present growth gaps, and compared to future sales growth projections (determined by the consolidated industry by industry analysis for each product line) to determine possible future growth gaps.

While careful price setting (as reviewed in the next chapter) is necessary for revenue and profit growth, the real key to continuous revenue and profit growth is a regular increase in unit sales volume. Sources of such unit sales volume increases are acquisitions, new products, and the expansion of sales volume of a firm's existing products (through means other than price changes).

REVIEW QUESTIONS

1. What are the major reasons why no firm can attain unlimited revenue growth?

2. Why is it advantageous for a firm to analyze its sales growth—past, present and future?

3. Can a firm have no revenue growth gap in relation to industry revenue growth but still have a revenue growth gap problem? Explain.

4. Should a firm be content if its revenue growth rate equals that of the industry as a whole?

5. What are a firm's major possible sources of future revenue growth?

NOTES

1. The simplicity of the equation belies the complexities of the relationships between price and volume (demand and demand curve analysis) and the relationships between costs and volume (cost and cost curve analysis). Nor does the equation recognize that a firm almost always sells more than a single product or

service and, therefore, faces multiple profit equations such as the one above. All in all, however, the simple equation above is quite adequate for pointing out the alternative means of effecting profit growth.

2.   For a description of Westinghouse's experience during the late 1960's and early 1970's, see *Wall Street Journal* (March 7, 1975), p. 1.

3

Converting Revenue Growth
Into Profit Growth

Up to this point, the emphasis has been upon developing revenue objectives and plans. Although necessary, continual revenue growth is nòt, however, a sufficient condition for achieving continual profit growth. As the basic profit equation indicates:

Profits = total revenue minus *total cost.*

In order to convert continuous revenue growth into continuous proﬁt growth, a firm must carefully watch its prices and its costs.

This chapter first considers the role of price changes as a source of revenue growth and profit growth. Following is a discussion of the importance of and methods of monitoring and controlling the firm's costs as part of the firm's quest for continual profit growth.

PRICE CHANGES AS A SOURCE OF
REVENUE GROWTH AND PROFIT GROWTH

The revenue component of the basic profit equation breaks down into *price times unit sales volumes.* Revenue can be increased, therefore, by changes in price and/or increases in unit sales volume (by acquisitions, adding new products internally, and/or increasing the sales volume of existing products).

PRICE/VOLUME RELATIONSHIPS

A demand curve represents the relationship between price and volume of units sold of a product in a particular operating period (e.g., a year). The typical relationship shows the volume sold increasing as price decreases and vice versa (see Fig. 3-1).

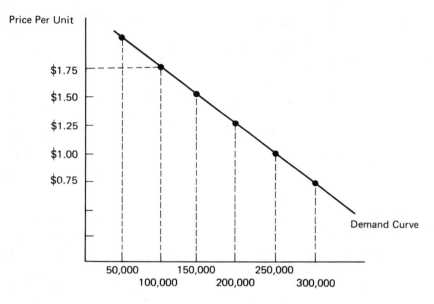

FIGURE 3-1.   Typical shape of a demand curve.

Note: A demand curve such as this is very difficult to derive. For a discussion of these difficulties, see W. J. Baumol, *Economic Theory and Operations Analysis* (Englewood Cliffs, N.J.: Prentice Hall, Inc., 1965). In addition, an actual demand curve is not apt to be linear like this. Also, the slope of the curve can vary significantly from product to product and industry to industry. Under certain circumstances, in fact, the demand curve or at least a section of it may show volume demand increasing as price increases. For a discussion of this phenomenon (e.g., S-shaped demand curve), see R. Leftwich, *The Price System and Reserve Allocation* (New York: Holt, Rinehart, Winston, Inc., 1971). Finally, this single diagram doses not recognize that a firm almost always sells more than a single product or service and, therefore, faces multiple demand curves such as the one in the exhibit. All in all, however, the diagram is quite adequate for pointing out the relationship of concern between price and sales unit volume.

By simply reducing price, the firm can achieve its goal of increasing unit sales volume—the lower the price, the higher the unit sales volume. Such a strategy (price reduction), however, can conflict with the firm's revenue growth goals and profit growth goals. Examining the relationship between price and total revenue serves as a good take-off point for considering those potential conflicts.

PRICE/REVENUE RELATIONSHIPS

The same curve that indicates the relationship between price and sales unit volume (i.e., the demand curve), also indicates the relationship between price and total sales dollars (i.e., total revenue).

For the example in Fig. 3-1, the total revenue achieved at each price indicated on the demand curve is

Price	×	Volume	=	Total Revenue
$0.75	×	300,000	=	$225,000
$1.00	×	250,000	=	$250,000
$1.25	×	200,000	=	$250,000
$1.50	×	150,000	=	$225,000
$1.75	×	100,000	=	$175,000

Figure 3-2 shows the resulting total revenue curve. The price at which total revenue is maximized, therefore, is somewhere between $1.00 and $1.25 (see page 39).

The exact *revenue maximizing price* is **$1.125,** at which price, the volume sold is 225,000 units and the total revenue equals $253,125. We next examine how this point is found.

FINDING THE REVENUE MAXIMIZING POINT. Choose two points on the demand curve and assign the relevant price and quantity of the first point the notations p_1 and v_1 and the second point the notations p_2 and v_2. The formula for the line in such a case is

$$p - p_1 = \frac{p_2 - p_1}{v_2 - v_1}(v - v_1)$$

In this case, let

$$p_1 = 1.00$$
$$v_1 = 250$$
$$p_2 = 1.50$$
$$v_2 = 150$$

Using the formula, we have

$$p - 1.00 = \frac{1.50 - 1.00}{150 - 250} (v - 250)$$

$$p - 1.00 = \frac{0.50}{-100} (v - 250)$$

$$p - 1.00 = -0.005v + 1.25$$

$$\boldsymbol{p = 0.005v + 2.25}$$

Since total revenue = price × quantity,

$$\text{TR} = (-0.005v + 2.25)\ v$$
$$\textbf{TR} = \textbf{-0.005}v^2 + \textbf{2.25}v$$

Total revenue is maximized where the slope of the TR curve = 0. The slope equals the first derivative of the total. The slope, therefore, $= -.01v + 2.25$. This $= 0$ when

$$0 = -0.01v + 2.25$$
$$0.01v = 2.25$$
$$v = \textbf{225,000 units}$$

To find the revenue maximizing price, return to the formula for price found above.

Therefore,

$$p = -0.005v + 2.25$$
$$p = -0.005\ (225) + 2.25$$
$$-1.125 + 2.25 = \textbf{\$1.125}$$

Total revenue at this revenue maximizing point equals

$$\text{TR} = p \times v$$
$$\text{TR} = \$1.125 \times 225,000 \text{ units}$$
$$= \textbf{\$253,125}$$

Points on the demand curve to the left of the revenue maximizing point are said to be on the "elastic" portion of the demand curve. When a firm is operating on this part of the demand curve, *a reduction in price*

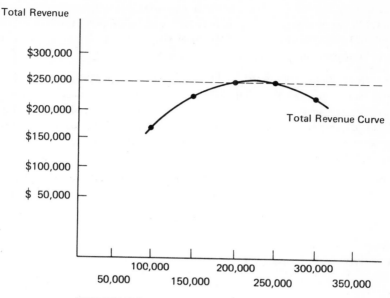

FIGURE 3-2. The total revenue curve.

results in an *increase in* volume and in *total revenue.* Points on the demand curve to the right of the revenue maximizing point are said to be on the "inelastic" portion of the demand curve. When a firm is operating on this part of the demand curve, a *price increase* results in an *increase in total revenue*—despite a reduction in volume sold.

Pricing a product to maximize unit sales volume, therefore, conflicts with a pricing strategy designed to maximize total revenue. Pricing strategies designed to satisfy either of the above goals are inconsistent with the goal of pricing to maximize profits—because these pricing strategies fail to take costs into consideration.

PRICE/PROFIT RELATIONSHIPS

When the firm's costs are also included in the analysis, the firm can determine the price(s) that is likely to yield the most profits for the firm in a given operating period. For example, assume that a firm manufactures and sells baseball bats and faces the demand curve in Fig. 3-1 for its bats.[1] Assume also that the fixed costs of the firm's operations are $100,000 and that the variable cost involved in producing and selling each bat is 40¢.[2]

Given that situation, the firm can maximize its profits at a *price* of $1,325—at which price, the *volume sold* is **185,000 units** and *profits* equal **$71,000.** Next we consider how this price is found (through the use of marginal analysis).

FINDING THE PROFIT MAXIMIZING POINT. Profit maximizing point is the point at which the difference between total revenue and total cost is the greatest. This is the point where the slopes of the two curves (total revenue curve and total cost curve) equal one another— i.e., where "marginal revenue" equals "marginal cost."

Marginal revenue is found by taking the first derivative of the total revenue curve. Given the total revenue curve of TR $= -0.005v^2 +2.25v$.

$$\textbf{Marginal revenue } = -0.01v + 2.25$$

Marginal cost is found by taking the first derivative of the total cost curve. Given the costs of:

$$\text{Fixed costs } = \$100,000$$
$$\text{Variable cost } = 40\cent \text{ per unit}$$
$$\text{the \textbf{total cost curve} } = \$100,000 + 0.40v$$

Given that total cost curve,

$$\textbf{Marginal cost } = 40\cent$$

Setting marginal revenue equal to marginal cost, we have

$$-0.01v + 2.25 = 0.40$$

The profit maximizing quantity, therefore, equals:

$$-0.01v = 0.40 - 2.25$$
$$v = \frac{-1.85}{-0.01}$$
$$v = \textbf{185,000 units}$$

To find the profit maximizing price, return to the formula for the demand curve, which in this case is

$$p = 0.005v + 2.25$$

Therefore, $p = - 0.005 \ (185,000 \text{ units}) + 2.25$

$$= 2.25 - 0.925$$
$$p = \textbf{\$1.325}$$

Total profits at this profit maximizing point are

$$\text{Profits} = \text{TR} - \text{TC}$$
$$= pv - [\text{FC} + vc(v)]$$
$$= \$1.325(185,000) - [\$100,000 + 40\%(185,000)]$$
$$= \$245,000 - (\$100,000 + 74,000)$$
$$= \$245,000 - \$174,000$$

Profits = $71,000

If firms did indeed face demand and cost situations as simple and straightforward as the one considered above, pricing would be a relatively easy task. Unfortunately, most demand and cost situations are very complex and not subject to that type of definitive profit maximizing analysis.[3]

Even if we set those difficulties aside, however, although careful price setting is necessary for a firm to realize continual revenue and profit growth, optimum price setting (optimum in terms of enabling the firm to maximize its profits) will not by itself yield revenue growth (except in inflationary situations, as considered below) or profit growth over the long run. Once optimum prices are set on a given sales unit volume of the firm's products (or services), any further price changes (increases or decreases) will result in declining rather than growing profits for the firm. *Pricing strategies—no matter how good they are—cannot yield long-run profit growth all by themselves.*

PRICE CHANGES AS A SOURCE OF REVENUE GROWTH IN INFLATIONARY TIMES

In inflationary times, demand curves shift outward in response to industrywide price increases. In such situations, firms can realistically plan to meet varying proportions of revenue growth objectives simply through the implementation of price increases.

In this regard, an important question should be considered: In inflationary times is revenue growth achieved by means of price increases an adequate form of revenue growth? The answer is an emphatic *NO*. In inflationary times the firm's costs are increasing also—often rising more rapidly than the firm can afford to or is allowed to (in cases where price controls are relevant) raise its prices. In such times, therefore, the incremental revenue realized through price increases is more often than not wiped out by the increased costs the firm is facing. Depending upon price increases as the major vehicle for achieving revenue growth in inflationary times may result in the firm's meeting its revenue growth objectives but will at the same time usually leave the firm far short in terms of meeting its performance (profit) objectives.[4]

Sources other than price increases must, therefore, be relied upon if a firm is simultaneously to meet both revenue growth and profit growth aspirations.

RELATIVE IMPORTANCE OF ALTERNATIVE SOURCES OF FUTURE REVENUE GROWTH

Despite the fact that a firm should not depend upon inflationary price increases as the sole or major source of revenue growth, the incremental revenue projected to result from such increases should be in the firm's overall revenue growth plan. In finalizing such a plan, the firm should very specifically differentiate among the exact growth strategies upon which it will depend for meeting its revenue growth objective.

For example, what proportions of the targeted growth will be met by price increases (in inflationary times), by acquisitions, by internally adding new products, and by increases in unit sales of established products? This might be done as in Table 3-1, which shows a firm projecting

Table 3-1
DIFFERENTIATING AMONG SOURCES OF
PROJECTED REVENUE INCREASES

	Present	*1978*	*1979*	*1980*	*1981*	*1982*	*1983*
Gross revenue goal	$220 million	253	291	335	385	443	509
Increase/Year		15%	15%	15%	15%	15%	15%
Source of Revenue Increase							
Price increases		6%	4%	3%	3%	3%	3%
Acquisitions		2%	3%	4%	4%	4%	4%
Internal product additions		4%	4%	4%	4%	4%	4%
Increased volume sales of established products (figured at current prices)		3%	4%	4%	4%	4%	4%

for 1978 a sales increase of 15 percent, accounted for to varying extents by each of four growth sources: price increases (6 percent), acquisitions

(2 percent), internally adding new products (4 percent), and increases in unit sales of the firm's established products—at this year's prices—(3 percent).

PERFORMANCE GAP ANALYSIS

As shown above, continual revenue growth is not sufficient for continual profit growth. The firm must also pay close attention to its costs. The relationship between a firm's profits and its costs are best captured and examined through *performance gap analysis*.

PERFORMANCE MEASURES

The firm has available a number of different possible measures for evaluating performance. The most common performance measures are profitability measures and include net income, operating profit margin, earnings per share, and return on investment. Other measures are also important to the firm—for example, liquidity ratios, leverage ratios, and activity or turnover ratios—and cannot be ignored in evaluating performance, but the profitability measures mentioned above offer the most direct and useful data for evaluating and projecting the firm's profits and profit growth.[5] Performance objectives are typically set, therefore, in terms of these profitability measures.

Of all the profitability measures available, one that is readily available and at the same time reflects the essence of performance as it relates to growth of both sales and profits is *operating profit margin (OPM)*. Operating profit margin equals the percentage of total gross sales revenue that remains after all cost and expenses other than those of a nonoperating nature, such as interest (except finance companies), minority provisions, and income taxes have been deducted. In its simplest sense, OPM equals before tax profits divided by sales. Operating profit margin data are readily available for publicly held corporations.[6]

MONITORING PERFORMANCE ON A
PRODUCT-BY-PRODUCT BASIS

A firm may desire a separate performance measure for each of its different products or product lines in order closely to monitor the profitability of its operations on a product-by-product basis, so that it may be more quickly alerted to profit problem areas. For such purposes, a firm may find it useful to develop a measure such as *margin after product expense* (MAPE). This measure may include the direct cost of manufacturing, distribution, and advertising for each separate product or product line but would not include any allocations of indirect costs such as depreciation, interest, general administrative overhead, and taxes. Miles Laboratories is one firm that uses this approach.

Firms desiring to use the *return on investment* or *return on assets employed* performance criterion as opposed to the return on sales criterion can similarly break down the return on investment measure among the firm's various product lines, or individual products—by determining the profits produced by each product line (or product) and then dividing that figure by the assets employed by and/or assigned to that product line (or product). International Harvester is one firm that uses this approach.

The principles for setting and evaluating performance objectives for individual product lines are essentially the same as those used for considering more generalized performance objectives for all of the firm's product lines combined.

SETTING PERFORMANCE OBJECTIVES AND EVALUATING PERFORMANCE

Two factors are particularly important in evaluating a corporation's performance over time by using the operating profit margin (OPM) measure. First, trends in the OPM are important. Has the firm's OPM been rising, falling, or steady over the past six to eight years? For example, Fig. 3-3 shows a firm in each of these situations (rising, falling, and steady OPM).

Second, what has the firm's performance been, compared with that of its major competitors and with the industry as a whole? No two firms have exactly the same mix of product lines or individual products, so strictly speaking it is difficult to compare the OPM of one firm with the OPM of another. With the exception of highly diversified conglomerates, however, most firms do concentrate production in a relatively small number of related product lines. Comparison with competitors and with the overall industry is, therefore, quite practicable for most firms.[7]

In setting performance objectives against which to compare its own performance, the firm should be concerned with both factors considered above—"trend in performance" and "performance relative to industry." A few examples can perhaps best show why both factors are important in evaluating performance.

Using the performance relative to industry criterion, a firm can be operating with a performance gap regardless of whether its own OPM is rising, falling, or steady. In Fig. 3-3, for example, if the average OPM for the industry has been a relatively steady 15 percent on a

Firm A.

Operating Profit
Margin <u>Rising</u>

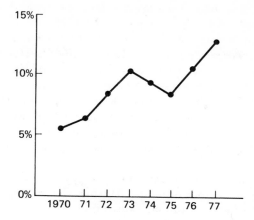

Firm B:

Operating Profit
Margin <u>Falling</u>

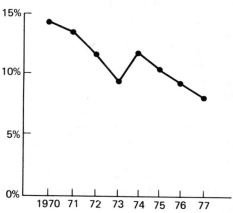

Firm C:

Operating Profit
Margin <u>Steady</u>

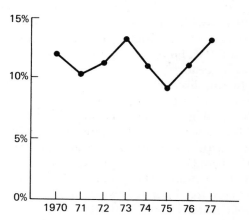

FIGURE 3-3.

year-by-year basis, then firms A, B, and C have all been operating with performance gaps over the past eight years.

Even meeting the average OPM of the industry, however, does not always preclude a firm from having a performance gap. For example, in particularly hard economic times or in times when an industry has reached its late maturity stage or saturation stage, a downward trend in OPM for the firm may be matched by a similar trend for the industry.[8] Under such circumstances a firm would be unwise to set its minimum performance standard equal to that of the industry average. A firm should not be satisfied with a steadily declining OPM under any circumstances.

The liquor industry provides a good example of such industrywide pressures on performance. During the latter half of the 1960's, unit volume grew at annual rates ranging from 5 to 7 percent. During the first half of the 1970's, however, unit volume growth averaged only 3 percent annually. Meanwhile, competitive pressures kept prices relatively stable (they rose less than 5 percent for the whole period), while the consumer price index rose approximately 65 percent (1965–74). Distillers' costs rose just as rapidly—with price rises in the first half of the 1970's alone amounting to 20 percent (glass), 38 percent (bottle caps), 20 percent (labels), 180 percent (sugar), 200 percent (fuel), 12.5 percent (labor), 50 percent (barrels), and 23 percent (rail freight). New cost-saving strategies and strategies designed to stimulate sales unit volume are currently being implemented by the liquor industry in an effort to reverse performance trends.[9]

An aggressive firm may set its performance objective equal *not* to the average firm in the industry, but equal to the OPM of the best-performing firm in the industry. For example, Ford Motor Company had maintained a relatively stable OPM throughout the latter 1960's and early 1970's—with an OPM at least as good as that of the automobile industry as a whole (ranging from 7 to 10 percent). Ford was dissatisfied with that OPM, however, because its major competitor, General Motors, consistently realized an OPM approximately five percent higher than Ford. In this instance, the firm (Ford) focused upon the performance of its most successful competitor in setting its own objective.[10]

In the domestic auto industry, General Motors has regularly maintained both the largest sales volume in the industry and the best OPM. The firm with the largest sales in an industry does not, however, always have the best OPM. In agricultural equipment, for example, the sales leader, International Harvester, has been faced with regularly declining performance for the past 10 years and is hard pressed to keep its operating profit margin above 5 percent, while its major competitors, Caterpillar and Deere, have both regularly maintained operating profit margins above the 10 percent level. In this instance, International

Harvester might well set its performance objectives in terms of the OPM's now achieved by Caterpillar and Deere.[11]

GENERAL PRINCIPLES FOR SETTING PERFORMANCE OBJECTIVES FOR THE FUTURE

Now that we have reviewed a few of the diverse types of situations under which both OPM trends and OPM performances relative to industry are important, a few guiding principles do emerge for determining whether/when a firm is operating with a performance gap. These principles include the following. A firm is operating with a performance gap if:

(a) The firm's OPM is consistently lower than that of the average for the industry as a whole.

(b) The firm's OPM is declining on a continual basis—whether or not the industrywide OPM is also declining.

(c) The firm aspires to have as good an OPM as its major competitor(s), regardless of what the average industry OPM is, but finds its OPM consistently falling short of that goal.

Figure 3-4 exhibits each of these three different OPM gap situations.

CLOSING PERFORMANCE GAPS

Performance gaps can be closed by changing prices, by reducing costs (by improving efficiency/productivity) or by some combination of these strategies. As considered above, price increases may or may not lead to improved performance, depending upon what the competitive conditions are and what happens to the firm's sales unit volume when prices are increased. Such price increases, if finally necessary, should only follow intensive efforts by the firm to cut back existing inefficiencies within the firm wherever possible.

Consider, for example, some of the strategies implemented in the performance gap situations described previously in the liquor industry, the automobile industry, and the agricultural equipment, trucks, and construction equipment industries.

LIQUOR INDUSTRY

Among the performance strategies being implemented in the liquor industry is lowering the proof of hard liquor and thus lowering taxes. Hard liquor is taxed at $10.51 per 100-proof gallon. A distiller can save

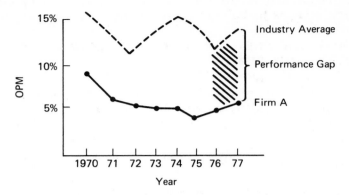

Firm A: Firm's OPM is consistently lower than the industry's average OPM

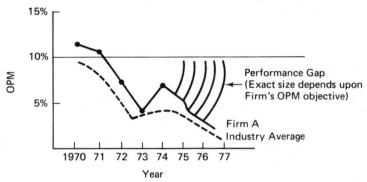

Firm B: Firm's OPM is declining on a continual basis (along with the industry)

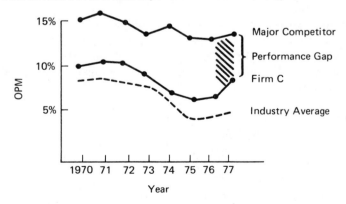

Firm C: Firm aspires to match OPM of its major competitor

FIGURE 3-4.   Performance gaps.

over 60¢ per gallon, therefore, by lowering the proof from 86 proof to 80 proof. Given the market pressures keeping liquor prices down, industry leaders feel longer-range profit growth is likely to depend upon growth of sales. With this point in mind, distillers are looking closely at export markets, are promoting bourbons as "mix-it-with-anything" liquors, are attempting to build a broader appeal for hard liquors such as tequila, and are sponsoring events covered by news media (especially sporting events), since hard liquor ads are banned from television.[12]

AUTOMOBILE INDUSTRY: FORD'S PERFORMANCE STRATEGIES

In Ford's strategy to improve its own OPM versus General Motors' OPM, Ford has taken three interrelated approaches: (1) cost cutting, (2) cutting back on low-performance operations, and (3) improving Ford's market share in the medium- and high-priced auto segments. Through its cost-cutting plan, Ford came up with 438 ways of improving efficiency and productivity, including launching new models over a weekend instead of after a two- or three-week closedown. On one model, as another money-saving example, Ford chopped two inches off the fender to make the vehicles fit better in boxcars and thus reduce shipping expense. "We use to ship a lot of air," said a Ford executive.

In cutting back on low-performance operations during the early 1970's, Ford dropped 18 money-losing or marginally profitable operations and targeted 50 more for a similar fate in the future. Dropped operations included Philco-Ford's microelectronics and laundry equipment. Finally, in an effort to stimulate sales in the high- and medium-priced auto segments—segments yielding greater profit margins—Ford rebuilt its Lincoln-Mercury division and has achieved significant sales success by aiming directly at the luxury car market with its Lincoln, Mark IV, and Thunderbird. New, more luxurious Mercury models were introduced to strengthen Ford in its move against entrenched medium-priced positions held by GM with its Buick, Pontiac, and Oldsmobile.[13]

AGRICULTURAL EQUIPMENT, TRUCKS, AND CONSTRUCTION EQUIPMENT INDUSTRIES: INTERNATIONAL HARVESTER'S PERFORMANCE STRATEGIES

In International Harvester's drive to improve performance, IH shut down seven marginal plants, planned to sell off its least profitable division (Wisconsin Steel), and cut back the number of models in its line of lightweight trucks from 65 to 30. Similar cutbacks took place through the divestiture of some company-owned outlets and in a sharp reduction in the number of district offices.

These economizing moves reflect a commitment on the part of IH top management to change the game from volume to performance. By ridding itself of marginal operations, assets were freed to help expand and modernize its more profitable product lines.[14]

RELATIONSHIPS BETWEEN REVENUE GROWTH AND PERFORMANCE OBJECTIVES/PLANS

Revenue growth and performance objectives should be set simultaneously because of their close interrelationship. It is most meaningful to consider that relationship over the long run as opposed to the short run.

In the short run, sales growth is not necessary to realize improved performance. Genesco, for example, cut back on both its investment and its sales volume in recent years in a direct attempt to improve its performance ratios. By selectively divesting itself of a number of low-performance subsidiaries, total investment was reduced, and return on investment figures for the overall firm perked up. Through those same divestitures and through selectively dropping low-performance products in existing lines, sales declined by nearly 20 percent, while profits declined very little—leaving Genesco with an improved overall operating profit margin.

During the economic hard times of the mid-1970's, many other firms also cut back on low-performance operations rather than entering the money market to finance such operations in order to carry them through hard times. Numerous examples reflect such strategies. Greyhound Corporation, the large bus company that has diversified into meat packing and other activities, liquidated its cattle-feeding operation, which lost over $10 million in 1974. Evans Products Company of Portland, Oregon, maker of transportation equipment and building products, agreed to sell a Far East ship-chartering operation and a new office building. Evans also sought to get out of the manufacturing and wholesale distribution of building materials. Alco Standard Corporation, a highly diversified mining, manufacturing and distributing company, sold a foundry business, and a wire and cable manufacturing operation in Canada. It also sold about half its United States mining operations to the steel companies that use the coal. Westinghouse Electric Corporation sold its $600-million-a-year appliance business to White Consolidated Industries, Inc. of Cleveland, ending an operating loss that ran into the millions.[15]

Although such strategies may hurt the firms' performance in the short run—particularly if assets are sold off at less than book value—over the longer run, firms feel that by pruning back on weak areas they can reduce interest costs and concentrate capital and management on ventures promising better revenue growth and performance in the future.

Such "cutting back" strategies alone, however, will not yield continual improvements year after year over the long run. Such long-run improvements are more dependent ultimately upon a regular expansion of the firm's sales.

At the same time, as has been emphasized above, a fixation on sales per se is just as inappropriate. In the agricultural equipment, trucks, and construction equipment industries considered previously, International Harvester is a sales leader, but International falls far behind its major competitors in terms of its OPM. In the words of International Harvester's president: "We became a sales-oriented organization, assuming the more volume we had, the more money we would make. We simply did not put sufficient emphasis on profitability." [16]

Sales growth objectives and performance objectives are, therefore, very closely interrelated and, as such, a firm should consider and set these objectives together in the firm's overall quest for long-run sales and profit growth.

THE ENVIRONMENTAL CONTEXT OF REVENUE AND PROFIT PLANNING DECISIONS

As emphasized throughout the past two chapters, a firm must make profits in order to ensure its long-term viability. This drive and quest for profits should not, however, blind the firm to its role and responsibilities as a social institution. With today's growth of consumerism, government regulation over consumer and industrial products, and the public's rising disenchantment with business in general, the need to maintain an awareness of this role is all too apparent.[17]

What is required today is an even closer monitoring of diverse and dynamic consumer demands. One scholar has described the growing complexity of the firm's task in terms of eight different types of consumer demand situations, each requiring a different corporate response. (See Table 3-2.)

Suffice it to say that a customer orientation is appropriate. The firm should concentrate upon monitoring the customer and adjusting strategies to ensure continual customer satisfaction. This importance of satisfying the customer should not, however, obscure the fact that a firm must realize revenue and profit growth over the long run if it is to survive and continue serving the customer.

Table 3-2
CORPORATE TASKS RELATING TO THE CONSUMER

Demand State	Corporate Task	Formal Name	Example
I. Negative demand	Disabuse demand	Conversional marketing	Dental work
II. No demand	Create demand	Stimulation marketing	Unfamiliar product
III. Latent demand	Develop demand	Developmental marketing	Low-tar, high-flavor cigarettes
IV. Faltering demand	Revitalize demand	Remarketing	Furs, hotels, autos
V. Irregular demand	Synchronize demand	Synchromarketing	Boats, hotels
VI. Full demand	Maintain demand	Maintenance marketing	Most products one time or another.
VII. Overfull demand	Reduce demand	Demarketing	Supply shortages
VIII. Unwholesome demand	Destroy demand	Countermarketing	Energy, cigarettes

Reprinted from *Journal of Marketing,* published by the American Marketing Association: Kotler, Philip, "The Major Tasks of Marketing Management," Vol. 37 (October, 1973), pp. 42–49.

SUMMARY

Achieving sales growth does not ensure the firm that it will also realize profit growth. To ensure continual profit growth, the firm must carefully watch its prices and costs.

Price changes can be used to increase a firm's volume, revenue, and/or profits. Price changes resulting in increased volume and/or revenue may, however, cause a decline in the firm's profits. Careful analysis of the relevant demand and costs involved in each market situation is required for optimum price setting.

Regardless of how successful a firm is in improving its total revenue (through unit volume increases and/or price changes), the firm's profits will not keep pace unless costs are watched very closely. Performance gap analysis is used as a tool for monitoring costs and setting overall cost and profit ratio objectives.

Operating profit margin (OPM) was suggested as one particularly useful performance measure for considering the firm's overall performance, because it is readily available and because it reflects the essence of performance as it relates to growth of both sales and profits. Measuring performance on a product-line-by-product-line basis is also very important and can best be done by using margin after product expense (MAPE) ratios or return on assets employed ratios.

In considering performance, the firm's performance trends and the firm's performance ratio(s) relative to industry ratios are both important. Three principles were presented for determining whether/when a firm is operating with a performance gap. A firm is operating with a gap if:

(a) The firm's OPM is consistently lower than that of the average for the industry as a whole.

(b) The firm's OPM is declining on a continual basis—whether or not the industrywide OPM is also declining.

(c) The firm aspires to have as good an OPM as its major competitor(s), regardless of what the average industry OPM is but finds its OPM consistently falling short of that goal.

Performance gaps can be closed by increasing prices, by reducing costs through improving efficiency/productivity, or by some combination of these strategies. The chapter reviewed several examples of such strategies.

The chapter concluded with a discussion of the interrelationships between revenue growth and performance objectives/plans and some comments on the environmental context of profit planning decisions.

REVIEW QUESTIONS

1. Does reducing a price usually increase or decrease:
   (a) Unit volume sold? Why?
   (b) The firm's total revenue? Why?
   (c) The firm's profits? Why?

2. Under what circumstances does an increase in price result in a decrease in total revenue?

3. Why is the revenue maximizing price usually different from the profit maximizing price?

4. Why is pricing *not* considered a long-term revenue and profit growth strategy?

5. Under what circumstances should a firm increase its prices during inflationary times?

6. What alternative sources of revenue growth should a firm include in its revenue growth plan?

7. What is operating profit margin and why is it a particularly valuable performance measure?

8. Can a firm be experiencing a performance gap despite steady improvement in the relevant performance measure (e.g., OPM)? Explain.

9. Why did Ford Motor Company consider itself to be operating with a performance gap?

10. Discuss how a firm can close its performance gap.

11. When is sales growth most important for improved performance? Why is sales growth not the end-all for achieving good profitability in both the long and short run?

12. Discuss the interrelationships between revenue growth and performance objectives.

NOTES

1. Because of the pricing markup structure through the distribution channel, the manufacturing firm receives only a fraction of the ultimate selling price—a larger or smaller fraction depending upon the number of and type of intermediaries the firm uses in its distribution channel(s) for the product. In this case, for example, the final consumer may pay (to the retailer) $4.00, the retailer may pay (to the wholesaler) $2.00, and the wholesaler may pay (to the firm) $1.25.

2. Fixed costs equal overhead expenses and other costs that the firm will have to incur regardless of the volume of the firm's products produced and sold—e.g., administrative overhead, property taxes, etc. Variable costs are costs related to the production and sale of incremental units of the firm's products—e.g., raw materials, labor, transportation, etc.

3. No attempt is made to discuss here in any depth the complexities of demand curve generation and analysis. The interested reader is referred to: D. S. Watson, *Price Theory and Its Uses* (Boston, Mass.: Houghton Mifflin, Inc., 1963), and W. W. Haynes, *Managerial Economics* (Homewood, Ill.: Dorsey Press, Inc., 1963). Nor is any attempt made here to discuss the complexities of cost curve generation and analysis. The interested reader is referred to: W. J. Baumol, *Economic Theory and Operations Analysis* (Englewood Cliffs, N.J.: Prentice-Hall, Inc., 1965), Chapter 11, and Lesourne, *Economic Analysis and Industrial Management* (Englewood Cliffs, N.J.: Prentice-Hall, Inc., 1967).

4. For an interesting discussion of some of the direct and indirect adverse effects of inflation upon corporate profits, see: "The Great Industrial Vanishing Act," *Business Week* (August 11, 1975), p. 48, and "Profits: The Illusion of a Boom," *Business Week* (August 10, 1974), p. 71.

5.   For a definition and discussion of the whole battery of finance ratios, see F. Weston, and E. F. Brigham, *Managerial Finance* (New York: Holt, Rinehart, and Winston, 1966), Chapter 4. For an enlightening discussion of the return on investment measure in particular, see F. W. Searby, "Return to Return on Investment," *Harvard Business Review* (March 1975), pp. 113–119.

6.   *Moody's Handbook of Common Stocks,* Introduction. For further elaboration, see Weston and Brigham, op. cit.

7.   It should be noted that accounting practices may vary significantly from firm to firm and from year to year for a specific firm—which in turn may distort the comparisons of one firm with another and/or one firm with itself on a year-to-year basis. For good examples of some of the distortions that may come up, see: "The Numbers Game—Paper Money," *Forbes* (July 1, 1975), p. 51.

8.   See the discussion of market structure profile life cycles in Part III of the text.

9.   "Liquor Men Feel Like the Morning After," *Business Week* (March 17, 1975), pp. 88–90.

10.   For a discussion of the Ford approach to improving its performance margin, see "Chasing G.M.," *Wall Street Journal* (May 15, 1973), p. 1.

11.   For a discussion of IH's problems and current strategies to overcome these problems, see "New Spur for a Sluggish Giant," *Business Week* (March 17, 1975), pp. 50–54.

12.   "Liquor Men Feel Like the Morning After," *Business Week* (March 17, 1975), pp. 88–90.

13.   "Chasing G.M.," *Wall Street Journal* (May 15, 1973), p. 1.

14.   "New Spur for a Sluggish Giant," *Business Week* (March 17, 1975), pp. 50–54.

15.   *Wall Street Journal* (March 17, 1975).

16.   "New Spur for a Sluggish Giant," *Business Week* (March 17, 1975), p. 50.

17.   For an enlightening discussion of these changes and businesses' response, see: "A Marketing Man Takes Marketers to Task," *Business Week* (July 28, 1975), pp. 42–43.

PART TWO

Building Market Structure Profiles

The firm's growth and performance perspectives constitute the focal point for its growth planning decisions and were the main topic discussed in the first part of the book.

Given certain growth and performance objectives, the firm then must come up with strategies to achieve those objectives. In Parts Two and Three, a new tool—*market structure profile analysis*—is offered to help the firm analyze the whole range of relevant growth opportunities and to select and design an appropriate mix of growth strategies.

In utilizing *market structure profile analysis*, (hereafter, MSP analysis), the firm develops a pragmatically oriented market structure profile for each relevant product line that the firm markets. These profiles themselves are policy oriented in that each profile suggests an appropriate mix of different growth strategies.[1]

The planner begins by estimating industry market potential (IMP) for the product line of concern. In MSP analysis, the words "industry" and "product line" are synonymous and are defined quite narrowly. An industry or product line is comprised of any and all products that do or can perform the same basic function. Industry market potential (IMP) is defined in terms of unit sales potential (versus dollar potential), and IMP equals the number of relevant consumers times the number of use occasions that arise per relevant consumer per operating period (usually one year).

WHY FIRM SALES FALL SHORT OF INDUSTRY MARKET POTENTIAL

Once IMP has been estimated, the task is to explain, in terms of market gaps and marketing gaps, exactly why the firm's own sales in that product line fall short of the IMP. Possible reasons include the following:

- *Lack of a full product line* within the relevant market.
- Absence of or *inadequate distribution* to or within the relevant market.
- *Less than full usage* within the relevant market.
- *Sales of directly competitive brands* within the relevant market.

For each market of concern, the planner attempts to quantify these various "reasons" and presents them in the form of a "market structure profile" such as the one in Figure IIa.

STRATEGIES TO CLOSE MARKET STRUCTURE PROFILE GAPS

Inferences for corporate growth strategies result from each market structure profile. A different type of corporate growth strategy is appropriate for closing each gap appearing in the market structure profile. Figure IIb lists some possible strategies and shows which gap each attempts to close.

As implied in Fig. IIb, market structure profiles can by themselves suggest what corporate growth strategies are most appropriate in individual markets (for each separate profile). As a general rule, strategies designed to close the largest market profile gaps will be the most marginally productive. That is, more sales per dollar of input are likely to result from strategies designed to close the larger market profile gaps. This generalization is certainly not true in every case but is logical and valid in most instances.

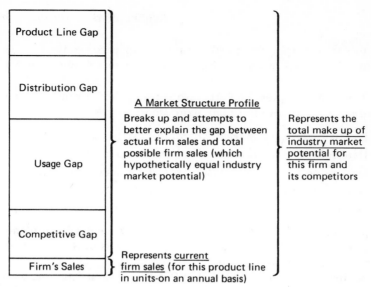

FIGURE IIa. Market structure profile example (would be expressed in units—on an annual basis).

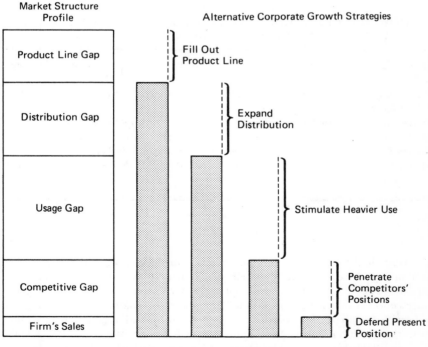

FIGURE IIb. Interrelationships between market profile gaps and corporate growth strategies.

Alternative corporate growth strategies, in turn, convert quite directly into the design of advertising themes and marketing programs in general.

The various chapters of Part Two consider how to develop market structure profiles. Involved are five basic steps:

- Estimate *industry market potential* (IMP) (Chapter 4).
- Determine size of *product line gap* (Chapters 5 and 6).
- Determine size of *distribution gap* (Chapters 7 and 8).
- Determine size of *usage gap* (Chapter 9).
- Determine size of *competitive gap* (Chapter 10).

These chapters include notes on the development and implementation of growth strategies relating to the various parts of the market structure profile under consideration.

The final section of the text, Part Three, considers specifically some of the many ways market structure profile analysis can be used to help a firm make better growth planning decisions. A summary of some of these uses appears in Table II.

Table II
HOW MARKET STRUCTURE PROFILE ANALYSIS CAN HELP A FIRM PLAN ITS FUTURE SALES VOLUME GROWTH

—Helps firm estimate incremental firm sales likely to result from taking advantage of each growth opportunity.
—Gives firm a new, supplementary structure for analyzing product and industry life cycles.
—Gives firm a new tool for predicting and analyzing competitive behavior.
—Is particularly helpful for comparing and analyzing international markets.
—Gives firm a new and meaningful basis for segmenting markets.
—Gives firm a common point of reference for comparing and evaluating different product lines.

NOTE

1.   Most of the logic and concepts involved in deevloping and using market structure profiles have been developed earlier—by other practitioners and scholars. The uniqueness of this tool centers about the integration of these older concepts into a new operational framework of analysis. The thoughts of Robert S. Weinberg were particularly influential and stimulating in providing an initial direction and mode of inquiry. See: Robert S. Weinberg, "Top Management Planning and the Computer," Chemical Marketing Research Association (December 1965 meeting, Cleveland, Ohio).

4

Industry Market Potential

The first task involved in building a market structure profile is to estimate the industry market potential (IMP) for the firm's relevant product line. In initially making IMP estimates, four precautions should be kept in mind:

(1) Define each product line narrowly.
(2) Make estimates in terms of unit sales rather than dollar sales.
(3) Develop initial estimates for one operating period (usually one year).
(4) Limit the IMP estimates to consideration of the United States market only (temporarily ignore the potentials in the international market).

A clarification of each of these precautions is necessary.

DEFINE EACH PRODUCT LINE QUITE NARROWLY

A broad or generic definition of industry is appropriate when a firm is concerned with defining its new product horizons. Chapter 1

61

elaborated upon this point. Recall, for example, the discussion under the section "Definition of a Firm's Business as a Synergistic Advantage."

When one is defining industry market potential (IMP), however, the terms "industry" and "product line" are synonymous, and both terms are defined more narrowly than in Chapter 1. In market structure profile analysis (hereafter MSP analysis), products included in one "industry" are all products (of this firm and of competitors) that do or can perform essentially the same function. Products that do not meet this criterion are not in that industry or product line for the purposes of MSP analysis. For example, a firm may describe particular divisions as a "baby products" division, a "food" division, a "household durables" division, an "office products" division, an "industrial" division, etc. All of these industry or product line definitions are much too broad for MSP analysis.

To estimate IMP for such divisions by using the principles of MSP analysis, these divisions must be broken down further into groups of products that perform the same function. For example, cotton swabs, baby shampoo, disposable diapers, baby powder, and baby oil are all "baby products," but they all fall into separate product lines because they are not functional substitutes for one another.

In line with this, it is important to note that a single product can fall into as many different industries as there are different uses for the product. For example, one can speak of cereal as a breakfast food (one industry) or as a snack (another industry). MSP-related industry or product line definitions will become more obvious as the reader moves through this chapter.

MAKE ESTIMATES IN UNITS, NOT DOLLARS

MSP analysis is concerned primarily with designing and selecting strategies to increase unit sales rather than dollar sales per se. Price change strategies per se are deemphasized so as to focus upon the firm's other growth strategy alternatives. Industry market potentials are defined, therefore, in terms of unit sales rather than dollar sales. One exception to this rule is discussed later in the chapter.

FOCUS UPON DATA FOR ONE OPERATING PERIOD

When estimating IMP for a product line, consider the potential for one operating period (usually one year) only. This becomes particularly relevant when one is estimating IMP for products with expected useful lives of greater than one year. Estimating IMP for such "long-lasting products" is treated later in this chapter.

INITIALLY LIMIT IMP ESTIMATES
TO THE UNITED STATES MARKET

MSP analysis is equally applicable in the United States alone or on a worldwide basis. Given the great diversity in various international markets, however, and inadequate consumer data in most of these markets, the text focuses upon IMP estimates and MSP analysis for the United States market only. MSP analysis for international markets is considered in Part Three (Chapter 13).

DEFINING INDUSTRY MARKET
POTENTIAL (IMP) AND FIRM
SALES (FS)

Industry market potential (IMP) for one use of a product equals the total number of units of the product that could be consumed during one operating period (e.g., one year) if the product were consumed in a full reasonable dose every time a "use occasion" occurred. If one firm sold enough of its own products to meet all of this demand, then that firm's sales (FS) would equal IMP. As one would anticipate, FS always falls short of IMP. One purpose of developing market structure profiles (MSP) is to explain in very graphic terms the assorted reasons why FS falls short of IMP in any given case. Assume, for example, that IMP equals 146 billion units but that FS equals only 8 billion units, as shown in Fig. 4-1. Through the use of MSP analysis, the overall gap between IMP and FS is broken up into a number of separate but interrelated subgaps, each one representing a separate growth opportunity.

ASSUMPTIONS FOR DERIVING IMP

A separate IMP should be determined for each use of the product. Three assumptions are made concerning usage of the product in order to derive IMP:

(1) *Everyone* who could reasonably be expected to use the product is using it.

(2) Everyone who is using it, is using it *on every use occasion.*

(3) *Every time* the product is used, it is used to the *fullest extent possible*—within reason (i.e.. in a full dosage, a full serving, etc.)

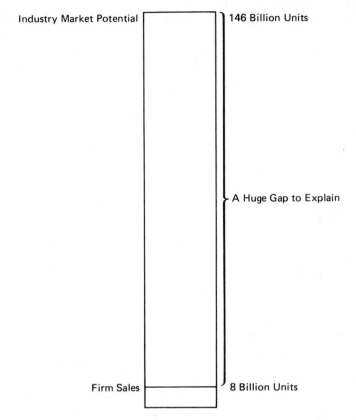

Industry Market Potential — 146 Billion Units

A Huge Gap to Explain

Firm Sales — 8 Billion Units

FIGURE 4-1.   Industry market potential (IMP) versus firm sales
(FS): a huge gap to explain.

As suggested above, it is highly unlikely that these assumptions will
hold for a firm for any of its product lines. *That these assumptions do
not hold is the very essence of and purpose of using IMP as the starting
point for developing a market structure profile.* The assorted reasons as
to exactly *why* one firm's sales (FS) fall short of IMP provide the logic
and basis for deriving the various subgaps in the market structure profile
for each product line of the firm.

Many other methodologies are available to the firm for estimating
market potentials.[1] One shortcoming that most other methods have in
common, however, is that they tend to consider current demand or current industry sales as upper limits to market potential for an individual
firm. Such bases severely underestimate the industry market potential—

particularly for product lines and products that are in early stages of their life cycles. The method of deriving IMP in this text overcomes this problem by considering market potential quite apart from actual sales at a given point of time. Only later on, when usage gaps are incorporated (a later chapter in Part Two), do actual sales come into the picture. Industry market potentials (i.e., IMPs) do, therefore, tend to be higher when one is using this approach to estimate market potentials than when one is using most other approaches.

ESTIMATING IMP IN THE SIMPLEST CASE

The simplest type of product for which to estimate IMP is a consumer product which has only one use and which is consumed in less than one year. Hamburgers, cigarettes, mouthwash, toothpaste, chewing gum, disposable diapers, beer, and innumerable other consumer nondurables fall into this category.

To derive IMP for any of these products, specific estimates must be made concerning the three assumptions mentioned above. Considering mouthwash, for example, how many "potential users" are there (assumption 1)? How many "use occasions" arise per user per year (assumption 2)? What is defined as "full use" for each use occasion (assumption 3)?

To help answer these questions, the firm has available United States census data, studies done by trade associations and commercial market research houses, the firm's own reservoir of previous research findings, and the firm's capabilities for doing new primary research or contracting such new research out to a market research house.[2] A high degree of accuracy in estimating IMP is *not necessary*. What is required is a *good ball park figure*, which can be adjusted later, if desired, to reflect subsequent findings.

Exhibit 4-1 presents an estimate of IMP for mouthwash.

ESTIMATING IMP FOR A PRODUCT WITH MORE THAN ONE USE

What is the IMP of cereal? As normally thought of, cereal is a breakfast food. It is not difficult to envision, however, a young child eating cereal as a snack after school. How much more difficult is it to imagine an adult munching on one of the many "natural" cereals while watching the late show? The point is, cereal has at least two separate potentials—one as a breakfast food, and another as a snack. A separate

Exhibit 4-1
ESTIMATING INDUSTRY MARKET POTENTIAL (IMP)
FOR MOUTHWASH

Number of Potential Users (Assumption 1)—*in United States only*
   —Assume that everyone 5 years and older is a potential user.
   —Five years and older = approximately 90 percent of the United States
   population (Source: *U.S. Statistical Abstract*)
   —United States Population = approximately 222 million (late 1970's—same
   source)
* —Number of potential users = 90% (222 m) = **200 million people**

Number of Use Occasions Per Year (Assumption 2)
   —Assume that each potential user can use mouthwash twice each day.
* —Number of use occasions per year
      = 200 million people × 2/day × 365 days
                      = **146 billion use occasions per year**
                      (in United States only)

Full Use on Each Occasion (Assumption 3)
   —Assume that full use (or full dosage) is one ounce per use occasion.
* —Total IMP = 146 billion ounces per year
      (at an average of 16 oz per bottle, this = 9.125 billion bottles)
* **Result: IMP = 146 billion units**

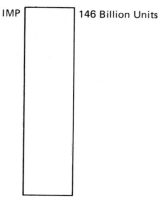

IMP | | 146 Billion Units

set of assumptions (numbers 1, 2, and 3) is necessary for determining each
IMP. Consider the assumptions presented in Table 4-1 for cereal as a
breakfast food and cereal as a snack. The resultant IMP's are presented
in graphic form in Fig. 4-2.

The reader may be inclined to now add the two IMP's to come up
with a total IMP for the product—cereal, in this case. This is not necessary, however, because a composite or total IMP for a product with
multiple uses has no functional value per se in market structure profile
analysis.

Table 4-1
ASSUMPTIONS FOR IMP's FOR CEREAL

Assumption	Cereal as a Breakfast Food	Cereal as a Snack
1. Number of potential consumers	220 million	220 million
2. Number of use occasions	7/week/person *	10/week/person *
3. Full serving size	approximately 1 oz	approximately 1 oz
IMP	200m × 365 × 1 oz = 80.3 billion oz	220m × 520 × 1 oz = 114.4 billion oz

* Estimated by the firm. Estimates on the number of potential use occasions typically start out quite high. This creates no problems or distortions for filling out the rest of the market structure profile (MSP), since these estimates can always be lowered later on, with the profile adjusted accordingly. *Note:* For certain products it is not feasible to attempt to estimate IMP for each possible "extended use." Chapter 9 deals with this problem and offers a pragmatic solution.

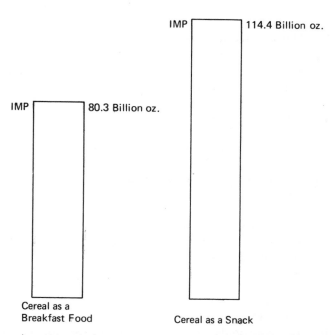

IMP ☐ 114.4 Billion oz.

IMP ☐ 80.3 Billion oz.

Cereal as a Breakfast Food

Cereal as a Snack

Example. Industry Market Potentials for Cereal (A Product with Multiple Uses)

FIGURE 4-2.   Multiple market structure profiles for a product with multiple uses.

ESTIMATING IMP FOR "LONG-LASTING" PRODUCTS

Deriving a useful IMP measure for products with an average useful life of longer than one year is somewhat more complex than the case considered above. Automatic dishwashers or electric garage door openers for household use serve as good examples. (Note, automatic dishwashers for institutional use in restaurants, hospitals, factories, etc. would have a separate IMP. See the previous discussion concerning products with multiple uses. The same principle holds for electric garage door openers and other long-lasting products.)

A problem arises because the firm wants to find IMP for one year at a time. For long-lasting products, IMP for one year is referred to as IMP-short run (or IMP_{SR}). In order to find an accurate IMP_{SR} for automatic dishwashers for the household, the firm must gather the following information:

a. The number of potential users (i.e., the number of households in this case).
b. The number of potential users presently having an automatic dishwasher.
c. The average useful life of an automatic dishwasher.
d. The number of automatic dishwashers sold in each past year covering the last X number of years, where X equals the average useful life of an automatic dishwasher.

Assume that the information gathered is as follows:

a. Number of potential users = 75 million households. (This equals IMP_{LR}—i.e., IMP-long run).
b. Number of households currently with automatic dishwashers. (Approximately 25–30 percent, according to *U.S. Statistical Abstract*—assume 28 percent in 1976. Therefore, automatic dishwashers are in 21 million households in the United States.)
c. Average useful life = 12 years (industry trade data).
d. Sales of automatic dishwashers over each of the past 12 years (see Table 4-2).[3]

The number of automatic dishwashers that could possibly be sold next year (i.e., IMP_{SR}) equals a potential *new user component* (i.e., the number of households not having automatic dishwashers now) *plus a replacement component* (i.e., the number of old household automatic

Table 4-2
ESTIMATED ANNUAL AUTOMATIC DISHWASHER SALES TO HOUSEHOLDS OVER PAST 12 YEARS

1965	1.0
1966	1.15
1967	1.30
1968	1.45
1969	1.60
1970	1.75
1971	1.90
1972	2.05
1973	2.20
1974	2.35
1975	2.50

dishwashers that can be expected to wear out next year). Therefore, IMP_{SR} for household automatic dishwashers equals **55 million units.** Derivation is presented in Table 4-3.

Table 4-3
ESTIMATED IMP (FOR NEXT YEAR) FOR AUTOMATIC DISHWASHERS FOR HOUSEHOLD USE

IMP_{SR} = new user component + replacement component
IMP_{SR} = [IMP_{LR} − units in use now] + replacement of worn-out units (i.e., the number of units sold 12 years ago)
IMP_{SR} = [75 million − 21 million] + 1.0 million
IMP_{SR} = 54 + 1 = **55 million units**

Note that the more mature an industry is and/or the shorter the average useful life is for the product, the more important the replacement component of IMP_{SR} becomes and the less important the new user component becomes.

In a mature industry, where sales have more or less peaked out for a "long-lasting" product and where sales have been steady on a year-to-year basis for some time, IMP_{SR} can be determined quite easily as follows:

$$IMP_{SR} = IMP_{LR} - \text{units in use now} + \frac{\text{units in use now}}{\text{avg. useful life}}$$

For many household durables, it is inaccurate to assume that "full use" means just one per household. The planner should bear this in mind when estimating "full use" in an effort to come up with an accurate IMP_{SR} for such products as refrigerators (what about that extra refrigerator in the basement or garage?), television sets (why not personal TV's?), radios, automobiles, etc.

ESTIMATING IMP FOR SPECIFIC SEGMENTS

One of the more useful tools that the firm has at its disposal today is segmentation. Many different kinds of segmentation have been developed, some of which overlap one another. The more popular forms of segmentation are

- Geographic segmentation
- Demographic segmentation
- Psychographic segmentation
- Segmentation by life styles
- Segmentation by benefits sought
- Customer type segmentation
- Product usage segmentation [4]

The closer a market moves toward maturity and the more competitors who enter the market, the more appropriate it is for a firm to divide the market into segments (using one or more of the segmentation bases listed above). Having done so, the firm studies the segments individually and selects one, two, or possibly all of the segments as "target markets." Subsequently, the firm develops a specific marketing program (i.e., product, distribution, price, and promotion) for each of the target markets.

If the firm has selected one (or more) segment(s) as the target(s) for the firm's marketing effort, it makes sense to separate it out in estimating IMP's as well. In this way, the discriminating power of the market structure profile (MSP) will be focused explicitly upon the target customers. The MSP for an individual segment provides a very useful guide for the firm in developing an overall marketing program for that segment. This point will become more vivid as the reader gains a better understanding of the development and interpretation of the concept of a market structure profile.

Geographic segmentation provides a relatively simple example of the case in point. Coors Beer chooses to limit its distribution to points west of the Mississippi. Coors, in effect, has chosen the western segment of the United States as its target market. The number of potential consumers that Coors uses in estimating its IMP is limited, therefore, to potential consumers west of the Mississippi. If by chance Coors should choose to expand its horizons by going after the eastern segment of the United States as well, Coors could then either group all potential United States beer consumers together into one IMP, *or* Coors could keep the western and eastern segments separate, with a separate IMP, a separate market structure profile (MSP), and a separate marketing program for each segment. This same principle applies regardless of the type of segmentation being used.

ESTIMATING IMP FOR LOCAL FIRMS AND IN OTHER SITUATIONS WHERE A FIRM HAS LIMITED GEOGRAPHIC MARKET HORIZONS FOR A PRODUCT LINE

Many business firms, either by choice or circumstances, face markets that are very limited in a geographic sense. Consider, for example, a local barber shop, a local independent car wash, or a local manufacturer of soft drinks who limits distribution to a 100-mile radius of his plant. It makes little sense for these local firms to define their IMP in terms other than their local market. In a sense, each has segmented the total market geographically and is aiming at a single geographic segment—the local segment.

Larger firms may quite consciously and permanently focus upon particular geographic segments of the market while excluding other geographic segments from their relevant market horizons. For example, a large firm may choose to overlook geographic segments where competition is extremely heavy and/or regions where very small proportions of IMP are located. The relatively heavy costs required to generate each sale in either of these two types of areas might simply not make it worth the firm's while to sell in such markets. When this is the case, these consciously excluded regions should *not* be included as part of the firm's definition of IMP.

If and when the firm's attitudes concerning the geographic limits of its potential market should broaden, then that firm's relevant IMP should expand accordingly.

ESTIMATING IMP WHEN SIGNIFICANT VARIATION OF PRICE EXISTS WITHIN THE RELEVANT PRODUCT LINE

Market structure profiles are intended primarily to offer new insights and perspectives to aid the firm in planning the growth of sales *unit volume*. As mentioned previously (precaution 2) concerning the estimation of IMP, the marketer should express IMP and the subsequent breakdowns of IMP into a market structure profile (MSP) in terms of units rather than dollars.

Given the narrow definition of an "industry" or product line when IMP is being estimated (precaution 1, according to which only products which perform essentially the same function are to be grouped into one "industry" or product line), the alternative elements or members of the product line typically do not vary "significantly" in terms of price.

For the purpose of estimating IMP, "no significant variation of price within a product line" implies that no single unit of one regular model of a product line is more than three or four times as expensive as one single unit of any other regular model of the same product line— with custom made (presumably relatively expensive) items excluded.

Because the prices of the various elements of any product line (as defined in MSP analysis) are not likely to vary significantly, the firm is relatively indifferent as to the product element makeup of unit sales volume growth realized, being primarily concerned with whether and to what extent *overall* unit sales volume growth does indeed occur.

Significant variation of price within the product line does, however, occur in certain instances. When this happens, the firm might desire to build into its MSP a preference for selling models on the higher price end of the product line, since these usually offer the seller greater profits per unit. Ford Motor Company, for example, would rather sell 100 Continentals than 100 Pintos because Ford can reasonably expect to make more in profits on the sale of each $11,000 Continental than on the sale of each $3500 Pinto.

When such variation of price does exist within a product line, the firm should estimate IMP in terms of dollar sales potential (using constant dollars, separating out any inflation component) rather than unit sales potential.

ESTIMATING IMP FOR INDUSTRIAL PRODUCTS AND SERVICES

The market potential for most industrial products and services is more difficult to estimate than the potential for consumer goods and services.

How, for example, can a firm estimate the potential for sheet metal, rivets, computers, machine tools, etc.? No simple solution exists for making such estimates.

The demand for industrial products that serve as components for ultimate consumer goods (e.g., auto steering wheels and brakes) is referred to as "derived demand"—i.e., the demand for the product (e.g., by auto manufacturers) is related directly to the actual demand for the relevant final consumer good. In estimating the market potential for such industrial products, projected demand (not potential) for the final consumer good *should be* considered a constraint. The process of estimating market potential for these industrial products, therefore, revolves around making and/or interpreting demand estimates for the relevant consumer good.

For other types of industrial products, the estimation of market potential can be much more complex.[5]

IMP-RELATED GROWTH OPPORTUNITIES

The firm has four growth opportunities related directly to IMP. These include:

(1) Natural changes in the size of IMP.
(2) Discovery of new uses or new user segments for existing products which can provide new IMP's for the firm's present products.
(3) Innovative product differentiations that can expand existing IMP's.
(4) Introduction of new product lines that provide new IMP's for the firm.

1. NATURAL GROWTH (OR DECLINE) OF IMP CUSTOMER POPULATIONS

Customer populations are in a continual state of flux. For example, Table 4-4(a) shows how the number of United States households has changed over the years. Table 4-4(b) shows variations in the size of different age groups in the United States over time.

As relevant customer populations change, IMP's change—sometimes providing new growth opportunities via "natural growth of IMP" [Fig. 4-3(a)] and at other times leading to a "natural contraction of IMP" [Fig. 4-3(b)].

What has happened to birthrates over the past 30 years provides a good example of the effects that natural changes in the size of IMP

Table 4-4

(a) *Number of U.S. Households Over Time*

% *Increase—10-year Periods*

1940	34.9 million	
1950	42.9	1940–1950 = 22.9%
1960	53.0	1950–1960 = 23.5%
1970	63.5	1960–1970 = 19.8%
1975	69.4	
1980	76.1	1970–1980 = 19.8%
1985	84.2	
1990	87.8	1980–1990 = 15.4%

(b) *U.S. Population by Age Group*

	1950	*1960*	*1970*	*Trend*
Under 5	16.2 million	20.3 million	17.2 million	↘
5–13	22.3	32.7	36.7	↑
14–17	8.5	11.2	15.9	↑
18–20	6.6	7.0	10.8	↑
21–24	9.3	8.6	12.9	↑
25–34	23.9	22.8	24.9	→
35–44	21.5	24.1	23.1	→
45–54	17.4	20.5	23.2	↑
55–64	13.3	15.6	18.6	↑
65 & over	12.3	16.6	19.9	↑
Total	151	179	203	

(Source: *Statistical Abstract of the United States*)

can have upon the marketer. The number of births per 1000 women of childbearing age (15–44) was 69.3 in 1974—down from 87.9 per 1000 in 1970 and 122.9 per 1000 in 1957, the postwar high. Reflecting this trend, Gerber's (baby food) sales dropped in 1973 for the first time in the company's history.

The effects of this decline in IMP for baby products today will be felt by IMP's for other products tomorrow. "There is a ripple effect working here," says William H. Francis, Gerber's resident demographer. "I have a friend at Upjohn who called the other day, and when I kidded him about his industry and its pill putting us out of business, he said, 'Sure, but remember that 20 years from now, we're out of business.' Eventually, everyone gets hit. You'll see it next in the nurseries, then the grade schools, high schools, colleges, in marriages, the furniture purchases for first homes, and so on. Today's birth dearth will have to pass through a whole generation before it works its way out and before the next population wave comes through, whatever that wave is." [6]

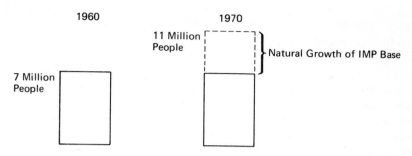

(a) Natural Growth of IMP Population Base for IMP's for Products for Age Group 18–20

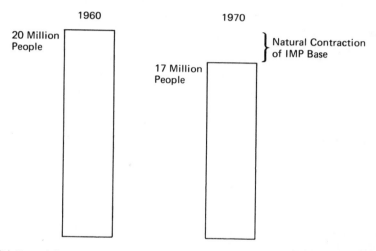

(b) Natural Contraction of IMP Population Base for IMPs for Products for Age Group 0–5

FIGURE 4-3.

AFFLUENCE: THE IMPORTANCE OF INCOME GROWTH AS A DETERMINANT OF IMP GROWTH. Recall assumption 1 in estimating IMP: "Everyone who could *reasonably* be expected to use the product." In coming up with a reasonable estimate of the number of potential customers, income of different consumers or groups of consumers can be an important consideration.

Income severely limits the IMP's of significant population segments —particularly in less developed and in developing countries—for a great number of products that most people in the United States regard as "necessities." While income is very obviously an IMP determinant for most products in such foreign markets, income can also be an important determinant for many products in the United States market. The economist typically refers to the relationship between income and the likely purchase of a particular product as the "income elasticity" of the product for people with particular incomes.

In estimating IMP's for particular products in the United States, excluding some income segments from IMP is realistic when the marketer has convincing evidence that the income of such segments is so limited that, despite the marketer's attempt to induce purchase, the purchase of the product by such segments is highly unlikely. The IMP's for leisure travel by air, central home air conditioning, legal services, movie cameras, and second homes serve as rather obvious examples. On the other hand, if the real incomes of these segments rise over time, then the seller of such products can appropriately recognize a growth in the IMP for his products in order to reflect the rising affluence of such segments.

Despite this point concerning the relevance of income as an IMP determinant, the firm developing MSP's should beware not to look at existing average demand levels for various income segments as a basis for estimating IMP for the various segments. Such an approach contracts IMP much too drastically and distorts the market structure profile. More specifically, that approach overlooks the possibilities of growth by means of stimulating the customer to spend a greater proportion of his income than he traditionally has on the relevant product line.

As a concluding note concerning the potential effect of personal income changes upon the size of IMP, in economic hard times when inflation and/or unemployment are on the rise and when real incomes are declining, the size of IMP's may contract as the number of relevant potential customers declines due to decreasing incomes.

2. NEW USES OR NEW USER SEGMENTS FOR EXISTING PRODUCTS MEAN NEW IMP's

NEW USES. Many products have more than one use. Firms can realize and take advantage of new opportunities by coming up with and promoting new uses for their existing products. Given the relatively narrow definition of "industry" or product line (as considered previously) when IMP is estimated, each alternative use for a product represents a separate IMP and a separate market structure profile. In effect, what the firm is doing is *segmenting* the market *in terms* of *product usage* and then treating each segment as a separate growth opportunity.

The sales of Arm & Hammer baking soda have been stimulated through the promotion of new uses for that product: "Back in 1971," says Arm & Hammer's marketing vice president, "we were in 92 percent of United States households, but our actual consumption as a baking ingredient had leveled off because baking itself had leveled off." So bginning that year, Arm & Hammer started promoting the cleansing and deodorizing values of its baking soda and advertised it first as a bath additive. Almost immediately, they experienced a 15 percent improvement in case sales. Next, the company began pushing Arm & Hammer as a kitchen cleaner, and sales jumped another 10 percent.

Since then, Arm & Hammer has been promoted for everything from deodorizing refrigerators, automobile ashtrays, and kitty litter boxes to controlling acidity in swimming pools. In some markets, each new application increased sales as much as 50 to 60 percent. "And this is just the beginning," says the marketing vice president, pointing to a doubling of sales since 1970 (to $44.7 million last year) and a tripling of profits (to $2.5 million). "We are still developing entirely new products," he says. "but in these times of inflation and shortages, you must also milk the products you already have out there. And that will be one of our prime avenues of growth through the 1970's." [7]

Clorox bleach (see Exhibit 4-2) and Real Lemon provide other examples of products that have been marketed with alternative uses being considered—i.e., additional IMP's and market structure profiles.

NEW USER SEGMENTS. The discovery of segments that heretofore have not been included in IMP estimates for a product also provides new growth opportunities for the firm in the form of new IMP's. The reaction of some "baby products companies" to the plight described previously provides a good example of this phenomenon. Faced with a decline in the size of the traditional market for its baby products, Johnson and Johnson began promoting its baby shampoo, baby oil, and baby powder to a new segment, the adult segment—a segment and a separate IMP which up to that time had not been explicitly recognized by Johnson and Johnson or other "baby products" firms in their growth strategies.

3. INNOVATIVE PRODUCT DIFFERENTIATION CAN EXPAND (OR CONTRACT) EXISTING IMP's

Before the introduction of the microelectronic chip into calculators, an IMP for "calculators for home use" (primarily mechanical adding machines) did already exist—along with an IMP for "calculators for business use." The invention of a low-cost, multiple-function electronic calculator was such a dramatic innovation and improvement (product differentiation) over mechanical calculators that the IMP for "calculators for home use" (i.e., potential of one per household) was expanded to an IMP for a "personal calculator" market (i.e., potential of one for each person able to use such a calculator).

Clorox. If you thought your sink was sunk.

Clorox gets out stubborn stains without scrubbing or scratching! Just run two inches warm water into sink, pour in ¾ cup Clorox® liquid bleach. Swish solution around, let stand 5 minutes. Then simply drain away many stubborn food stains—even tea and grape juice—as well as germs and odors.

Remove coffee and tea stains from coffee pots, tea pots and cups. Just soak 5-10 min. in solution of 3 tbs. Clorox to quart of hot water. Rinse. (Not for metal pots.)

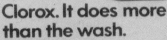

Clorox. It does more than the wash.

©1974 The Clorox Company.

What happened in effect in the calculator market was that the product differentiation was significant enough and attractive enough to justify a change in the derivation of IMP for the calculator market. This change increased the number of potential buyers as a proportion of the population because of the vastly improved price/performance of the new electronic calculator versus the older mechanical adding machine.

At various points of time historically, similar differentiations have occurred in the production and operating technologies for radios, television sets, and other electronic household products. In each case, sometimes gradually and sometimes rapidly, an expansion of the definition of IMP for the relevant product has been justified, thus reflecting a new growth opportunity for the relevant industry.

In the case of long-lasting products (i.e., products with an average useful life of greater than one year), significant product differentiations not only add to the "new user component" of IMP_{SR} (review the section covering IMP for long-lasting products) but can also increase the size of the replacement component of IMP_{SR}. The logic is that the new differentiation may stimulate present users to replace their old model with the new model while the old model is still quite functional. Color television sets, solid state television sets, pot-scrubbing dishwashers, energy-saving dishwashers, high-mileage automobiles, etc. serve as possible examples of this phenomenon.

Significant product differentiations can sometimes result in the erosion of IMP rather than resulting in new growth opportunities through increasing IMP. This is particularly true in mature markets and applies equally as well to both long-lasting products and products with an average useful life of less than one year. In mature markets for these products, most potential users are already using the product. Look at the kinds of differentiation that frequently occur in such markets. Gillette comes out with a stainless steel blade, a platinum blade, etc.—each "differentiated" blade giving more shaves than its predecessor. Goodyear comes out with a 50,000-mile tire. In these cases, the differentiation is introduced in an effort to grow via defending present market share or via capturing a greater market share of the existing mature market—without much hope of bringing about an increase in IMP and a related increase in firm sales. Such differentiations, related to building more durability into the relevant product(s) in mature markets, erode rather than expand IMP.[8]

4. NEW PRODUCT LINES MEAN NEW IMP'S

As discussed in Chapter 1, when a firm's present sales and its sales projections leave the firm short of its overall sale and profit growth goals, the time may have come for the firm to consider venturing into new product lines. Each new product line introduced represents a new IMP and a new market structure profile—possibly a number of IMP's depending upon whether and to what extent the firm recognizes multiple uses for and/or user segments of the new product.

In providing the firm with a new IMP, each new product line introduced by a firm represents a new growth opportunity. In response to declining potentials in the baby market, Motherhood Maternity Shops introduced a new line of nonmaternity clothes for women, adding to its promotion campaign the note, "You don't have to be pregnant to shop at Motherhood." In response to those same pressures, Gerber has entered the single-serving foods market (with "Singles") and other adult food markets, including peanut spread and catsup.[9]

Because of the very real phenomenon of product and industry life cycles, very few firms can achieve continual growth of sales and profits over the long run without adding new product lines (and, therefore, new IMP's) with some regularity. This is true for large firms and for smaller firms.

SUMMARY

Estimating industry market potential (IMP) is the first step to take in building a market structure profile (MSP).

A number of precautions should be taken in developing IMP estimates. Each product line should be defined narrowly. Potential should be defined in terms of units rather than dollars and should be estimated for one operating period (e.g., one year). Finally, IMP estimates in this chapter were confined to the United States market only.

An IMP estimate itself is made by assuming that:

(1) Everyone who could reasonably be expected to use the product is using it.
(2) Everyone who is using it is using it on every "use occasion."
(3) The product is used to the fullest extent possible (within reason) —i.e., full serving or full dosage—every time is it used.

The first example presented was the estimation of IMP in the simplest case—where a product has only one use and is consumed in less than one year. IMP estimates followed for products with multiple uses, for "long-lasting" products, for specific segments, for local firms, for situations where significant variation of price exists within the relevant product line, and for industrial products and services.

The chapter concluded with a discussion of four IMP-related

growth opportunities, including: natural changes in the size of IMP, discovery of new uses or new user segments for a firm's existing products, innovative product differentiations, and a firm's introduction of new product lines.

REVIEW QUESTIONS

1. In market structure profile (MSP) analysis, how broadly should a product line be defined?

2. How can personal income affect the estimation of the number of potential customers for a product?

3. For MSP analysis, should the user add up the IMP's for all of the various possible uses and/or segments recognized? Explain.

4. Why and how does the estimation of IMP for long-lasting products differ from the estimation of IMP for products normally consumed during a single operating period?

5. Under what circumstances should a firm define separate profiles for different segments of a market?

6. How does the estimation of IMP differ for local firms as opposed to national or regional firms?

7. Under what circumstances should IMP and the breakup of the market structure profile be defined in terms of dollars, rather than units?

8. How does the estimation of IMP differ for industrial products as opposed to final consumer products?

9. Under what circumstances might IMP decrease over time?

10. How can personal income affect the estimation of the number of potential customers for a product?

11. Should a firm recognize a separate IMP and MSP for every single possible "extended use" of a product?

NOTES

1. For examples of other methodologies for estimating market potentials for consumer markets, see: H. D. Wolfe and D. W. Twedt, "Establishing Market Potentials," Chapter 6 of *Planning and Managing the Promotional Mix* (Madison, Wis.: Wolfe and Twedt, 1967), pp. 93–110; P. Kotler, "Market Measurement and Forecasting," Chapter 7 of *Marketing Management* (Englewood Cliffs, N.J.: Prentice-Hall, Inc., 1972), pp. 355–63; and John J. Brion, *Corporate Marketing Planning* (New York: John Wiley & Son, Inc., 1967). For methodologies estimating market potentials in industrial markets, see: *Appraising the*

Market for New Industrial Products (New York: National Industrial Conference Board, 1968), especially pp. 65–98; M. E. Stern, "Assessing Market Opportunities" in *Market Planning* (New York: McGraw-Hill, Inc., 1967); P. Kotler, op. cit., Chapter 7; H. D. Wolfe and D. W. Twedt, op. cit., Chapter 6; J. J. Brion, op. cit., pp. 364–74; and *Sales Analysis* (New York: National Industrial Conference Board, 1969), especially pp. 18, 25, 34.

2.   For quick access to demographic data such as the number of people of certain ages, living in certain places, etc., see the annual edition of the *U.S. Statistical Abstract*. For industry reports, consult the *F & S Index* at the library and/or contact industry trade sources for references to additional trade or commercial studies of various markets.

3.   If b and c are correct, the average yearly sales over the past 12 years have been 1.75 million units per year (i.e., 21 m ÷ 12 years = 1.75 m). Industry data show accelerating sales over the past 12 years. In 1965, only approximately 10 percent of the households had automatic dishwashers. That figure rose to 17 percent by 1970 and approximately 28 percent by 1976. Given those figures, annual automatic dishwasher sales can be estimated.

4.   For discussions of the motivation, methodologies, and uses of segmentation as a marketing strategy, see: W. Smith, "Product Differentiation and Market Segmentation as Alternative Marketing Strategies," *Journal of Marketing* (July 1956), p. 108; J. F. Engel, et al., eds., *Market Segmentation: Concepts and Applications,* Holt, Rinehart, and Winston, 1972; and R. E. Frank, et al., *Market Segmentation,* Prentice-Hall, Inc., 1972.

5.   No attempt is made to cover the wide range of techniques used for estimating market potential for these other types of industrial goods and services. The interested reader should refer to the sources mentioned in footnote 1, which do present many methods of making such estimates.

6.   "The Lower Birthrate Crimps the Baby Food Market," *Business Week* (July 13, 1974), p. 45. Similar changes take place in the IMP for industrial products as the economy moves through economic cycles and buyers change their desired inventory levels.

7.   "Toward Higher Margins and Less Variety," *Business Week* (September 14, 1974), p. 100.

8.   Recall that IMP is defined in terms of units. Increased prices of the new product versus the old can offset the decline in IMP if IMP were expressed in terms of dollars. It is also important to note in considering differentiation as a growth tool that the differentiated product may eat into the firm's own present product sales. For example, did Ford Pinto capture sales from the import auto market or from the Ford Mustang and the Ford Fairlane market? This possible phenomenon of "cannibalism" must be carefully considered in evaluating the overall net results of a new product introduction. The next chapter considers this phenomenon in greater depth.

9.   Op. cit., *Business Week* (July 13, 1974), pp. 45–50.

5

Product Line Gaps:
Description and Measurement

One reason why an individual firm's sales fall far short of its IMP's is because each firm has product line gaps of one sort or another. This chapter examines the various types of product line gaps and their measurement. The following chapter (Chapter 6) discusses the firm's growth opportunities relating to either directly closing product line gaps or to creating new product line elements through innovation or significant product differentiation.

DIFFERENT TYPES OF PRODUCT
LINE GAPS

As many different types of product line gaps exist as there are methods of expanding present product lines. In considering the various types of product line gaps below, keep in mind the relatively narrow definition of "product line" used when market structure profiles are developed. Briefly recall that definition from Chapter 4: Products falling into an individual "industry" or product line are those products that do or can perform the same functions.

As a general principle, the more mature an industry becomes in terms of its industry life cycle, the more different types and variations of a product emerge. Related directly to this point, the generalization can be made that the more mature an industry becomes, the more different variations of a product an individual firm must come up with in order to avoid an expansion in its product line gap. For example, when microwave ovens for household use were first introduced, there was little "differentiation" in the market. Each competitor marketed a single model or possibly two models and regarded its major marketing task as that of informing and convincing nonusers of the advantages of microwave ovens versus traditional ovens. As significant blocks of consumers were "converted," it became important for individual competitors to differentiate their products (and later to aim at specific individual segments of the market) in order to ensure the firm of a share of the growing market. The differentiation itself led to the expansion of product lines in terms of size, color, options, and price.

Similar phenomena occur in other markets. In the late 1960's and early 1970's, Gillette began promoting the "Dry Look" for men—the first task being to get men to use a hair spray. By 1974, Gillette had expanded their "Dry Look" line to include an After Shampoo Control, and the Dry Look spray came with an adjustable spray valve and in three types: Regular, Extra-Hold, and the Dry Look for Oily Hair.

SIZE-RELATED PRODUCT LINE GAPS

Perhaps the most generalizable of all product line gaps are gaps related to product size. As markets mature, product size can become an important competitive tool for differentiating the products of one competitor from those of other competitors.

Product "size" can be defined along many different dimensions. Product size can refer to the *container size* for consumables such as soft drinks or detergents, to *capacity* for durables such as refrigerators, water heaters, or computers, or to *power* for lawn and garden tractors, automobile engines, or industrial machinery. A firm interested in defining its "size-related product line gaps" or interested in differentiating its own product(s) by expanding its product line(s) in terms of sizes offered should closely consider all of the possible dimensions of size in making such calculations or decisions.

OPTIONS-RELATED PRODUCT LINE GAPS

In consumer durables, an almost unlimited variation and number of optional features can be offered by a firm desiring to cater to specific demands of individual customers. By making such features available, the firm differentiates its products from competitive products.

Automobiles serve as one good example of the case in point. Ford's options, for example, relate to engine, transmission, rear-end gear ratio, differential, suspension system, brakes, power assists, comfort and convenience features, seating (upholstery and type of seats), floor covering, special instruments, external trim, tires, luggage rack, and other equipment. In addition to variations in these options, Ford makes available automobiles in different sizes (subcompact, compact, etc.), types (two-door sedan, two-door hardtop, etc.) and colors. The various sizes are treated as potential product line gaps separate from options per se. Given all of the product option categories and the variety of choices available in each, Ford can produce tens of thousands of automobiles, each one in some way different from every other one.

Similar sets of options are available in other consumer durables such as refrigerators, projectors, televisions, etc. Many options are attractive to marketers not only because they provide more thorough product line coverage but also because they offer an opportunity for incremental revenues. Consider the $400 for air conditioning, or $200 for automatic transmission on automobiles, for example.

Attachable options are particularly attractive because they do not have to be purchased all at one time by the consumer. Simplicity markets a whole line of "quick-switching attachments" for its lawn and garden tractors, including rotary mowers (of various sizes), rotary tillers (of various sizes), a cultivator, a spring tooth harrow, a weed cutter, a lawn roller, a vacuum collector, a dozer blade/snow plow, a dump cart, a front-end loader, a leaf mulcher, wheel weights and counterweights, and others. Each of these attachable options represents potential additional revenue for Simplicity, and at the same time enhances the attractiveness of the basic product (the tractor) itself. "You are buying a lot more than a lawn mower when you purchase the Simplicity tractor."

STYLE-, COLOR-, FLAVOR-, AND FRAGRANCE-RELATED PRODUCT LINE GAPS

Other product line gaps that a firm can face are related to style, color, flavor, and/or fragrance, depending upon the nature of the product.

Style and color can be important in customer purchases of clothing and consumer durables such as furniture, appliances, and automobiles. Footjoy, for example, has expanded its golf shoe product line to include 62 separate styles and colors. Texture can also be an important variable in purchasing decisions regarding fabrics (e.g., clothing and furniture). In the case of consumables, such as food and drink products, liquors, tobaccos, toiletries, etc., flavors and fragrances can become important means of expanding product lines for individual firms—and, therefore, creating product line gaps for other firms. Multiple-flavored Koogle peanut spreads, Jello gelatin, Hi-C soft drinks, Campbell's soups, Sealtest ice cream, and Post cereals serve as examples for everyday food and drink products. In other product areas, multiple flavors and/or fragrances are just as important: Borkum Riff markets bourbon, cognac, rum, cherry liqueur, and champagne pipe tobacco; Liroux markets 48 flavors of "international liqueurs"; Rise markets regular, menthol, and lime shaving creams; and English Leather markets a whole line of different after-shave fragrances, etc.

FORM-RELATED PRODUCT LINE GAPS

Individual customers or groups of customers may find one *form* of a product more attractive than another. Each different form of the product available represents a new possible product line gap for any firm selling that product. Possible dimensions of form include:

(1) Method or principle of operation.
(2) Range of operation.
(3) Product format.
(4) Product composition.
(5) Form of container.

Most products are defined along more than a single one of these form dimensions. Most product lines, therefore, have many possible form-related product line gaps.

The first form dimension, *method or principle of operation,* has a different meaning for different products. Lawn mowers can be reel or rotary, power or nonpower. Power mowers can be gasoline or electric, walking or sitting. Electric power mowers can be cord or battery. All of these represent different forms of the product—in terms of different principles of operation—and as such, different potential product line gaps.

Pencils, fountain pens, ball points, eversharps, and felt tips all perform the same basic function or task. Each product, however, accomplishes the task through a slightly different principle or method of operation. The same generalization is true for other products such as shaving systems (bonded blade systems, twin edge systems, injector systems, razor band systems, traditional safety razor systems, and electric razors of varying types) and tires (two-ply, four-ply, belted, radials). Each product type relies upon a slightly different technology for accomplishing the same basic task.

Another dimension of form for some products is *range of operation*. Range here is *not* meant to have a quality connotation (i.e., the mileage range of a tire). Range here refers rather to the range of variation in the *type* of product performance desired. Shock absorbers are available in a range from those delivering a soft ride to those delivering a harder ride, yet more stable handling. Golf club shafts are available in a flex range from light to extra stiff. Shampoos are available for hair ranging from dry to oily, and so on.

A third dimension of form relevant for many products is *product format*—i.e., in what format the product is available. Desenex (for athlete's foot) comes in powder, ointment, or spray-on form. Antacids come in chewable (Rolaids), swallowable (Di-Gel), liquid (Pepto Bismol), effervescent powder (Bromo Seltzer), or effervescent tablet (Alka Seltzer) form. Dog food comes in cans (Alpo), nuggets (Purina Dog Chow), or individual servings (Gaines Burgers). Margarine is available in tubs or sticks, in whipped form or solid form.

Product composition is a fourth dimension of form. Margarine can vary in composition (corn oil, vegetable oil, etc.). So too can the composition of many other products such as skis (wood, steel, fiberglass, plastic, nylon), razor blades (steel, stainless steel, chromium, platinum, Teflon-coated), and many others.

A final dimension of form that can cause product line gaps is related to *product containers*. Soft drinks come in resealable bottles, nonresealable bottles, returnable bottles, throwaway bottles, easy-open cans, and regular cans. Window cleaners are available in finger sprayer or a trigger sprayer, etc. Reusable containers (e.g., the jelly jar that becomes a glass) are an additional possible container form dimension.

As mentioned above, more than a single one of these form dimensions may be relevant for a single product line. A firm marketing a product line may, therefore, face several different types of form-related product line gaps.

QUALITY-RELATED (AND PRICE-RELATED) PRODUCT LINE GAPS

The range of quality and price within a product line provides yet more potential product line gaps for a marketer.

"Price lining" has long been a popular practice used by marketers to provide consumers with a choice of products differentiated from one another by overall quality. Items on the high end of the price line are presumably (from the manufacturer's, the marketer's, and the consumer's point of view) of higher overall quality than items on the lower end of the price line. *Figure 5-1*, for example, shows suit brands sold by

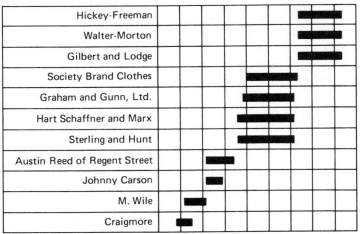

	$50	75	100	125	150	175	200	250	300	350
Hickey-Freeman								████		
Walter-Morton								████		
Gilbert and Lodge								████		
Society Brand Clothes					████					
Graham and Gunn, Ltd.				████						
Hart Schaffner and Marx				████						
Sterling and Hunt				████						
Austin Reed of Regent Street		██								
Johnny Carson		██								
M. Wile	██									
Craigmore	██									

Source: Hart Schaffner and Marx (Chicago), Annual Report, 1972. p.6.

FIGURE 5-1.

Hart Schaffner & Marx and its manufacturing subsidiaries and is arranged in terms of price and quality. Other apparel manufacturers do the same.

Sporting goods manufacturers market tennis rackets, golf clubs, basketballs, etc. in a range from beginner's models (low price) up to professional models (high price). Brewers do the same with their beers. Anheuser Busch, for example, markets Michelob, Budweiser, and Busch. Carpet manufacturers produce and sell carpets that look quite similar but actually vary significantly from one another in terms of density of the pile (and, therefore, in price as well).

DISTRIBUTOR BRAND-RELATED PRODUCT LINE GAPS

Many well-known manufacturers realize significant proportions of their sales through selling to retailers (or occasionally wholesalers) who then put their own brand names on the products. Major tire manufacturers (e.g., Goodyear) make "Atlas Tire" for Standard Oil. Major appliance manufacturers (e.g., Whirlpool) make Kenmore appliances for Sears. Major food producers and processors (e.g., Heinz) produce private labels for A & P, Kroger, Safeway, etc.[1] These are all examples of "dealer" or "distributor" brands and represent another type of sales growth opportunity for manufacturers.

Many manufacturers regard such private brands strictly as competition and refuse to produce such brands. For manufacturers with this attitude (e.g., Maytag and Polaroid), private brands *do not* represent a product line gap. For manufacturers who recognize the private brand market as a separate segment, however (e.g., General Electric and Kodak), private brands certainly *can* account for product line gaps. Levis might increase their sales significantly if they distributor-branded through Sears as well as selling under their own Levis brand name. The advantages and disadvantages of attempting to expand sales in such a fashion have been discussed in depth elsewhere.[2] Suffice it to say here that such possibilities can constitute yet another form of product line gap.

SEGMENT-RELATED PRODUCT LINE GAPS

A firm using segmentation divides the market into separate segments based upon one of the alternative segmentation dimensions or methods reviewed in Chapter 4. The firm then develops a special marketing program (product, distribution, promotion, and price) for each segment that it chooses as a "target market." For each segment recognized, the firm defines a separate IMP—as indicated in· Chapter 4. A firm has a product line gap equal to IMP for any segment for which the firm does not have a product [e.g., the anticavity segment for Lever Bros.—Fig. 5-2(a)]. For segments to which the firm does offer a product,

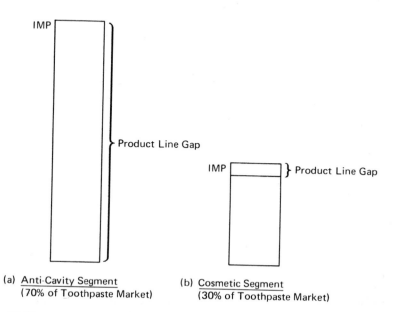

(a) Anti-Cavity Segment
(70% of Toothpaste Market)

(b) Cosmetic Segment
(30% of Toothpaste Market)

FIGURE 5-2. Lever Bros. product line gaps in the toothpaste market before introducing Aim.

it is possible for the firm to have any of the various kinds of product line gaps discussed above. The following example clarifies this point.

One way to segment the toothpaste market is by "benefits sought." [3] Typical segments are the "anticavity" segment (approximately 70 percent of the market) and the "cosmetic" segment (approximately 30 percent of the market). Up until the mid-1970's, Lever Bros. had two entries for the cosmetic market (Pepsodent and Close-Up) but did not have a product for the anticavity segment—which represents a separate IMP. For the anticavity segment, therefore, Lever Bros. had a 100 percent product line gap. [See Fig. 5-2(a)].

In the cosmetic segment, Lever Bros. may well have had a product line gap as well, but such a gap would have been related to size or flavor—not to the absence of any market entry whatsoever for the segment. For example, see the small gap depicted in Fig. 5-2(b) for Lever Bros. in the cosmetics segment. By introducing Aim toothpaste in 1974, Lever Bros. closed most of its product line gap in the anticavity segment. Note that a product line gap still may have existed (see Fig. 5-3(a)) because of size, flavor, or texture gaps (e.g., Aim was marketed as a "gel" as opposed to paste).

Similar analyses are not difficult to envision for soft drinks (e.g., sugar segment versus sugar-free or diet segment), cigarettes (e.g., flavor segment versus low tar segment), and so on.

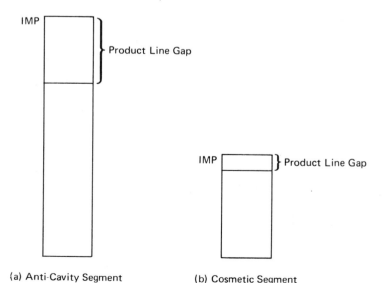

(a) Anti-Cavity Segment   (b) Cosmetic Segment

FIGURE 5-3.   Lever Bros. product line gaps in the toothpaste market after introducing Aim.

ESTIMATING THE SIZE OF PRODUCT LINE GAPS

A firm faces a potential product line gap for each IMP that is relevant for the firm. A product line gap is expressed as a proportion of IMP. The derivation of the product line gap constitutes the second step in building a market structure profile (MSP).

The firm begins deriving a product line gap by specifying the alternative elements that it recognizes in the product line. For a particular product line, elements of the product line can be defined along any of the different dimensions reviewed in the first part of the chapter. Size, options, style, color, flavor, form, quality and/or distributor brand-related product line gaps may exist for each IMP that a firm recognizes.

In enumerating the possible elements of a product line, a firm that is just adding the relevant product line (e.g., firm A) should focus on one or two basic dimensions—whichever ones are most meaningful for the particular product. Flavor, for example, might be the most important dimension for a firm adding cereal as a new product line.

A firm that has been selling cereal for some time, however, (e.g., firm B) should include more dimensions in its enumeration of possible elements of the product line. Relevant dimensions for this firm for the cereal market might include flavor, size (box size), product composition, and others. Exhibit 5-1 enumerates the possible elements as they might be viewed by these two firms—one that is just now adding the product line [5-1(a)] and another that has marketed the product line for some time [5-1(b)] (see page 92).

Keep in mind in the analysis that each separate use of the product has a separate IMP. In this case (cereal), the IMP used in the following example is the IMP for cereal as a breakfast food (i.e., excluding other uses for cereal—e.g., cereal as a snack).

Frequently, firm sales breakdowns and/or industrywide sales breakdowns along the product line dimension desired by the firm may simply not be available or may be too expensive to generate or acquire. In such cases, *data availability may become the key criteria for selecting the relevant dimension(s)* for differentiation among product line elements.

ESTIMATING THE SIZE OF THE FULL PRODUCT LINE GAP (FPLG)

The next step is to estimate the market potential for each product line element recognized by the firm (e.g., regular, sugar-coated, and natural cereals). Since present industrywide sales fall short of IMP,

Exhibit 5-1
ENUMERATING THE ELEMENTS OF THE
PRODUCT LINE: EXAMPLE—CEREAL

(a) *Elements for a Firm Just Adding Cereal as a Product Line*
Relevant Product Line Dimension: Flavor
Three Alternatives: a. Regular Nonsugared Cereal
b. Presweetened Cereals
c. Natural Cereals

(b) *Elements for a Firm Already Selling Cereal for Some Time*
Relevant Product Line Dimensions

Flavor	*Size*	*Product Composition*
a. Regular	d. Individual Size Boxes	g. Wheat-based
b. Presweetened	(1 ounce)	h. Oat-based
	e. Regular Size Boxes	i. Corn-based
	(12 ounce)	j. Rice-based
	f. Family Size Boxes	k. Other
	(18 ounce)	

Listing of 45 Possible Combinations

gad, gae, gaf, gbd, gbe, bge, gcd, gce, gcf
had, hae, haf, hbd, hbe, hbe, hcd, hce, hcf
iad, iae, iaf, ibd, ibe, ibe, icd, ice, icf
jad, jae, jaf, jbd, jbe, jbe, jcd, jce, jcf
kad, kae, kaf, kbd, kbe, kbe, kcd, kce, kcf

Visually Perceived: 45 Possible Alternatives

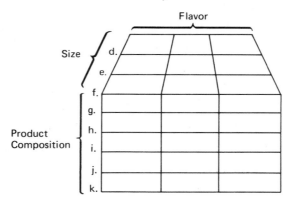

present sales for any individual element of the product line cannot be used as a measure of potential sales for that element. What measure then can be used?

One alternative measure is to use the individual elements' proportions of current industry sales as a basis. Assume, for example, that firm A (the one adding cereal as a new product line) desires to measure its product line gap. Exhibit 5-2 shows an estimate of current industry sales (in terms of unit sales, where one unit equals one ounce —i.e., one full serving) for cereal as a breakfast food, broken down into the three product elements relevant for firm A. If it is assumed that potential sales would match current industry sales in terms of the proportion of sales accounted for by each product line element, firm A has a product line gap equal to 20 percent of IMP, since it sells elements a and c but not element b (presweetened cereal). If an IMP of 80.3 billion units is assumed for cereal as a breakfast food, as derived earlier (see Chapter 4), firm A's full product line gap (FPLG) for cereal as a breakfast food = 20 percent times 80.3 billion = 16.1 billion units.

Exhibit 5-2

FIRM A'S FULL PRODUCT LINE GAP FOR CEREAL
AS A BREAKFAST FOOD

IMP equals 80.3 billion units—derived originally from Table 4-1:

Assumptions	*Cereal as a Breakfast Food*
Number of potential consumers	220 million
Number of use occasions	7/week/person
Full serving size	approximately 1 oz
IMP =	220m × 365 × 1 oz
	80.3 billion oz

Product line gap equals 20 percent of IMP—derived as follows:

Product Line Elements	*Current Industry Sales (in UNITS—where one unit = 1 oz) Cereal as Breakfast Food*	% of Current Industry Sales	Our Firm Sells
(a) Regular cereal	9.375 billion units	50%	x
(b) Presweetened cereal	3.750 billion units	20%	No
(c) Natural cereal	5.625 billion units	30%	x
Total	18.75 billion units	100%	80%

Full product line gap = 100% − 80% = **20% of IMP**

20% of IMP = 20% (80.3 billion units) =
16.06 billion units

Exhibit 5-2 *(Continued)*

Market Structure Profile Reflecting This Gap

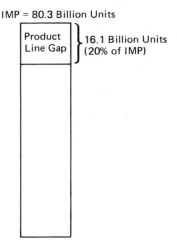

IMP = 80.3 Billion Units

ESTIMATING FULL PRODUCT LINE GAP WHEN A RECENT INNOVATION OR SIGNIFICANT PRODUCT DIFFERENTIATION IS ONE OF THE PRODUCT LINE ELEMENTS

Under certain circumstances, the firm may not want to use product line elements' present proportions of current industry sales as the basis for estimating the potential sales for each element. In cases where a new innovation or significant product differentiation has recently entered the market as a new product line element, the proportions of current industry sales achieved by each product line element may overestimate or underestimate the correct proportions of industry market potential which should be assigned to each product line element. In such cases, proper adjustments should be made.

Envision, for example, the change that took place along these lines when low-priced (under $50) electronic calculators were introduced in the early 1970's. Table 5-1 exemplifies this point. In that case, a firm not producing low-cost mechanical adding machines but producing the other two product line elements would face a product line gap equal to 20 percent, not 80 percent, regardless of the current proportions of industry sales. On the other hand, a firm producing the low-cost mechanical adding machine, but not the other two product line elements, would face a product line gap equal to 80 percent, not 20 percent. (Keep in mind that such innovations can so dramatically improve the price/

Table 5-1

ESTIMATING PROPORTIONS OF IMP FOR
NEW INNOVATIONS OR SIGNIFICANT
PRODUCT DIFFERENTIATION

*Example: % of Current Industry Sales Versus % of IMP for the
Personal Calculator Market in 1972*

Product Line Elements	A % of Industry Sales in 1972 *	B % of Industry Market Potential in 1972 *
1. Mechanical Low-cost Adding Machines	80%	20%
2. High-cost Electronic Calculators w/Tape Printout	2%	5%
3. Low-cost Electronic Calculators	18%	75%

* All figures are estimates.

Interpretation:

When innovation or significant product differentiation is not yet reflected in the proportion of current industry sales (column A), the firm should estimate the proportion of future IMP *likely to be* garnered (column B) by each existing product line element. In this case, note the large difference between columns A and B for product line element 3, low-cost electronic calculators.

performance of the relevant product that industry market potential may also be increased—as considered in Chapter 4.)

The low-cost electronic calculator was a real innovation and revolutionized the market for personal calculators. Other innovations or product differentiations are less revolutionary in their effects on their relevant markets—but at the same time may make it unrealistic to directly use the proportion of current industry sales achieved by each existing product line element to estimate the proportion of IMP to assign to each product line element. Consider, for example, how 120 mm cigarettes (introduced in 1974) and personal luxury cars (introduced in the mid-1960's) expanded those product lines. The year before introduction, such new product line elements accounted for no industry sales. When introduced, however, they certainly did deserve a proportion of IMP. Exactly what proportion of IMP to use is determined by the firm's realistic outlook and projections concerning what proportion of total industry sales will eventually be accounted for by sales of the new product line element. In making such projections, sales relevant are sales not just for the first firm's model, but sales for all models (including the competitors') that are based upon the same differentiation.

The more mature an industry becomes, the more innovations and significant product differentiations are likely to appear. As a market matures, therefore, a firm must incorporate such new innovations into its estimates of market shares for the various elements of the firm's product lines.

Similar adjustments may be called for if a firm feels that product line elements that it does market can penetrate the sales positions of product line elements that it does not market—*even when its own product line elements represent no innovation or significant new product differentiation.* Chapter 10 (on "Competitive Gaps") considers this case in greater depth.

SUMMARY

This chapter examined the various types of product line gaps and their measurement.

The firm begins deriving a product line gap by specifying the alternative elements that it recognizes in the product line. For a particular product line, elements of the product line can be defined along any of the different dimensions reviewed in the first part of the chapter. Size, options, style, color, flavor, form, quality, segment and/or distributor brand-related product line gaps may exist for each IMP that a firm recognizes.

In enumerating the possible elements of a product line, a firm that is just adding a product line should stick to one or two basic dimensions—whichever ones are most meaningful for the particular product and ones for which industry sales data are readily available. A firm that, on the other hand, has been selling a product line for some time should include more dimensions in its enumeration of possible elements of the product line.

In most instances, the proportion of current industry sales accounted for by each element gives an appropriate estimation of the proportion of IMP to assign to each product line element. In cases where a new innovation or significant product differentiation has recently entered the market as a new product line element, the proportion of current industry sales achieved by each product line element may overestimate or underestimate the correct proportion of industry market potential which should be assigned to each product line element. In such cases, proper adjustments should be made.

REVIEW QUESTIONS

1. From your own experience, give an example of each of the product line dimensions defined in the chapter.

2. How many separate elements of a product line should a firm recognize?

3. If IMP is 100 billion units and firm A sells product line elements for which industrywide sales account for 75 percent of total industry sales, what size is firm A's product line gap?

4. In Question 3 above, under what circumstances might the firm make different estimates of its product line gap? Give examples from your own experience.

NOTES

1. In the food market, such labels now account for approximately 13 percent of all food sales. "Marketing Trends," *Boardroom* (November 15, 1974). For discussion of dealer branding and the controversy surrounding it, see: L. Morse, "The Battle of the Brands," *Dun's Review* (May 1964), p. 98; V. J. Cook and T. F. Schutte, *Brand Policy Determination* (Boston, Mass.: Allyn and Bacon, Inc., 1967); and T. F. Schutte, "The Semantics of Branding," *Journal of Marketing* (April 1969), pp. 5–11.

2. For example, see E. J. McCarthy, *Basic Marketing,* 5th ed. (Homewood, Ill.: Richard D. Irwin, 1975).

3. One marketer divides the market into four "benefit segments": flavor segment, brightness segment, decay prevention segment, and a price segment. See R. I. Haley, "Benefit Segmentation: A Decision-Oriented Research Tool," *Journal of Marketing* (July 1968), pp. 30–75. Others prefer to consider only two benefit segments: a cosmetic segment and an anticavity segment. See, for example, M. E. Bale, "Market Segmentation" in L. Adler, ed., *Plotting Marketing Strategy* (New York: Simon and Schuster, 1967), pp. 100–102. For another discussion of benefit segmentation, see C. R. Wasson, et al., *Competition and Human Behavior* (New York: Appleton-Century-Crofts, Inc., 1968), pp. 12–13.
   For enlightening discussions of alternative segmentation methods and principles, see: "The Positioning Era," *Advertising Age* (April 24, 1972, May 1, 1972, and May 8, 1972); "Positioning Ads," *Wall Street Journal* (December 13, 1972), p. 1; F. Bass, et al., "Market Segmentation: Group Versus Individual Behavior," *Journal of Market Research* (August 1968), pp. 264–70; J. T. Plummer, "The Concept and Application of Life Style Segmentation," *Journal of Marketing* (January 1974), pp. 33–37; and J. F. Engel, et al., *Market Segmentation: Concepts and Applications* (New York: Holt, Rinehart, and Winston, 1972).

6

Product Line Gap-Related
Growth Strategies

PRODUCT LINE GAP-RELATED
GROWTH STRATEGIES

Chapter 4 included a description and analysis of four alternative growth strategies related directly to industry market potential (IMP). It was shown that the firm could grow by means of:

(1) Natural changes in the size of IMP.

(2) Discovering new uses or new user segments for existing products to provide new IMP's for the firm's present products.

(3) Introducing innovative product differentiations and thus expanding existing IMP's.

(4) Introducing new product lines to provide new IMP's for the firm.

The concepts and analysis presented in this present chapter concerning product line gaps provide the firm with two more growth strategy alternatives. These are:

(5) Filling out existing product lines.

(6) Creating new product line elements through innovation or significant product differentiation.

FILLING OUT EXISTING PRODUCT LINES

One growth alternative that the firm can pursue is to fill out existing product lines by adding elements which up until this time the firm has not sold. Each of the various types of product line gaps described in Chapter 5 represents a potential growth opportunity. Mercury filled in a size-related product line gap with its Bobcat, Ford with its "precision size" Granada. Simplicity filled in an options-related product line gap by expanding its line of garden tractor options. Lancers filled in a taste- or flavor-related product line gap by adding Lancers' Rubeo. Form-related product line gaps were filled by Personna with its twin double-edge blade and by Cross with its felt tip pen. Bouchard filled in a price-related product line gap by adding a low-priced wine.

In the cereal example presented in Chapter 5, firm A could fill in its 16.1-billion unit product line gap by starting to sell presweetened cereals in addition to its regular and natural cereals. Firm B (see Exhibit 5-1) could fill out part of its product line gap by adding any of the 45 possible product line elements that it recognizes [in Exhibit 5-1], but does not currently sell.

CREATING NEW PRODUCT LINE ELEMENTS THROUGH INNOVATION OR SIGNIFICANT PRODUCT DIFFERENTIATION

As considered in Chapter 4, innovations or significant product differentiations can expand existing IMP's and as such represent a means of potential growth (growth alternative 3).

Regardless of whether such innovation or differentiation provides a growth opportunity through operating to expand existing IMP's, those same new product line elements (innovations, etc.) do offer a growth opportunity in the form of potential displacement and take-over of the position(s) of one or more existing product line elements.

The introduction of the "Trac II" by Gillette, for example, was a significant product differentiation. That product (Trac II) probably did not constitute a growth opportunity for Gillette in terms of increasing IMP, but the Trac II did provide a growth opportunity for Gillette by displacing entrenched industry market share positions held by existing product line elements such as injector systems, bonded systems, band blades systems, traditional double-edge systems, etc. Gillette, of course, was more interested in displacing product line elements where Gillette itself had no entry (e.g., bonded systems) or a relatively weak entry (e.g., injector systems). Care certainly must be taken in adding any new product line elements so as to avoid "cannibalizing" one's own present strong product line elements instead of competitive elements. The second section of this chapter ("Cautions and Complexities") elaborates upon this point.

Inexpensive Kodak "Instamatic" cameras took over market share from old box-type cameras. Later on, Kodak's pocket instamatics and Polaroid's inexpensive Square Shooter-Two squeezed into the same market, moving other camera types aside. Low-tar cigarettes wedged into the cigarette market. Many other examples of this phenomenon occur each year—graphite golf shafts, felt tip pens, push button telephones, "diet" beer (e.g., Miller's Lite), etc.

CAUTIONS AND COMPLEXITIES

Care should be taken in selecting and designing product line gap-related growth strategies. Among the points to *keep in mind* in considering such strategies are the following:

A NARROW DEFINITION OF PRODUCT LINE IS REQUIRED FOR BUILDING MEANINGFUL MARKET STRUCTURE PROFILES

The marketer should remember the relatively narrow definition of "product line" when he is considering possible strategies related to "filling out the product line." The breadth of the product lines implied by advertisements for such product lines as Faberge's "Nail Care Products" (including a whole range of nail care products—'enriched cuticle remover,' 'ceramic glaze basecoat,' 'nail spray,' 'nail glaze remover,' and 'nail treatment cream') or General Tire's "Complete Tennis-Line" (including balls, rackets, covers, braces, shoes, etc.) for example, are far too broad for defining product line gaps and discussing the possibilities of filling in such gaps. Such broad definitions are related more closely to the analysis of IMP (refer to Chapter 4).

COMPETING FIRMS FACE THE SAME IMP BUT DIFFERENT MARKET STRUCTURE PROFILES— THIS BEGINS WITH DIFFERENT PRODUCT LINE GAPS

It is not at all likely that any two firms selling a given product line will market exactly the same product line elements, have the same distribution gaps, and have the same firm sales. Although two or more firms may indeed face the same IMP(s) for a given product line, they will not face the same market structure profiles for that same line. The implications of market structure profiles differ, therefore, from firm to firm—even for firms marketing essentially the same product.

PRODUCT AND/OR INDUSTRY LIFE CYCLES SHOULD AFFECT THE EVALUATION OF PRODUCT LINE GAP-RELATED GROWTH STRATEGIES

As the life cycle of a product line moves into its growth phase, an individual competitor is likely to offer differentiated version(s) of the product in order to establish a uniquely attractive position(s) in the marketplace. With many competitors following this same strategy, the number of different possible product line elements grows rather quickly, making it more difficult and more expensive for any individual competitor to keep up with such proliferation.

In the late growth and maturity phase, individual competitors segment the market and develop special marketing programs, including special products at times, for segments selected as target markets. The number of possible product line elements continues to grow, therefore, well into the maturity and saturation phases of the life cycle.

The product line gap for an individual firm is likely to grow in complexity as new product line elements are added to the industrywide product line. Depending upon the industry sales captured by each new product line element, and upon the substitutability of the firm's offerings for new competitive offerings, this growth in product line complexity may or may not imply a growth in the size of an individual firm's product line gap. What product line gap does remain for a firm, however, generally becomes more and more difficult and expensive to close as the product line life cycle matures.

FILLING OUT A PRODUCT LINE IS OFTEN AN INAPPROPRIATE STRATEGY CHOICE—CUTTING BACK ON A PRODUCT LINE CAN AT TIMES BE AN APPROPRIATE STRATEGY CHOICE

In times of such expansion, filling out a product line or attempting to maintain a completely full product line can often be an inappropriate strategy. In such cases, established firms are usually better off to concentrate on the elements where the industrywide volume is and/or where their individual firm's strengths lie. Firms newer to and less well-established in the industry are often better off to avoid direct competition with established firms by focusing upon particular segments of the market or in other ways seeking out their own specialized market niche.

A strategy choice to attempt to "maintain a full product line" may be dysfunctional in many other situations as well because costs are involved in providing each variation of a product. With this point in mind, many competitors consciously choose to market only certain elements of a product line—desiring each element to carry its "own weight" in terms of revenue generated versus incremental costs incurred in producing and marketing that separate element. This strategy can become particularly important when costs are rising rapidly.

During inflationary times in the early 1970's, for example, paper mills dropped cheaper grades of paper, and chemical firms discontinued low-profit specialized products and other low-volume products that were not returning a good profit on investment.[1] Manufacturers catering directly to final consumers at the retail level sometimes follow similar "cutting back" strategies. As mentioned earlier, for example, Castle and Cooke cut back the number of types and sizes of Dole pineapple that it marketed from 27 to 10 in a move to economize during the early 1970's. Other consumer goods manufacturers implemented similar strategies.[2]

CONSIDER THE POSSIBLE "CANNIBALISTIC" EFFECTS OF NEW PRODUCT LINE ELEMENTS

Expansion of a firm's product line must be planned carefully lest the firm's new entries cannibalize sales of the firm's present market entries. Analysts of the American automobile industry agree that Ford's Falcon and Chevrolet's Corvair, introduced in the early 1960's, ate more into Ford's and Chevy's own full and midsize car sales than into the sales of imports—the target of these United States "compact" cars. Any firm considering the expansion of an existing line must carefully avoid a similar fate.

A time when such cannibalism may be acceptable is when the firm is merely beating a competitor to the punch in an attempt to defend the firm's present position against an actual or potential competitive entry that would severely endanger the firm's present market share or position. Certainly Gillette has cannibalized its own position in its razor system product line many times. The point in this case is, however, that if Gillette had not done so with continual changes and improvements in razors and blades, a competitor such as Shick certainly could have been more successful in penetrating Gillette's position.

When significant competition against one or all of a firm's established markets is not threatened, however, cannibalism can indeed be very undesirable. In such circumstances, the key question for the firm to consider in deciding whether or not to introduce a new element of the product line is whether or not that expansion will attract new sales for the firm, rather than replace old sales. Later chapters covering "Usage Gaps" and "Competitive Gaps" expand upon this point.

In certain situations ethical implications may be very relevant in such decisions and cannot be ignored. Assume, for example, that IBM is—as is the case—the dominant competitor and technological leader in the computer industry. What if IBM comes up with a technology which it could make operational in one year and which would reduce computing costs by 90 percent? If it is assumed that the present price/performance of IBM installations is very competitive and is in no immediate threat of being surpassed by any competitor, the introduction of the new computer generation would surely cannibalize the position of IBM's own existing equipment before allowing it to run its projected life cycle. Should IBM move ahead today with the new technology to make it operational as quickly as possible? This is a complex question with no simple answer.

SOME FACTORS WORK IN FAVOR OF MAINTAINING A "FULL PRODUCT LINE"

Countering some of the forces mentioned above, which may make it unwise or otherwise difficult for an individual firm to maintain a full product line, other forces or pressures make it advisable for a firm to maintain a full product line. These forces come primarily from customers—be they industrial customers or final consumers, be they wholesale buyers or retail buyers.

A full complement of products can be very important to the customer. Consider an industrial customer who may require three or four different sizes of fork lifts or a dozen grades or sizes of a particular new input such as steel. This customer would like to buy in quantity from a single manufacturer in order to get a price break, so he searches out a manufacturer with a broad product line who can fill all of his wide-ranging needs. This also facilitates followups with the manufacturers for such operations as servicing, maintenance, adjustments, etc. A full complement of product line elements may be just as important to final consumers as to industrial customers. The housewife wants a matching set of different size cookware; the handyman may want a matching set of screwdrivers of different sizes, and so on.

The importance and difficulties of establishing and then maintaining good distribution coverage, intensity, and exposure cannot be over-emphasized as a key to successful marketing. Chapters 7 and 8 elaborate considerably upon this point. One of the wholesaler's functions is to buy from various manufacturers and then to provide a full line of assorted products to retailers, thus simplifying the retailers' buying task. Understandably, a wholesaler's job is simplified in similar fashion if he can buy a full line of a product from a single manufacturer, rather than being forced to search out and pull together a full product line through buying from various and assorted manufacturers. As a result, the manufacturer with a full product line is frequently in a more advantageous position than a limited line manufacturer to be able to pick and choose the best wholesalers for his product.

Many retailers today, especially discount houses and national retailers (e.g., Sears and J.C. Penney), but more and more other retailers as well, prefer to bypass the wholesaler and buy directly from the manufacturer in order to obtain better prices and better service—directly from the manufacturer. The manufacturer with the full product line is attractive to such retailers, because this manufacturer reduces the number of contacts that the retailer must maintain. Offering a full product line also may in and of itself swing a retailer to purchase directly from a manufacturer, stimulating the retailer to bypass the wholesaler altogether for the relevant product line. This phenomenon can also help the manufacturer in terms of gaining expanded distribution.

Should the manufacturer, then, maintain a full product line? As seen in the previous discussion of cautions, no simple answer to this question is possible. Forces exist in most instances working both for and against maintaining a full line. Perhaps the most realistic generalization to make is that a firm which maintains a reasonably full product line without worrying about matching competitive differentiations that fail to capture significant market shares will usually be in a position to realize most of the advantages of a completely full product line without suffering its disadvantages (cost and complexity).

As indicated above, exceptions to this generalization apply for less well-established firms and for firms getting into a product line quite late in the line's life cycle. In these cases, the firm is better off with a limited line focused upon particular segments or in other ways oriented toward a specialized niche in the market.

SUMMARY

Chapter 6 considers product line gap-related growth strategies and the cautions and complexities that one should keep in mind when selecting and designing these strategies.

The concepts and analysis presented concerning product line gaps provide the firm with two more growth strategy alternatives. These are

- Filling out existing product lines.
- Creating new product line elements through innovation or significant product differentiation.

The strategy "filling out the existing product line" is straightforward. The second strategy (innovations, etc.) offers a growth opportunity in the form of potential displacement and take-over of the position(s) of one or more existing product line elements.

Keep in mind the following points when selecting and designing product line gap-related growth strategies:

- A narrow definition of product line is required for building meaningful market structure profiles.

- Competing firms face the same IMP but different market structure profiles—this begins with different product line gaps.
- Product and/or industry life cycles should affect the evaluation of product line gap-related growth strategies.
- Filling out a product line is often an inappropriate strategy choice; cutting back on a product line can at times be an appropriate strategy choice.
- There are possible cannibalistic effects of new product line elements.
- Important factors work in favor of maintaining a full product line.

REVIEW QUESTIONS

1. From your own experience, can you think of any new product line elements that have expanded IMP and penetrated the market share positions of older product line elements? How about new product line elements that penetrated market share positions of older elements but did not expand IMP?

2. Why should a firm be careful not to define its product line too broadly when using MSP analysis?

3. Do all firms selling a certain product line face the same market structure profile? Explain.

4. As a product line moves through an industry life cycle, how should a firm's product line gap-related growth strategies change? Why?

5. Under what circumstances is cutting back on the number of product line elements offered an appropriate strategy choice? Explain.

6. What is the cannibalistic danger of adding new product line elements? Should a firm ever move ahead with introduction despite the likelihood of such cannibalism?

7. In the hypothetical IBM case mentioned in the chapter, discuss the question: "Should IBM move ahead today with the new technology to make it operational as quickly as possible?"

8. What forces suggest that a manufacturer (or a firm in service industries) should maintain a full product line?

NOTES

1. "Demand, Controls Spur Many Concerns to Drop Bottom-of-Line Goods," *Wall Street Journal* (August 28, 1973) p. 1.

2. "Toward Higher Margins and Less Variety," *Business Week* (September 14, 1974), p. 100.

7

Distribution Gaps: Description and Measurement

The product line gap provides one reason why a firm's actual sales in a given product line fall short of the firm's potential sales in that product line. A firm cannot sell a product that it does not offer in its product line. Distribution gaps of various types provide additional explanations for the overall gap between actual firm sales and potential firm sales. Very simply put, a firm cannot *sell* a product when it does not *distribute* that product.

This chapter defines three different types of distribution gaps and discusses the explicit measurement of these gaps. The following chapter examines strategies that a firm can use to close distribution gaps.

THREE TYPES OF DISTRIBUTION GAPS

Sales of an individual product line of a firm can be adversely affected by any or all of three different types of distribution gaps: *coverage* gaps, *intensity* gaps, and *exposure* gaps.

COVERAGE GAP

A *distribution coverage gap* exists when a firm does not distribute the relevant product line or any individual element thereof in all geographic regions desired. The size of the gap is measured as a proportion of industry market potential (IMP) accounted for by the regions where any or all of the elements of the product line are not distributed.

The firm's own definition of "complete distribution" is essential for the derivation of all three different types of distribution gaps. If a firm regards the whole United States as its potential market and distributes a product in areas containing 90 percent of the total United States IMP for the product, the firm faces a *10 percent coverage gap*.[1]

INTENSITY GAP

Within those geographic regions where a firm does distribute its product, the firm may still face a *distribution intensity gap*. A distribution intensity gap exists when a firm's entire product line or individual elements thereof are distributed in an inadequate number of outlets—within a geographic region where the firm does have distribution coverage.

A distribution intensity gap is measured as a ratio of the outlets through which the firm does distribute the relevant product line (within a given geographic region) versus the "ideal universe" of outlets through which the firm desires to distribute that product line (within that same region). The firm defines its ideal universe of outlets through defining "complete distribution" for the relevant product line.

For example, if a firm's product line is available in outlets handling 70 percent of the volume handled by the ideal universe of desired outlets (as specified in the firm's own definition of "complete distribution") in a geographic region, then the firm has a *30 percent intensity gap* for this product line in that region.

EXPOSURE GAP

Within outlets where the firm does have distribution of the relevant product line, the firm can still face a *distribution exposure gap*. A distribution exposure gap exists when a firm's entire product line or individual elements thereof have poor or inadequate shelf space, location, displays, etc.—within outlets where the firm does have distribution for the product.

As with the estimation of the distribution coverage gap and the distribution intensity gap, the estimation of the *distribution exposure gap* depends upon the firm's own definition of "complete distribution" for the relevant product line. Complete exposure desired can be meaningfully expressed as a function of the exposure received by the leading competitive brand(s) of the same product.

For example, if the firm's product line has the same general location and types of shelf/display space in most outlets as major competitive brands, but on average has only 80 percent as many facings as the major competitive brand, the firm might estimate a *20 percent exposure gap* for that product line.

ESTIMATING THE SIZE
OF DISTRIBUTION GAPS

The degree of accuracy with which the size of the three distribution gaps can be estimated depends to a considerable extent upon the resources that the firm is willing to expend to obtain reliable measurements. As considered below, a number of commercial services are available that facilitate the accurate estimation of distribution gaps. Either additionally or alternatively, the firm can directly sponsor such field research either by its own distribution sales force or by outside commercial parties. Other firms may prefer to rely upon armchair estimates by the best-qualified and most widely experienced members or affiliates of the firm.

As in the cases of measuring IMP and product line gaps, the incremental costs involved in obtaining absolutely accurate measurements will often outweigh the incremental benefits to be derived from such definitive measures. In many cases, ball park estimates can be generated quite inexpensively and will prove quite satisfactory for the purposes of generating useful market structure profiles.

The first task involved in estimating the size of distribution gaps for one product line of a firm is for the firm explicitly to *define* for itself what it regards as *complete distribution* for this product line.

DEFINING COMPLETE DISTRIBUTION

The definition of "complete distribution" can differ dramatically from firm to firm for a given product line and from product line to product line for a given firm. What is regarded as "complete distribution" for a specific product line of a single firm is determined primarily by: (1) the firm's geographic market horizons, (2) the relevant customer's willingness to shop for the product, and (3) the relevant customer's brand recognition, image of the brand, and brand preference.

(1) The firm's geographic market horizons. Factor 1, the firm's geo-

graphic market horizons, focuses upon the individual firm's definition of "complete geographic coverage." Despite the growing dominance in the United States of large corporations as opposed to small corporations in terms of dollar sales, the vast majority of all United States corporations are still quite small both in terms of total revenues generated and in terms of geographic market horizons. This is true for most firm services (e.g., restaurants, laundries, retailers, movie houses, consultants, legal services offices, etc.) but is just as true for a very large number of manufacturers of industrial and/or consumer goods.

Distribution coverage falling outside of the geographic market horizons of a firm does *not* show up as a distribution gap if IMP has been properly defined for that firm. As seen in Chapter 4, a firm with local market horizons has in a very real sense segmented the overall United States market geographically and is aiming at one of those segments. The only relevant IMP for that firm is the IMP located within that geographic segment. The same principle is true for any firm, small or large, that has limited geographic market horizons for a product line.

The important point to keep in mind in considering geographic market horizons is that IMP falling outside of a firm's self-imposed limit on its relevant geographic boundaries should not be included as part of that firm's IMP and does not, therefore, constitute part of a distribution coverage gap for the firm. Because Coors chooses not to market Coors beer east of the Mississippi, IMP for beer falling east of the Mississippi is not part of the IMP for Coors and the East is not part of Coors' distribution coverage gap.

This does not imply that a local or regional firm cannot have a coverage gap, however, since the firm may have a geographic market horizon larger than its present geographic coverage. "National firms" frequently have important distribution coverage gaps. The exact measurement of geographic coverage gaps is discussed below following the considerations of customer's willingness to shop and brand recognition, brand image, and brand preference.

(2) Customer's willingness to shop. The less willing the customers in the relevant market are to shop for a particular product, the broader a firm's distribution must be to achieve *complete distribution intensity* within those geographic areas where the firm does have distribution coverage. More intensity means more of and possibly a greater variety of distribution locations or outlets within a given geographic area.

In defining complete distribution intensity for a particular product line, therefore, the firm should closely study and analyze just how much shopping its relevant customer group is willing to do to find and purchase the product.

Different customers may show varying degrees of willingness to shop for the same product. Such differences may be caused by variances in income, attitudes, intended use of the product, or any number of other reasons. The firm should study each customer group for which it has defined a separate IMP and should attempt to generalize concerning the willingness of each group to shop around for the product. This, in turn, is an important guide for defining exactly what "complete distribution intensity" means for each customer group for which a separate IMP has been defined for the relevant product line.

For the purpose of defining complete distribution intensity, placing products along a spectrum of "willingness to shop" for the relevant customer group is more appropriate than attempting to classify products flatly into certain types, as suggested by some authors.[2] This is exemplified below, where distribution gap measurement is considered.

(3) Brand recognition, brand image, and brand preference are three different yet closely related factors, all of which affect the definition of complete distribution to a relevant customer group for a given product line of a firm.

Brand recognition can be very important in defining complete distribution intensity and exposure. A brand that is not familiar to a target customer group requires more intense distribution (i.e., more outlets) and better exposure (i.e., better in-store space and promotion) than a brand that is quite familiar to the relevant customers. This does not imply that all brands which have achieved good recognition do not require a demanding definition of complete distribution intensity and exposure.[3]

Brand image can also be important in defining complete distribution and exposure. A particular manufacturer's (or distributor's) brand of a product line may be well recognized but at the same time may have a relatively poor image with a given customer group. For example, most people recognize the two brand names, K-Mart and Kodak. Both brands have achieved high recognition. It is safe to say, however, that Kodak photographic products have a better image with most customer groups than do simliar products marketed under the K-Mart brand name. This may or may not be justified as a result of comparing just the quality of the two brands, but customer psychological and sociological factors can also affect the image of a particular brand for any given customer group.

Good overall brand image makes it easier for the manufacturer to improve distribution intensity and exposure, because retailers are usually also aware of the brand's good image. When the good image results in relevant customers' preference for the brand, the manufacturer sometimes may cut back his definition of complete distribution.

Brand preference means that the customer may be willing to search for this particular brand. In such instances, the manufacturer may be able to define complete distribution intensity and exposure in a less demanding fashion. As considered below, however, brand preference does not always imply a greater willingness to shop.

For some customer groups, good overall brand image does not result in customer preference for the brand—as expressed in the purchase of that brand. Mercedes automobiles have an excellent overall brand image with most automobile customer groups, but financial constraints preclude most would-be customers from expressing a purchase preference for Mercedes. Most customers express a brand preference for less expensive autos. *Brand image* focuses, therefore, upon overall quality, while *brand preference* considers the total product package—including price.[4]

For a particular relevant customer group, therefore, the better the brand recognition and image, and the stronger the brand preference, the more favorable position the firm is in to make its definition of complete distribution intensity and exposure less demanding—*provided that* the willingness-to-shop rating for the product for the customer group is not near the zero end of the willingness-to-shop spectrum. The section below on "measuring distribution gaps" makes this more explicit.

As in measuring and describing "willingness to shop," measuring and describing brand recognition, brand image, and brand preference should also be accomplished along a spectrum, rather than by using a few artificial categories. As was also the case for "willingness to shop," different relevant customer groups may occupy different positions along these brand spectrums for a single one of the firm's product lines. Part of the firm's task is to study its customer target group(s) in order to be able to make accurate generalizations concerning relevant customer groups' brand recognition, image of the brand, and brand preference.

ESTIMATING THE SIZE OF DISTRIBUTION GAPS

Somewhat standardized data are quite readily available for estimating the size of the three types of distribution gaps for a firm's individual product lines. Examples of such data are presented below. The individual firm's interpretation of such data for the purpose of developing quantitative distribution gap estimates is not standardized, however; it is an individualized task for each firm. Two firms with the same product line and same distribution patterns can quite easily come up with different distribution gap estimates. This can happen because each firm may have a separate definition of "complete distribution" and/or because each firm prefers a different interpretation of quite similar distribution gap data.

In attempting to determine the size of the various distribution gaps, *exact measurement* of the three distribution gaps is *not* required—a good estimate will be adequate in many instances for most firms. Over time, as the firm's experience with developing market structure profiles grows, the firm will develop new and more accurate measures for complete distribution and for the distribution gaps themselves. Most firms using market structure profiles for the first time will find that their first distribution gap estimates are quite meaningful in terms of providing the overall growth planning perspectives for which these profiles are intended.

A market structure profile mirrors the market structure for one product line of one firm. An individual firm may find it meaningful in some instances to generate two or more market structure profiles of the same product line and same relevant customer group, reflecting different assumptions for the firm's definition of complete distribution or different estimates of the distribution gaps themselves. The firm can then sit back and gain considerable insight from analyzing the market structure profiles resulting from the different assumptions or estimates. This is most likely to be a worthwhile exercise when the firm has considerable doubts as to what specific assumptions, measures, and/or estimates to use in quantifying its distribution gaps for a particular product line.

SIZE OF DISTRIBUTION COVERAGE GAP. The distribution coverage gap can be measured and expressed either as a proportion of the IMP remaining after the product line gap has been subtracted from IMP or as a direct proportion of total IMP. The firm developing the market structure profile must keep in mind that it makes little sense to consider a distribution gap for product elements that the firm does not sell. The product line gap reflects zero distribution for those elements not sold by the firm.

The firm's first task in determining the size of the distribution coverage gap is to find a measure that can accurately reflect the geographic dispersion of IMP. The "number of potential customers" used in defining IMP (refer to Chapter 4) usually provides an appropriate measure. The relevant question is "How are these potential customers dispersed geographically?" Once that question is answered, distribution coverage gap estimation is a relatively simple task.

In mapping out the geographic location of potential customers, the firm is often best off to break the total relevant geographic market horizon into a number of relatively large geographic territories or segments. Such an approach is particularly appropriate for describing large geographic areas falling within the firm's geographic market horizons but where the firm does not yet distribute the relevant product line or product line element. One fairly typical scheme divides the United States into ten geographic market territories.[5] See Fig. 7-1.

Government census data for each region are available for households, individuals, household heads, or housewives. Sex, age, occupation, education, color, income, family size, home ownership, dwelling characteristics, and marital status are among the demographic characteristics

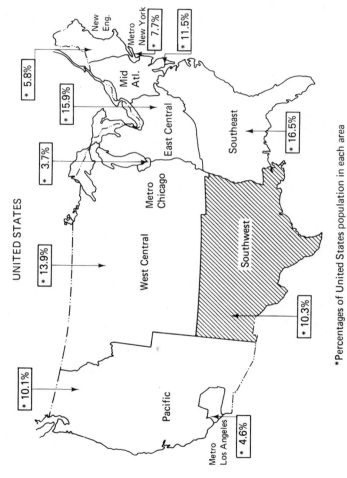

UNITED STATES

New Eng.

* 5.8%

Metro New York

* 7.7%

* 11.5%

Mid Atl.

* 15.9%

East Central

Southeast

* 16.5%

* 3.7%

Metro Chicago

West Central

* 13.9%

Southwest

* 10.3%

Pacific

* 10.1%

Metro Los Angeles

* 4.6%

*Percentages of United States population in each area

FIGURE 7-1.   A. C. Nielsen Territories.

for which cross-tabulations are available for determining the size of the relevant customer population in each of these geographic areas. Compilations of selected census data such as the above are available annually in the *Statistical Abstract of the United States.*[6] Detailed census data are available in other published sources [7] and on magnetic tape. These data are readily available and relatively inexpensive to acquire.

For industrial markets, the *United States Census of Business, Census of Manufacturers, Census of Mining Industries, Census of Agriculture,* and *Census of Transportation* may be particularly useful for estimating the size of IMP in different geographic areas.

For product line elements that the firm has been distributing for some time, the firm is better off to break the ten larger regions referred to above into smaller regions. United States census figures are available for standard metropolitan statistical areas (SMSA's) of varying sizes ranging from 50,000 to 99,999 on up to SMSA's of 4,000,000 or over. Cross-tabulations on the wide variety of demographic characteristics referred to above are available for each of these areas, individually and in aggregate form. A firm may find it most realistic to key in on SMSA's or counties of a minimum specified size to start with and then expand to broader distribution coverage as time passes. Market research firms provide similar data for major markets—keyed to particular product lines. Table 7-1, for example, shows A.C. Nielsen's 32 major market areas.[8]

As an alternative to focusing upon major metropolitan areas, a firm can subdivide a large region by state, county, or any other basis that it finds convenient and/or particularly useful. A wide variety of census data is available by state and by counties—individually or classified into four size groups.

As a simple and direct example of the quantification of a distribution coverage gap, assume that the proportion of IMP in each geographic area is the same as the proportion of population in each area.[9]

Assume also that the firm's geographic market horizon includes the entire United States (except Alaska and Hawaii), that the firm has no product line gap, and that the firm's product line is available in all areas except the Southwest. In this case, where IMP for the firm's product line elements is distributed the same as population, the firm's distribution coverage gap equals:

Area	% of IMP for the Firm's Product Line Elements
Southwest	10.1%
Distribution coverage gap =	**10.1% of IMP**

Table 7-1
THE NIELSEN MAJOR MARKETING AREAS

The marketing areas covered by NMMS provide a wide variation relative to size, geography, climate and general demographic composition. On a combined basis, they provide insight into the grocery buying habits of over 121 million people. Singly or in combination, these markets offer the means to probe virtually every aspect of drug and grocery marketing preferences.

	% of U.S. Grocery Sales	% of U.S. Drug Sales	% of U.S. Populations
Atlanta	1.4	1.3	1.3
Boston	3.2	3.0	3.2
Buffalo	0.9	0.9	0.9
Chicago	3.7	5.0	3.7
Cincinnati	1.4	1.3	1.3
Cleveland	2.3	2.1	2.3
Dallas/Ft. Worth	1.4	1.9	1.5
Denver	0.8	0.9	0.8
Detroit	3.3	3.6	3.0
Houston	1.3	1.2	1.3
Indianapolis	1.3	1.7	1.3
Jacksonville	0.5	0.7	0.5
Kansas City	1.0	1.3	1.1
Los Angeles	5.4	6.1	4.7
Louisville	0.7	0.7	0.7
Memphis	0.9	0.8	1.0
Miami/Ft. Lauderdale	1.5	1.8	1.2
Milwaukee	0.9	0.8	1.0
Minneapolis/St. Paul	1.2	1.3	1.4
Nashville	0.8	0.7	0.8
New York	7.7	6.5	7.9
Oklahoma City	0.6	0.5	0.6
Omaha	0.5	0.6	0.6
Philadelphia	3.6	3.0	3.7
Phoenix	0.7	0.9	0.7
Pittsburgh	2.1	1.7	2.1
Portland	1.1	1.0	1.0
Rochester	0.5	0.5	0.5
St. Louis	1.4	1.3	1.4
San Francisco/Oakland	2.7	3.3	2.4
Seattle/Tacoma	1.3	1.3	1.2
Washington/Baltimore	3.2	4.4	3.2
Total	59.3	62.1	58.3

If the firm had a real product line gap of 20 percent of IMP (as in the previous case of firm A for breakfast cereal) and the different possible elements of the product line were spread evenly from a geographic point of view, then the firm's distribution coverage gap would equal 8.1 percent of IMP. See Table 7-2 for the calculation.

Table 7-2
SIZE OF DISTRIBUTION COVERAGE GAP WHEN FIRM
ALSO HAS A PRODUCT LINE GAP

Product Line Element	% of IMP (based upon current proportion of industry sales)	Distribution Coverage for the Firm (expressed as a % of total U.S. Mkt.)	Distribution Gap (expressed as a % of IMP)
A	20%	0% (product line gap)	
B	80%	100% − 10.1% = 89.9%	(80%) × (10.1%) = 8.1% of IMP

Different distribution coverage gaps for different elements of the product line. Firms can have different distribution coverage gaps for different elements of the same product line for two reasons. First, as United States markets have become more competitive, more and more firms segment markets geographically (and by other means) in an attempt to develop and offer individualized marketing programs for each segment and thus to establish a better competitive position in each segment. The growing geographic regionalization of broadcast and print advertising media has aided this process, as has the growing availability of more regionalized data.[10] Segmentation in general has led to the proliferation of product line elements and individualized marketing programs.

Second, because of the dynamics of the marketplace, most firms are continually adding and deleting elements of each individual product line. One study revealed that in 1975 more than 80,000 items were being offered to food stores in the United States and that the number was expanding—despite the discontinuance of approximately 15,000 items in that same year.

Because of these two factors (the narrower segmented approach of marketing programs and the rapid turnover of elements in a given firm's product line), firms today quite often have a different distribution coverage gap for separate elements of the same product line.

An element that has been sold by the firm for some time is likely to have a smaller coverage gap than an element just introduced. Expanding distribution coverage for a new product line element takes time.

The product may first be test-marketed in a small region.[11] If the test market results are satisfactory, manufacturing capacity has to be built for the product. Then wholesalers and retailers in various regions must be convinced and/or stimulated to add the product line. All of these processes are time consuming. The firm may prefer a gradual move into one region after another in order to learn from its mistakes in early regional markets and thus be more effective in entering later markets.

SIZE OF DISTRIBUTION INTENSITY GAP. The firm experiences a *distribution intensity* gap only in those geographic regions where it does distribute the product, i.e., where it has distribution coverage. Distribution intensity is defined as a proportion of the sales volume of outlets through which the firm is distributing the product line versus the total sales volume of all the outlets through which the firm would like to be distributing its product. The firm's ideal number and mix of outlets are defined directly as a function of the firm's own definition of "complete distribution." [12]

The firm's first task in estimating the distribution intensity gap is to quantify "complete distribution." Once again, the greater the willingness to shop and the stronger the brand recognition, image, and preference, the fewer outlets a firm needs to include in its definition of complete distribution. Willingness to shop is the key variable. Brand image and preference *can* improve willingness to shop, but a low willingness to shop may still exist despite strong brand preference for certain products, especially for low-priced drug and/grocery items.

Exhibit 7-1 shows the relationships between willingness to shop and brand preference and the extent of distribution intensity required for a product if it is to meet its definition of complete distribution intensity. Given a universe of possible sales outlets for a product line, the definition of complete distribution intensity for a product line falling into Quadrant IV of Exhibit 7-1 would include a very high proportion of, if not all, possible outlets. The definition of complete distribution intensity for a product line falling into Quadrant III would include a lower proportion of all possible outlets than that for one in Quadrant IV. Product lines in Quadrant II require yet fewer outlets for complete intensity, and those in Quadrant I can meet their complete distribution intensity definition with relatively exclusive distribution.

Different target market can mean a different quadrant and a different definition of complete distribution intensity. It should be noted that one product line (or an element of same) may fall into a different quadrant in Exhibit 7-1 and therefore have a different definition of complete distribution intensity for two or more different markets for which the firm has defined separate IMP's (and, therefore, separate market structure

Exhibit 7-1
DISTRIBUTION INTENSITY CLASSES

Quadrant	*Definition of Complete Distribution Intensity*
I.	Relatively exclusive distribution is adequate for complete distribution intensity
II.	Requires more outlets for complete distribution intensity (selective distribution)
III.	Requires wide distribution within a given geographic area for complete distribution intensity (somewhat intensive distribution)
IV.	Requires distribution in every possible outlet for complete distribution intensity (intensive distribution)

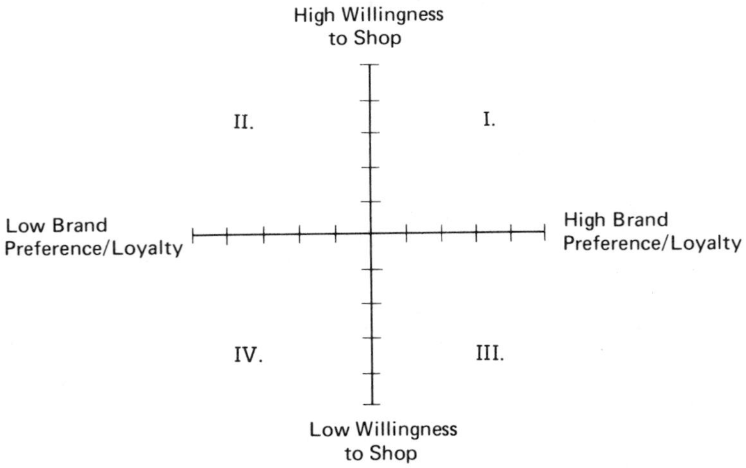

profiles). A candy bar manufacturer, for example, may consider his brand-loyal customers as one segment (in Quadrant III) to continue satisfying and those who do not now eat candy bars as another segment (in Quadrant IV) to try to capture.

What types of outlets? In order to quantify complete distribution intensity, the firm first specifies the types of potential outlets for its products. For final consumer goods, relevant outlets may include a variety of different types of retail stores plus vending machines, direct mail, and/or wholesale discount houses. Special definition of complete distribution intensity must be devised for services and industrial products.[13]

Since the text focuses upon final consumer goods, it is appropriate to consider outlets for such goods in greater depth. Retail outlets for final consumer goods may be classified along any of a variety of dimensions, including extent and type of merchandise handled, size, ownership, and location. In quantifying complete distribution intensity for final consumer goods, all of these dimensions may be relevant. The firm might begin by listing the types of outlets through which it could possibly sell this product line *by extent of merchandise handled*.[14] In doing so, the firm lists store types such as food stores, drug stores, discount stores, department stores, etc.—all the kinds of outlets through which the firm would like to sell this particular product line. The firm may also want to classify stores along some of the other dimensions mentioned above.

Which particular outlets? Having specified the types of relevant outlets for the product line, the firm next determines through which particular types of sales outlets it would like its product sold. This selection process is based primarily upon which quadrant of Exhibit 7-1 (distribution intensity class) is relevant for this particular product line of the firm. More of the different possible outlet types would be relevant for a situation in Quadrant IV than for one in Quadrant I.

Once a list of relevant types of outlets within each relevant geographic area has been drawn up, the firm then selects the specific *number* and *location* of outlets of each type (e.g., by type of merchandise handled) that will constitute complete distribution intensity for the particular product line of concern. The ideal *number* and *location* of each type depend again upon willingness to shop and brand preference and/or loyalty. Depending upon potential *customers' willingness to shop for the product* (specified in Exhibit 7-1), the firm may feel that it has to have the product available within a *certain number of miles or minutes* of each potential customer. The greater the willingness to shop, the greater the number of miles or minutes. Depending upon potential customers' *brand preference and/or loyalty,* the firm may feel that it has to have its product available *wherever competitive brands are sold.* The greater the preference and/or loyalty for its brand, the lower is this need. Actually mapping out relevant geographic areas with the location of IMP centers and the firm's outlets marked for each area helps the firm quickly find distribution intensity gaps.

Including an ownership dimension in the classification and selection of outlets can often be very helpful. Does the firm desire distribution for the relevant product through corporate chains, through franchised systems of independent stores, and/or through independent stores? To define this dimension of complete distribution, the firm must consider the patronage habits of its potential customer. Failure to distribute through stores of a particular ownership type which are patronized regularly by customers for the relevant type of product may leave a large distribution intensity gap.

Assign a potential to each outlet. Having specified the number, location, and ownership of each type (by extent of merchandise) of outlet desired for the product line in each relevant geographic area, the firm then assigns a sales potential to each outlet included in its definition of complete distribution intensity. The total sales potential for each area of concern is the proportion of IMP (minus the product line gap) located in the relevant geographic area. All relevant outlets within the area are not assigned the same sales potential. Rather, the firm should weight each outlet as a function of its current total sales volume, or, better yet (if data are readily available), as a function of each outlet's current (or potential) sales volume of products in the relevant product line.

Example of measuring a distribution intensity gap when no product line gap exists and no distribution coverage gap exists. Assume that the relevant product is breakfast cereal and that the firm defines complete distribution intensity as a desire to sell its product through every store that sells food as a main or major line in each relevant geographic area. Assume also that the firm divides the United States into the ten geographic areas depicted in Fig. 7-1 and that the firm has some distribution in each of the ten areas. This firm's total distribution intensity gap equals the summation of the intensity gaps that it has in each geographic area.[15]

From United States census data or from a commercial research house, the firm can find that there are approximately 260,000 stores that sell food as a main or major line in the United States. Column one of Table 7-3 shows how these are distributed among the ten geographic areas described in Fig. 7-1.

To determine the intensity gap in one geographic area—New England, for example—the firm would first have to know in which of the 11,443 relevant outlets its product line was available. Commercial store audit services such as the syndicated services of A. C. Nielsen, Market Research Corporation of America, or the store panel services (e.g., store audits) of such firms as Market Facts, Ehrhart-Babic Store Audits, or Burgoyne Retail Sales Studies can provide such information, or the firm can attempt to gather these data through its own salesmen and/or its wholesale and/or retail contacts. In gathering or procuring such information, data on overall store volume (turnover) should also be kept, for a low-volume store does not contribute as much to distribution intensity as a high-volume store.

In the present case, assume that the firm has no product line gap and no distribution coverage gap and that the firm's product line is available in 9500 of the 11,443 target outlets in New England and that these 9500 outlets account for approximately 90 percent of the store volume (turnover) of the 11,443 stores. This leaves the firm with a *10 percent distribution intensity gap in the New England area.* If IMP is assumed

Table 7-3
FINDING THE DISTRIBUTION INTENSITY GAP

Area	1 Percentage of IMP Here = % of Total Dollar Food Sales	2 Percentage of Food Sale ($) in Each Area Accounted For By Stores Where This Product Line Is Available	3 Distribution Intensity (as % of IMP)	4 Distribution Intensity Gap (as % of IMP)
New England	6.0%	90%, 6% × (90%) =	5.4%, 6% — 5.4% =	0.6%
Metro New York	7.6	90	6.8	0.8
Middle Atlantic	11.8	90	10.6	1.2
East Central	17.0	80	13.6	3.4
Metro Chicago	4.0	90	3.6	0.4
West Central	12.7	80	10.2	2.5
Southeast	15.1	90	13.6	1.5
Southwest	9.7	70	6.9	2.8
Greater Los Angeles	5.5	90	5.0	0.5
Remaining Pacific	10.6	50	5.3	5.3
	100.0%		Total distribution intensity gap =	19% of IMP

to be dispersed geographically in the same way as dollar food sales, then 6 percent of IMP is in New England (see Table 7-3, Column 1). As a percentage of IMP for the whole United States the 10 percent intensity gap in New England converts to $10\%(6\%) = \%_{10}$ **of 1% (i.e., 0.6%) of IMP** for the whole United States.

Table 7-3 also provides an example of how a firm can determine its total distribution intensity gap for the whole United States. In that example, the firm has its weakest intensity in the Pacific (50% of 10.6% of IMP = **5.3% of IMP**), in the East Central (20% of 17%= **3.4% of IMP**), the Southwest (30% of 9.7% = **2.8% of IMP**), and the West Central (20% of 12.7% = **2.5% of IMP**). The firm's *total distribution intensity gap equals 19.0 percent.*

Distribution intensity gap where a product line gap and a distribution coverage gap exist. Assume that a firm has a 20 percent product line gap (therefore, 80 percent of IMP product line coverage) and that the firm has no distribution coverage in the Southwest (9.7 percent of IMP), Greater Los Angeles (5.5 percent of IMP), or the Remaining Pacific (10.6 percent of IMP). In this case, the firm's *distribution coverage gap* equals 80 percent of (9.7% + 5.5% + 10.6%) = 20.7 percent of IMP and the *intensity gap now equals 8.32 percent of IMP*—that is, the total of the distribution intensity gaps of the other seven regions times the percent of IMP in each region times the product line coverage in each region. Table 7-4 shows the calculations and the resulting market structure profile.

Different intensity gaps for different product line elements. As discussed in the previous section on measurement and estimation of distribution coverage gaps, product line elements do not all necessarily have the same distribution coverage. The narrow segmented approach to marketing and the rapid turnover of elements in a given firm's product line were mentioned as causes of this phenomenon.

Just as those factors can leave a firm with different coverage gaps for different elements of a product line, they also frequently result in different intensity gaps for the different product line elements. A firm may be successful in gaining some distribution coverage in a geographic area (e.g., Metro New York) for a new product line element, thus closing a coverage gap there. The number of outlets distributing the new element, however, is likely to be small at first in comparison with the number of Metro New York outlets distributing the more established elements of the firm's product line. Distribution channel members (wholesalers, retailers, etc.) do not accept every new product element that comes along. They must be convinced and stimulated to take on each new one. It is highly unlikely that they will expand their stores, their display space, their storage facilities, etc. for a new product line element. What they

Table 7-4

1	2	3	4	5	6	7	8
Area	% of IMP	Product Line Coverage	Distribution Coverage	Distribution Coverage Gap as % of IMP	Distribution Intensity Gap	Distribution Intensity Gap as % of IMP	Resulting Market Structure Profile
Southwest	9.7% ×	80%		= 7.8%			IMP
Greater L.A.	5.5% ×	80%		= 4.4%			
Remaining Pacific	10.6% ×	80%		= 8.5%			
New England	6.0% ×	80%	X	1	× 10%	= 0.48%	20% of IMP } Product Line Gap
Metro N.Y.	7.6% ×	80%	X	1	× 10%	= 0.61%	
Mid Atlantic	11.8% ×	80%	X	1	× 10%	= 0.94%	20.7% of IMP } Distribution Coverage Gap
East Central	17.0% ×	80%	X	1	× 20%	= 2.72%	
Met. Chic.	4.0% ×	80%	X	1	× 10%	= 0.32%	8.3% of IMP } Distribution Intensity Gap
West Cent.	12.7% ×	80%	X	1	× 20%	= 2.04%	
Southeast	15.1% ×	80%	X	1	× 10%	= 1.21%	

Product Line Gap = 20% of IMP

Total Distribution Coverage Gap = 20.7% of IMP

Total Distribution Intensity Gap = 8.32% of IMP

generally have to do in order to take on a new element is to drop an old one. An average food store sells less than 10,000 different items—yet more than 50,000 items are fighting for positions in that outlet.

SIZE OF THE DISTRIBUTION EXPOSURE GAP. The firm can experience a distribution exposure gap only in those outlets where its relevant product line is sold. For consumer goods, distribution exposure refers to the shelf space, facings, location, displays (size and frequency), other store-related promotions (such as special prices and/or local advertising) and inventory per store for the firm's relevant product line.[16]

In order to measure or estimate exposure gap size, a firm must *develop a meaningful exposure index* and *then define* what it means by *complete distribution exposure* for the relevant product line in terms of that index. For consumer goods, the index and the definition of complete exposure may differ for different types of product lines. Complete exposure may mean one thing for autos, another for refrigerators, another for candy bars, another for cereal, etc.

Defining complete distribution exposure is similar to defining complete distribution intensity in that willingness to shop and brand recognition, image, and preference are critical determinants. The marketer should consider what willingness to shop and what brand preference exists for his product for the relevant customers. When Quadrant I (of Exhibit 7-2) is relevant, the definition of complete distribution exposure is not very demanding, since the customer is willing to search out the product and brand. Exposure equal to that of competitive brands constitutes complete distribution exposure for products in Quadrant II. Prime location in the outlet is of paramount importance for items in Quadrant III; the loyal customer will buy it if he sees it, but will not go out of his way to look for it. Items in Quadrant IV need heavy exposure—the definition of complete exposure for these products is very demanding.

Different target market can mean a different quadrant and a different definition of complete distribution exposure. As seen when we defined complete distribution intensity earlier, different customer groups for which different IMP's and different MSP's are generated may have different degrees of brand preference and willingness to shop for the same product line of the firm. As a result, the relevant product can fall in a different quadrant of Exhibit 7-2 and require a different definition of complete distribution exposure as well.

Setting up an exposure index. The method used to set up an index against which to determine the exposure gap in each outlet is quite arbitrary for each firm. The definition of complete distribution exposure,

Exhibit 7-2
DISTRIBUTION EXPOSURE CLASSES

Quadrant	*Definition of Complete Distribution Exposure*
I.	*Little exposure* needed in the outlet. Consumer is willing to look for the product and brand.
II.	Exposure required for a firm's product in Quadrant II depends upon exposure of *competitive brands.* Heavy exposure is usually *not* required.
III.	Need better exposure in the store than for Quadrant I. Customer will not look all over for the product type. Given *good location* in the store, high brand preference implies that a great amount of shelf space, facings, in-store promotion, etc., is not necessary if aiming at current brand-loyal customers. Better exposure is required if aiming at new customers who are loyal to a competitive brand.
IV.	Definition of exposure here is *very demanding.* Shelf location, space, and facings are very important, as are in-store promotions (displays, specials, coupons, etc.).

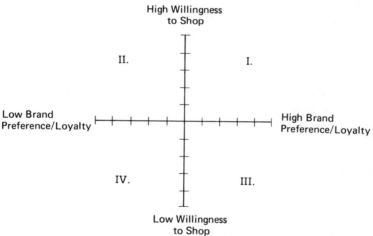

therefore, may vary from firm to firm, no matter how similar these firms, their product line(s), and their customer groups.

One way to set up an index is first to prepare a check list and then to take a sample audit of the firm's outlets to ascertain the level of current exposure for the firm's relevant product line and that of the major competitor. Exhibit 7-3 presents a sample check list. The six different

Exhibit 7-3
DISTRIBUTION EXPOSURE CHECK LIST

Store Name: _____

Store Location: _____

Store Size—Volume: _____
          —Square Feet of Shelf and Display Space (excluding aisles, stockroom,
          checkout, etc.): _____

Relevant Product Line Element(s) _____

1	2	3	4	5
		Goal	*Our*	
Weight for		*(Ideal*	*Product*	*Major*
this Product	*Exposure Factor*	*Exposure)*	*Line*	*Competitor*
	—Location			
	—Shelf Space Occupied			
	—Number of Facings			
	—Displays			
	—Other In-store Promotion			
	(Specify)—Special Price			
	—Local Advertising			
	—etc.			
	—Amount of Inventory on			
	Hand			

Exposure Rating for this product line of this firm for this outlet: _____
     (Present Exposure Versus Ideal Exposure)

exposure factors listed in the audit form (Exhibit 7-3) can each have a
different rating of importance (Column 1) from product line to product
line and/or from relevant customer group to relevant customer group—
depending upon which quadrant (of Exhibit 7-2) is relevant for the particular product line and target market.

If the firm does not have a direct sales organization capable of per-
forming such an audit efficiently, the audit can be contracted out to a
marketing research firm which does custom retail audits or which uses
store panels of dealers. Burgoyne, Ehrhart-Babic, and Market Facts are
among the firms that provide such services. Market Research Corporation
of America (MRCA) regularly audits over 2000 key supermarkets in 50
major metropolitan areas and reports on stocks and shelf-space assign-
ments. A. C. Nielsen provides regularly syndicated services reporting on a
variety of distribution exposure factors.

To save time and money, a firm may prefer to do a few random audits and then generalize these audits to cover the whole proportion of the firm's outlets. Such a method, however, leaves a great deal of uncertainty in the resulting index.

After the firm has the basic audit information on hand on its own product line and that of the major competitor(s), it can draw up an ideal exposure profile for the product line. The ideal exposure profile for *space, facings,* and *inventory level* should be stated as a *percentage* of the feet of shelf and/or display space and storage space each outlet has available. The comparative space, facings, and inventory levels of the major competitor can be used as a yardstick if the product is in Quadrant II (of Exhibit 7-2). More demanding goals for space, facings, and inventory levels should be set if the product is in Quadrant IV or if it is in Quadrant III and the firm is attempting to win over customers currently loyal to another brand.

The ideal exposure profile should also include quantitative and/or qualitative ideals for in-store location, displays, and promotions. Good locations, displays, and other *in-store promotions* (coupons, specials, bonus packs, etc.) are particularly important for products in Quadrants III and IV (Exhibit 7-2). A product on display, for example, will usually sell much better (frequently many times better) than when it is not on display. Products on the right-hand side (to the flow of store traffic), at the periphery of the store, and/or at eye level also tend to turn over faster than products placed in locations less conspicuous and less convenient for the potential customer. Location, display, and in-store promotion data should, therefore, be included in the original audit, in the ideal exposure index, and in subsequent audits.

Having set up an ideal exposure profile, the firm then rates its current exposure versus the ideal exposure. Since many qualitative factors can be involved (e.g., location in the store), a definitive quantitative rating as a ratio of the ideal exposure is not easily forthcoming. It is functional, however, to use the audit data (Column 4 of Exhibit 7-3) and compare it with the ideal exposure profile (Column 3 of Exhibit 7-3) in order to come up with such a quantitative estimate. Shelf space, facings, and stock-on-hand are easily compared quantitatively. For location, displays, and in-store promotions (for which no natural quantitative measure exists), the firm can devise whatever kind of quantitative rating scheme that it feels gives meaningful data for comparing ideal exposure with the relevant product line's current exposure.

Variations in exposure gaps for different product line elements, for different outlets, and/or for different geographic regions. As with distribution coverage and intensity gaps, distribution exposure gaps can vary from product line element to product line element within a given product line. Exposure gaps can also vary from distribution outlet to distribution outlet, although the marketer will usually find it more useful to generalize for each of the different types of outlets and/or geographic regions in which he is selling the relevant product line.

The distribution gap is expressed as a ratio or percentage of existing exposure versus ideal exposure. Table 7-5 is an expansion of Table 7-4 and provides an example of determination of a firm's distribution exposure gap on a regional basis and for the United States as a whole. In the exhibit, the total distribution exposure gap for this one product line of the firm works out to equal **11.1 percent of IMP.**

SUMMARY

This chapter defines three different types of distribution gaps: coverage gaps, intensity gaps, and exposure gaps. A consideration of the explicit measurement of the size of distribution coverage gaps and intensity gaps follows.

A *distribution coverage gap* exists when a firm does not distribute the relevant product line or any individual element thereof in all geographic regions desired. A *distribution intensity gap* exists when a firm's entire product line or individual elements thereof are distributed in an inadequate number of outlets—within a geographic region where the firm does have distribution coverage. A *distribution exposure gap* exists when a firm's entire product line or individual elements thereof have poor or inadequate shelf space, location, displays, etc.—within outlets where the firm does have distribution for the product.

The firm's own definition of complete distribution coverage, intensity, and exposure is essential if the sizes of the various distribution gaps are to be estimated. Complete distribution for a particular product line is defined as a function of three factors: (1) the firm's geographic market horizons; (2) the relevant customer's willingness to shop for the product; and (3) the relevant customers' brand recognition, image of the brand, and brand preference.

Given the firm's definitions of complete distribution coverage and intensity, the size of the *distribution coverage gap* is measured as a proportion of the industry market potential (IMP) accounted for by regions where any or all of the elements of the relevant product lines are not distributed. The size of the *distribution intensity gap* is measured as a ratio of the outlets through which the firm distributes the relevant product line (within a given geographic region) versus the "ideal universe" of outlets through which the firm desires to distribute that product line (within that same region).

Table 7-5
FINDING THE DISTRIBUTION EXPOSURE GAP

1	2	3	4	5	6	7	8	9
Area	% of IMP	Product Line Coverage	Distribution Intensity	Distribution Intensity as a % of IMP	Distribution Exposure as a % of Ideal Distribution Exposure	Distribution Exposure as a % of IMP	Distribution Exposure Gap as % of IMP	Resulting Market Structure Profile
New England	6.0% ×	80% ×	90% =	4.32% ×	75% =	3.24% from 4.32 =	1.08%	IMP
Met. New York	7.6% ×	80% ×	90% =	5.47% ×	75% =	4.10% from 5.47 =	1.37%	20% of IMP } Product Line Gap
Mid Atlantic	11.8% ×	80% ×	90% =	8.50% ×	75% =	6.38% from 8.50 =	2.12%	
East Central	17.0% ×	80% ×	80% =	10.88% ×	90% =	9.79% from 10.88 =	1.09%	20.7% of IMP } Distribution Coverage Gap
Met. Chicago	4.0% ×	80% ×	90% =	2.88% ×	90% =	2.59% from 2.88 =	0.29%	
West Central	12.7% ×	80% ×	80% =	8.13% ×	90% =	7.32% from 8.13 =	0.81%	8.3% of IMP } Distribution Intensity Gap
Southeast	15.1% ×	80% ×	90% =	10.87% ×	60% =	6.52% from 10.87 =	4.35%	11.1% of IMP } Distribution Exposure Gap
					Total Distribution Exposure Gap =		11.1 %	

(Assume no coverage in Southwest, Greater Los Angeles, and the Pacific.)

129

Different coverage gaps and different intensity gaps can exist for separate elements of a single product line. A firm can also face different intensity gaps for different target markets of a single product line, because the willingness to shop and/or brand preferences may vary from target market to target market.

As with the estimation of the distribution coverage gap and the distribution intensity gap, the estimation of the *distribution exposure gap* depends upon the firm's own definition of "complete distribution" for the relevant product line. The firm begins by setting up an exposure index. With the aid of the index, a firm's distribution exposure can be meaningfully expressed as a function of the exposure received by the leading competitive brand(s) of the same product. Different exposure gaps can exist for a single product line for different target markets. Different exposure gaps can also exist for different elements of a single product line within a given outlet.

REVIEW QUESTIONS

1. In your own words, explain what is meant by each of the three different types of distribution gaps.

2. Can a firm have no distribution (and no sales) in the Southern United States (or any other large geographic area) and not be faced with a distribution coverage gap? Explain.

3. Why might different groups of consumers have a different willingness to shop for the same product?

4. Why might a single customer have a greater brand preference for one product (e.g., cigarettes) than for another product (e.g., beer)?

5. Why can two firms with the same distribution for a given product line face different size distribution gaps?

6. If customers show high willingness to shop and low brand preference, should the product be available in more or fewer outlets than if customers show low willingness to shop and high brand preference? Explain.

7. Why should a firm not attempt to get distribution of its product(s) in every possible outlet?

8. Might the distribution exposure required vary from candy bar manufacturer to candy bar manufacturer? Explain.

9. Why might a firm face different exposure gaps for different elements of a single product line?

NOTES

1.   Treated separately below are the firm's development of a meaningful definition for "complete distribution" and the firm's exact measurement of its distribution coverage gaps.

2.   One popular goods classification scheme separates products into four categories: unsought goods, convenience goods, shopping goods, and specialty goods. Relevant customers exhibit a low willingness to shop for goods they view as "convenience" goods or "unsought" goods and a greater willingness to shop for products they view as "shopping" or "specialty" goods. For elaboration, see McCarthy, op. cit., pp. 265–75.

3.   Good brand image can lead to a less demanding definition of complete distribution. Whether it does or not depends upon whether the good brand image results in an expression of brand preferences as well.

Even when such brand preference does exist, the firm sometimes cannot justify a less demanding definition of complete distribution. Whether or not he can depends ultimately upon the relevant customer group's willingness to shop for the preferred brand. Back we are again to the importance that willingness to shop plays in defining complete distribution. Regardless of brand preference, most customer groups are not willing to put much time or effort into shopping for such products as regularly purchased low-priced grocery and drug items. For more expensive and more irregularly purchased products, however, brand preference may indeed stimulate a customer group to shop around for a desired brand—sometimes much more, depending upon the degree of brand preference and the importance of the purchasing decision to the customer group.

4.   Ibidem.

5.   A. C. Nielsen scheme, using United States Bureau of Census Data.

6.   For a guide to census data available, see the *Catalog of U.S. Census Publications,* which is issued quarterly.

7.   For a brief description of each source, see: H. Boyd and R. Westfall, *Marketing Research* (Homewood, Ill.: Richard D. Irwin, 1972), pp. 249–51.

8.   A. C. Nielsen, *Summary for U.S.A. Market,* 1975.

9.   For a large number of final consumer goods, this population basis provides a good measure for the geographic dispersion of IMP. The dispersion of United States food sales varies slightly from the dispersion of population. Column 1 of Table 7-3 presented later in the chapter shows the proportion of total United States food sales accounted for by each region of the country. For example, the Southwest accounts for 10.1 percent of the United States population but only 9.7 percent of all United States food sales.

For industrial products or for final consumer goods for which IMP varies by geographic region—e.g., ski equipment, boats, air conditioning, etc.—the dispersion of population can be radically different from the dispersion of IMP.

10.   E.g., Nielsen's "Major Market Areas."

11.   For example, A. C. Nielsen has approximately 300 special test marketing areas.

12.   No substitutability of product line elements is assumed in this case.

13.   For service industries (e.g., restaurants, laundries, hotels, etc.) distribution intensity is defined in terms of the location of service outlets. For industrial products, distribution intensity is defined in terms of an optimum number of contacts between the firm's salesmen and potential customers.

14.   In doing so, keep in mind that relevant geographic areas falling outside of the firm's present geographic coverage are part of the firm's distribution coverage gap—not part of its distribution intensity gap.

15.   Alternatively in this case, because the firm has full distribution coverage, the firm could simply define one overall intensity gap for the whole United States. This, however, might prove a clumsy figure to work with when strategizing to close intensity gaps in specific geographic areas.

16.   For industrial products and service industries, the meaning of distribution exposure varies considerably from the above description. Distribution exposure is not a relevant concept—and, therefore, no exposure gaps exist—for industrial products and services sold through personal selling direct to the customer. Distribution exposure gaps for service industries can include such factors as inadequate display facilities for a retail outlet, inadequate table space for a restaurant, an inadequate number of teller windows for a bank, or inadequate or inappropriate hours of business for any such service businesses.

8

Distribution Gap-Related Growth Strategies

DISTRIBUTION GAP-RELATED GROWTH STRATEGIES

Previous chapters enumerated six alternative growth opportunities and discussed how they interrelate with each other in terms of the overall framework provided by the concept and formulation of a market structure profile. These six growth opportunities were

(1) Natural changes in the size of IMP.

(2) Discovering new uses or new user segments for existing products to provide new IMP's for the firm's present products.

(3) Developing innovative product differentiations to expand existing IMP's.

(4) Introducing new product lines to provide new IMP's for the firm.

(5) Filling out existing product lines to close product line gaps.

(6) Creating new product line elements through innovation or significant product differentiation.

The three types of distribution gaps provide three additional growth opportunities or strategies for the firm. There are opportunities to grow through:

(7) Expanding geographic distribution coverage.

(8) Expanding distribution intensity (i.e., the number of outlets for the relevant product in each geographic area where the firm now distributes the product).

(9) Expanding distribution exposure (i.e., to improve the exposure of the firm's relevant product line within individual outlets).

EXPAND GEOGRAPHIC DISTRIBUTION COVERAGE

Of the three distribution gap-related growth strategies, expanding geographic distribution coverage is the least complex. What is involved basically is a move on the part of the firm to begin distributing and selling the firm's product line in geographic areas where, heretofore, this product line of the firm has not been available.

As pointed out in the discussion in the previous chapter, any number of phenomena can account for a "distribution coverage gap." Expanding distribution coverage closes part (or all) of that coverage gap. For example, assume that the firm faces the coverage gap derived in Chapter 7 (as displayed in the market structure profile in Table 7-4). In this case, the firm faces a distribution coverage gap equal to 20.7 percent of IMP, because the firm does not distribute the product line in the Southwest (7.8 percent of IMP—see Column 5 of Table 7-4), greater Los Angeles (4.4 percent of IMP), and the Remaining Pacific (8.5 percent of IMP). Assume that the firm now begins to distribute the product line in the Southwest. This immediately reduces the size of the firm's overall distribution coverage gap for this product line by 7.8 percent of IMP. As a result, the firm's coverage gap is reduced from 20.7 percent of IMP to 12.9 percent of IMP.

EXPAND DISTRIBUTION INTENSITY

A firm expands distribution intensity by gaining new distribution outlets in any given geographic area. As considered earlier, the type and number of distribution outlets desired by the firm for "complete distribution" of that product line are specifically defined by the firm as the first step in determining the size of the distribution intensity gap. A certain proportion of IMP is assigned to each outlet falling within the "complete distribution" definition. The summation of the IMP in outlets where the firm does not yet have distribution equals the distribution intensity gap for that particular geographic region.

Since outlets can vary in type and size from geographic region to geographic region, the definition of "complete distribution" in terms of the types and numbers of desired outlets can also vary from region to region. For example, the Southeast has many more food outlets than the Pacific region. Including Los Angeles, the Pacific has 9.3 percent of all food outlets in the United States, whereas the Southeast has 24.6 percent of the United States food outlets. The Southeast, however, accounts for fewer food outlet sales than the Pacific region (15.1 percent of all United States food sales are accounted for by the Southeast region versus 16.1 percent by the Pacific region). For complete distribution in the Southeast for most food product line elements, therefore, a firm would presumably have to be in a larger number of outlets than in the Pacific region.

In the example of the determination of an intensity gap presented in Chapter 7 (Table 7-4), the firm distributed its product line (i.e., had distribution coverage) in all areas except the Southwest, Greater Los Angeles, and the Remaining Pacific. Of the areas where it did have distribution coverage, the firm had its weakest intensity (20 percent intensity gap—see Column 6 of Table 7-4) in the East Central (intensity gap = 2.72 percent of IMP).

By expanding distribution intensity (i.e., by getting the firm's relevant product line into new outlets) in any or all of the geographic areas where the firm presently has distribution coverage, the firm closes part of its distribution intensity gap. Assume, for example, that the firm in Table 7-4 expanded its intensity in the East Central from the current 80 percent intensity up to 100 percent intensity. The result would be a reduction of that firm's distribution intensity gap from 8.32 percent to 5.6 percent of IMP.

EXPAND DISTRIBUTION EXPOSURE

Expanding distribution exposure for a product line means improving in-store factors such as shelf space, facings, location, displays, inventory, etc., in individual outlets. As indicated in Chapter 7, the firm must develop a meaningful exposure measurement index for rating exposure in individual outlets. The firm then defines complete exposure as a certain rating on that index and proceeds to generate an exposure rating for outlets of various types and/or in various locations. (See Exhibits 7-2 and 7-3, and Table 7-5, for example.)

A firm can have an exposure gap only in outlets where the firm's relevant product is available for sale. In the example presented in the previous chapter (Table 7-5), the firm was shown to have a total distribution exposure gap of 11.1 percent of IMP. By gaining more shelf space, more facings, more displays, better location, etc., the firm improves its exposure and reduces its exposure gap. The firm of concern in Table 7-5 had an exposure gap equal to 4.35 percent of IMP in the Southeast alone —reflecting an average exposure rating per outlet equal to 60 percent (Column 6 of Table 7-5) of the firm's ideal or target exposure.

By improving its exposure in the Southeast from 60 to 90 percent of ideal, the firm's overall distribution exposure gap would decline by 30 percent times 10.87 percent of IMP (which is the percent of IMP in the firm's outlets in the Southeast—Column 5 of Table 7-5), which equals 3.26 percent of IMP. The exposure gap is, therefore, reduced from 11.1 percent of IMP to 7.8 percent of IMP.

CAUTIONS AND COMPLEXITIES IN CONSIDERING DISTRIBUTION GAP-RELATED GROWTH OPPORTUNITIES

As in the case of the growth opportunities and strategies considered in Chapters 4 and 6, the firm should be aware of a number of cautions and complexities in the actual design and implementation of distribution gap-related growth strategies. Included are the following:

EXPANDING DISTRIBUTION OR MAINTAINING COMPLETE DISTRIBUTION IS NOT ALWAYS AN APPROPRIATE STRATEGY

Chapter 6 pointed out that the contraction of a particular product line is sometimes more appropriate than filling out or expanding that product line. The same principle sometimes holds with regard to expanding or contracting distribution for a product line. The most obvious situation when contraction of distribution is preferred to expansion is when a product line is being phased out—for any of the reasons discussed in earlier chapters. Contraction of distribution *coverage* may also be appropriate at other times; for example:

> One product manager was able to convince his management that to market nationally, as they had been doing for decades, was foolish. It was a close-to-commodity category supporting but one major brand in any market and having heavy private label influence. Where they were not the major brand, they had little hope of successful marketing. However, they found they could very profitably produce the private label in these areas and are now so doing. They are concentrating all their marketing funds in the markets where they can get a return.[1]

Living with distribution *intensity* gaps as opposed to closing such gaps is also appropriate in many instances. For example, marketing dollars assigned to building distribution intensity can frequently be spent most productively if the firm concentrates its dollars and efforts on improving intensity in high-population-density areas. Census data show, for example, that while the largest size counties (size A) have less than 30 percent of the food outlets, these stores account for over 40 percent of all sales of food outlets nationwide.

The same principle applies regarding the desirability and productivity of focusing efforts on building distribution intensity in high-volume stores and/or in areas where fewer stores handle a greater percentage of the total volume. As mentioned earlier, for example, the Southeast has over 24 percent of all the United States food outlets, but these stores account for only approximately 15 percent of the national food outlet volume. In contrast, the Far West has approximately only 9 percent of all the United States food outlets, but these account for more than 16 percent of the United States food outlet volume.

Again and again the same point is relevant. The key criterion in deciding whether contraction or expansion is appropriate is the firm's goal of maximizing its return on its investment dollars. This criterion holds whether the firm is concerned with adding or deleting product lines or product line elements or whether the firm is concerned with expanding or contracting distribution coverage, intensity, or exposure. In view of that goal, a major concern in considering alternative distribution gap-related strategies and opportunities is to consider and compare the individual cost-benefit trade-offs of the various alternatives available to the firm so as to maximize the productivity of limited funds available.

AVOID WASTING DISTRIBUTION DEVELOPMENT DOLLARS

A firm has no need for greater distribution intensity and/or exposure than is called for by the willingness to shop and the brand preferences of its relevant customers for the firm's product line. A careful analysis of the relevant market situation is very worthwhile in order to determine what realistically constitutes "complete distribution" for the firm's product line of concern.

Distribution development dollars can be spent much more productively elsewhere than on expanding the distribution intensity and/or exposure of a product line that is close to or is already at or beyond complete distribution according to the firm's well-thought-out definition of complete distribution for the relevant product line and market.

SELLING TO NATIONAL OR REGIONAL ACCOUNTS

Selling to national and/or regional accounts can also be a very productive way for the firm to spend distribution development dollars. For industrial goods firms, this means selling to large national firms that individually represent huge potential sales volume. For consumer goods firms, corporate retail chains such as K-Mart, Kroger, J.C. Penney, etc. and/or manufacturer-sponsored (Midas Muffler, MacDonald's, Holiday Inn), wholesale-sponsored (Ace Hardware, Western Auto, Walgreen Drugs), and retail-sponsored (Associated or Certified Grovers) systems of independent stores offer very lucrative potential sales. From the point of view of firms desiring to spend distribution development dollars productively, those chains or systems of stores are most attractive which buy from manufacturers (or their intermediaries) on a national or regional basis as opposed to buying on a local, store-by-store basis.

USING DEALER BRANDING TO IMPROVE DISTRIBUTION COVERAGE, INTENSITY, AND EXPOSURE

A dealer selling products under his own private label or private brand name will usually give that brand excellent *exposure* in his outlet(s).

Many dealers and dealer chains (or franchised systems of independent stores) prefer selling their own private labels over selling products under manufacturers' brand names. The motivation for and evolution of this phenomenon has been described well elsewhere.[2] Suffice it to say that dealers buy these products for less and therefore can sell them for less and/or receive a higher markup on these products. At the same time, these dealers use private labels to help build store traffic and loyalty.

The only way to get distribution in some chains is through private branding. Sears, for example, places a heavy emphasis upon offering products under its own label. Many times the only way to expand *intensity* to cover outlets that have such a philosophy is to go the private brand route.

A number of dealer chains and systems of independent stores have better brand recognitions, image, and preference than do many manufacturers—especially smaller, less well-known manufacturers. Such manufacturers may find that the most efficient and productive way to improve distribution coverage, intensity, and exposure is to emphasize private branding as opposed to attempting to distribute the product under the firm's own less well-known brand name.

As indicated in Chapter 4, the firm may consider distributor or dealer brands as an entirely separate IMP and market structure profile, or may integrate these outlets into the IMP(s) for all different types of outlets together. Whichever alternative is chosen, growth potentials related to dealer branding should not be overlooked.

CHANGING A FIRM'S DEFINITION OF GEOGRAPHIC REGIONS AS THE FIRM'S DISTRIBUTION EXPANDS

As soon as a firm begins distributing in an area—regardless of the number of outlets through which the firm's relevant product line is distributed (even a single outlet)—the entire distribution coverage gap for that area for the firm's relevant product line is closed.

As mentioned in Chapter 7, a firm can change its definition of geographic regions as it expands its distribution coverage. For example, if a firm distributes only east of the Mississippi, the firm might prefer to classify all of the IMP falling west of the Mississippi as belonging in one region, the "West." If the firm then begins distributing the relevant product line in one state of the West, say California, the firm would now recognize no coverage gap.

In view of this possibility, the firm might find it useful to adjust its definition of geographic regions and split the West into a number of regions (or by state). In the case above, the firm would be shown still to have a significant coverage gap in the area west of the Mississippi—with the exception of having coverage in California or in the subwestern region covering California.

DIFFERENT DEFINITIONS OF COMPLETE DISTRIBUTION FOR DIFFERENT TARGET MARKET SEGMENTS

Because different customer segments may be different in terms of their "willingness to shop" and "brand preference" characteristics, the appropriate definition of complete distribution can vary from segment to segment. Given such a variation in the definition of complete distribution, a firm with certain degrees of distribution coverage, intensity, and exposure for a particular product line may at the same time face different size distribution coverage, intensity, and exposure gaps for that product line for each different customer segment.

As seen in Chapter 4, this problem can be handled by generating a separate IMP and a separate market structure profile for each customer segment recognized and sought out by the firm. For a single product line, therefore, a firm may face two or more separate market structure profiles —such as those presented in Exhibit 8-1.

Contrasting market structure profiles such as those in Exhibit 8-1 can also exist for two firms with identical product lines and identical distribution patterns. Two such firms can face different size distribution gaps because of contrasting definitions of "complete distribution" and/ or because of varying interpretations of the same distribution gap data.

Exhibit 8-1
A SINGLE FIRM MAY FACE AS MANY DIFFERENT
MARKET STRUCTURE PROFILES (AND DIFFERENT
DISTRIBUTION GAPS) AS THE NUMBER OF
SEPARATE CUSTOMER SEGMENTS THE FIRM RECOGNIZES

Firm: xxxx
Product Line: I

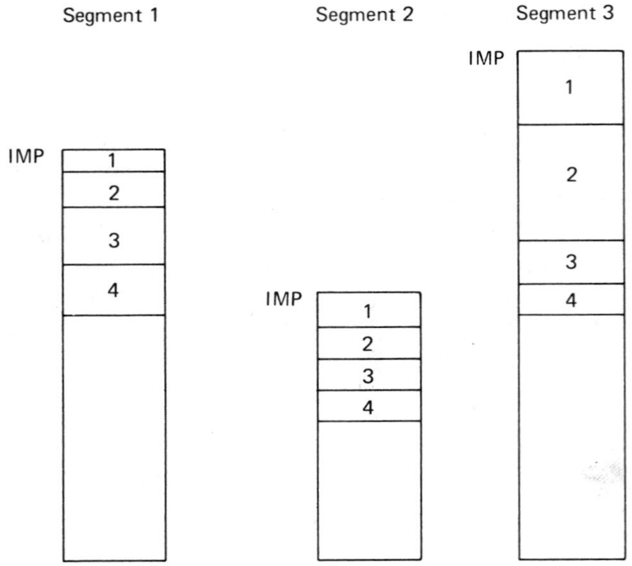

Gaps
1. Product Line Gap
2. Distribution Coverage Gap
3. Distribution Intensity Gap
4. Distribution Exposure Gap

SOMETIMES DIFFERENT TYPES OF OUTLETS ARE APPROPRIATE TO IMPROVE DISTRIBUTION INTENSITY

The proportions of total sales achieved currently through various types of outlets can properly be used in many instances to assign IMP to different outlets in an attempt to estimate the size of the distribution intensity gap for a particular product line of a firm. Earlier in the text, for example, a distribution intensity gap was developed for firm XYZ for cereal—*as a breakfast food. What about for cereal as a snack?* Cereal

has a separate use as a snack food and a separate IMP and market structure profile reflecting this separate use (recall—new use for existing product as growth opportunity 2). Where should snacks be distributed to
have complete distribution? In the same stores as breakfast food, yes,
but in many, many other locations as well. Why not in the vending
machines and at the theater like other snacks?

For cereal as a breakfast food, the proportion of sales achieved
presently by different types of outlets can properly be used for assigning
proportions of IMP to each different type of outlet. For cereal as a snack,
this is not the case. Reflecting this, Exhibit 8-2 shows two contrasting
market structure profiles for cereal as a breakfast food and a snack. Note
how much more important the intensity gap is for cereal as a snack. Different IMP's and different product line gaps could also exist, but are
omitted in the Exhibit in order to emphasize the contrasting intensity
gaps.

Exhibit 8-2
DIFFERENT INTENSITY GAPS AS A FUNCTION OF
ALTERNATIVE PRODUCT USE

Firm: xxxx
Product Line: A — Cereal as a Breakfast Food
              B — Cereal as a Snack

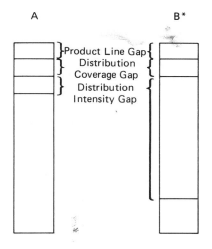

* Different IMPs and different product line gaps
could also exist but are omitted in the Exhibit
in order to emphasize the contrasting intensity gaps.

THE DYNAMICS INVOLVED IN CLOSING
DISTRIBUTION GAPS

The relationship between a firm closing its distribution gaps and realizing an increase in the firm's sales of the relevant product line is indirect rather than direct. The gap that a firm closes by expanding distribution coverage, intensity, and/or exposure does not convert totally into increased firm sales.[3]

Exhibit 8-3 displays the dynamics of a market structure profile as a firm hypothetically expands first its distribution coverage (part B), then

Exhibit 8-3
DYNAMICS OF A MARKET STRUCTURE PROFILE (MSP)
AS VARIOUS DISTRIBUTION GAP-RELATED
STRATEGIES ARE IMPLEMENTED

A	B	C	D
Profile Before Distribution Strategies are Implemented	Coverage Gap is Partially Closed	Intensity Gap is Partially Closed	Exposure Gap is Partially Closed

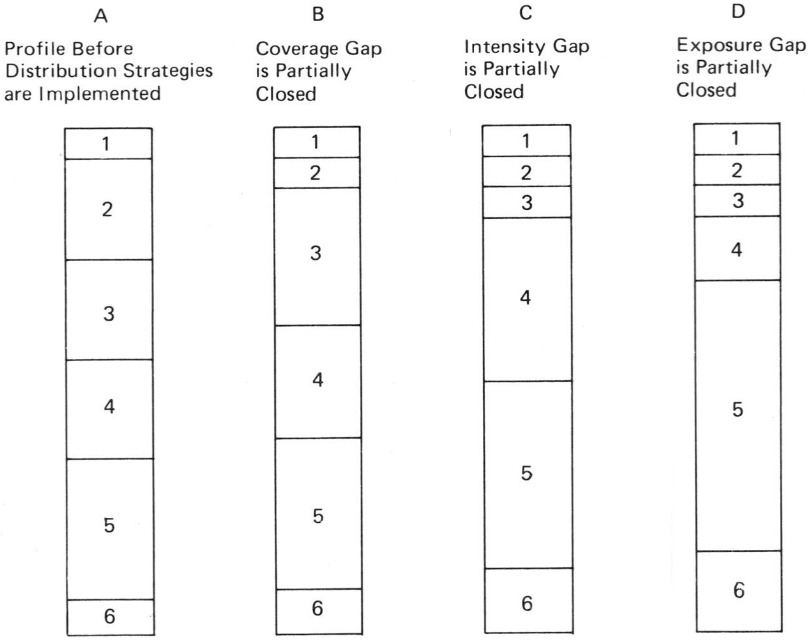

Gaps
   1. Product Line Gap
   2. Distribution Coverage Gap
   3. Distribution Intensity Gap
   4. Distribution Exposure Gap
   5. Usage and Competition Gaps
   6. Firm Sales

its distribution intensity (part C), and then its distribution exposure (part D). Note how the intensity and exposure gaps increase (as a percentage of IMP) as the coverage gap is closed (part B). This is because a firm moving into a new geographic area generally begins with poor intensity and poor exposure. In part C, as the intensity gap is closed, the exposure gap increases. This is because the firm is moving into new outlets and generally will not have very good exposure in these outlets initially. In part D, as the intensity gap is closed, the usage and competitive gaps become very important. Later chapters discuss these gaps in detail.

A slight increase in firm sales has been indicated (in Exhibit 8-3) as each strategy is implemented. Well-planned strategies such as these should yield such increased firm sales.[4] In actual practice the firm may well end up implementing all three of these distribution strategies at one time. Exhibit 8-3 separates the strategies in time in order to show the dynamics of the market structure profile as various distribution strategies are implemented.

SUMMARY

Chapter 8 examined distribution gap-related growth opportunities and strategies.

The three types of distribution gaps provide three growth opportunities or strategies for the firm. These are opportunities to grow through:

- Expanding geographic distribution coverage.
- Expanding distribution intensity (i.e., the number of outlets for the relevant product in each geographic area where the firm now distributes the product).
- Expanding distribution exposure (i.e., to improve the exposure of the firm's relevant product line within individual outlets).

Cautions and complexities to keep in mind when considering these distribution gap-related growth opportunities or strategies are the following:

- Expanding distribution or maintaining complete distribution is not always an appropriate strategy.
- Closely consider the willingness to shop and brand preferences of customers when thinking about expanding distribution intensity and/or exposure.

- Selling to national or regional accounts can be a very productive way to spend distribution development dollars.
- Going the dealer brand route is sometimes the best way to improve distribution coverage, intensity, and/or exposure.
- Expanding distribution coverage may call for a redefinition of the firm's geographic regions.
- Different target market segments may require different definitions of complete distribution.
- Different types of outlets may be appropriate for expanding distribution intensity for different uses or user groups of a product.
- Closing one distribution gap usually has direct effects upon the size of other distribution gaps.

REVIEW QUESTIONS

1. Why is it often inappropriate to attempt to build or maintain complete distribution?

2. What is a national account?

3. What are some advantages and disadvantages of using dealer branding as a vehicle for expanding distribution?

4. Why might it be appropriate for a firm to change the definition of its geographic regions as the firm expands its geographic coverage?

5. Why can different market segments require different definitions of complete distribution?

6. What is likely to happen to the intensity gap and exposure gap when the coverage gap is closed? Explain.

NOTES

1. SAMI, Inc., Case Study.

2. For example, see, E. J. McCarthy, *Basic Marketing*, 5th ed. (Homewood, Ill.: Richard D. Irwin, Inc., 1975).

3. Part Three of the book examines much more specifically the process of estimating incremental firm sales likely to result from implementing various alternative growth strategies.

4. Ibidem.

9

Usage Gaps

In originally estimating industry market potential (IMP), as discussed in Chapter 4, three assumptions are made concerning the usage of the product or service. The three assumptions concerning each use or user segment for the product or service are

(1) Everyone who can reasonably be expected to use the product or service is using it.
(2) Everyone who is using it, is using it on every "use occasion."
(3) Every use is a "full use" (e.g., full serving).

These usage assumptions hold in very few market situations. Usually many potential users are not using a product. Many of those who do use the product do not use it on every "use occasion." Finally, many uses of most products are not "full" uses. For each assumption that does not hold for a firm in a given market situation, that firm faces a usage gap.

Reflecting the three complete usage assumptions made in estimating IMP, the firm can face three separate but interrelated usage gaps for each IMP that the firm recognizes. The three usage gaps are referred to as: *the nonuser gap,* the *light user gap,* and the *light usage gap.* These usage gaps provide yet three more reasons or explanations why the firm's sales in this product line fall so short of IMP.

The reader should note that usage gaps are not determined until first the firm's product line gap and then the distribution gaps have been subtracted from IMP. The logic involved in subtracting the gaps in this particular order is that usage gaps are irrelevant for product line elements that the firm does not produce and for distribution coverage, intensity, and exposure that the firm does not have. Part Three of the text discusses the logic and implications of this point in greater detail.

The first section of this chapter considers in greater depth the exact meaning of each of the three different types of usage gaps. Following this is a discussion of the measurement of these three gaps and then a brief review of usage gap-related growth opportunities. The chapter concludes with notes on some cautions and complexities to keep in mind when evaluating, designing, and implementing usage gap-related growth strategies.

TYPES OF USAGE GAPS

In addition to being adversely affected by a product line gap and by distribution gaps, sales of an individual product line of a firm can be adversely affected by three different types of usage gaps: a *nonuser gap*, a *light user gap*, and a *light usage gap*.

NONUSER GAP

A *nonuser gap* refers to the proportion of IMP (the product line gap, if any, and distribution gaps having already been subtracted) accounted for by customers who could potentially use the product but are not using it.

Carefully defining the group of potential customers is at the heart of accurately estimating IMP and subsequently determining the size of the relevant usage gap in a given market situation. As we saw in Chapter 4, anyone who could "reasonably" be expected to use the product is included in the universe of potential customers. The word "reasonably" makes it realistic to exclude certain subgroups of the relevant population because of such consumption constraints as income, age, location, etc.

As also mentioned in Chapter 4, however, an aggressive (more inclusive) definition of the group of potential customers is suggested—especially when one is initially drawing up a market structure profile for a product line. Later on, in a matter of minutes, a firm can generate additional profiles for the same market situation, with the additional profiles reflecting varying definitions of the group of potential customers. The firm can then compare the different profiles, simulate closing particular gaps in the profiles, and estimate the likely effects on the other gaps and upon the firm's own sales. Part Three discusses this type of analysis in greater depth.

LIGHT USER GAP

A *light user gap* refers to the proportion of IMP (the product line gap, the distribution gaps, and the nonuser gap having already been subtracted) accounted for by those who do use the product but do not use it on every "use occasion."

What is the number of use occasions per potential user per year (i.e., one operating period) for the relevant product line? As in the case of estimating the number of potential users (which is used as the basis for determining the nonuser gap), the number of use occasions per potential user per year is originally estimated when the IMP is derived for the product line. Again, a "reasonable" estimate must be made, but, it is suggested that the estimate be somewhat aggressive—especially when one is initially drawing up the market structure profile.

How many use occasions arise per potential user per year for consumables such as a soft drink, a window cleaning agent, or a tennis ball? How many uses per potential user for more durable products such as an automobile, a stereo system, or a set of golf clubs? These are some of the difficult kinds of questions that the firm must attempt to answer in order first to come up with a realistic IMP estimate and then later to determine the size of the light user gap.

With reference to Chapter 4 and the discussion of growth opportunity 2—new uses for the product—each different use for a product (sometimes referred to as "extended uses") can and most of the time should be dealt with as a separate IMP and separate market structure profile. Following this principle facilitates the process of estimating the number of use occasions per potential user per year. At times, primary research will have to be done to come up with a realistic estimate. The section below, "Measuring the Size of Usage Gaps," elaborates upon this point.

LIGHT USAGE GAP

A *light usage gap* refers to the proportion of IMP (the product line gap, the distribution gaps, the nonuser gap, and the light user gap having already been subtracted) accounted for by use occasions met with a use of the relevant product—but less than a "full use."

Exactly what a full use is, when a use occasion arises, must be defined originally when IMP is estimated. How much time on a single long distance call should the phone company define as one full use? How large an insurance policy is one full use? How much sun tan lotion is one full use? How much beer is one full use? These are the kinds of questions that the firm must answer when first estimating IMP if the firm expects to come up with a realistic estimate of the size of the light usage gap for the relevant product line.

MEASURING THE SIZE OF USAGE GAPS

As when measuring the size of product line gaps and distribution gaps, the degree of accuracy with which the size of the three usage gaps can be estimated depends to a considerable extent upon the resources the firm is willing to expend in order to obtain accurate measurements.

Much national and regional data desired for estimating product line gaps and distribution gaps are available on a regular basis from commercial research houses which provide syndicated product line and distribution data services, as reviewed in previous chapters. In contrast, however, data on usage and nonusage of products are generally less readily available—without the firm's doing primary research studies on its own or contracting out such studies to a commercial market research house.

In many instances, data on usage may be available from industry-wide sources such as industry trade associations, from academic research studies, or from governmental sources.[1] In such instances, however, the data frequently are defined along parameters different from those the firm desires or are not as complete as the firm desires. Such secondary data on usage can, nevertheless, enable the firm to make at least ball park estimates regarding usage gaps for the relevant product line(s).

The question for the firm then becomes whether the costs involved in generating more definitive usage data through running or contracting out a primary research study are worthwhile in terms of the incremental benefits to be derived. A large proportion of the time, a firm may be better off to stick with the ball park estimate when first generating a market structure profile for a product line and then, later on, when trying to establish and use market structure profiles for more exacting long-range growth planning, seriously to consider investing in primary market research to develop more definitive data.[2]

SIZE OF NONUSER GAP

As indicated above, usage data are available from secondary public sources for some products. Exhibit 9-1, for example, suggests the proportions of households that are nonusers, light users, and heavy users of

Exhibit 9-1
VOLUME PURCHASED BY DIFFERENT USER GROUPS

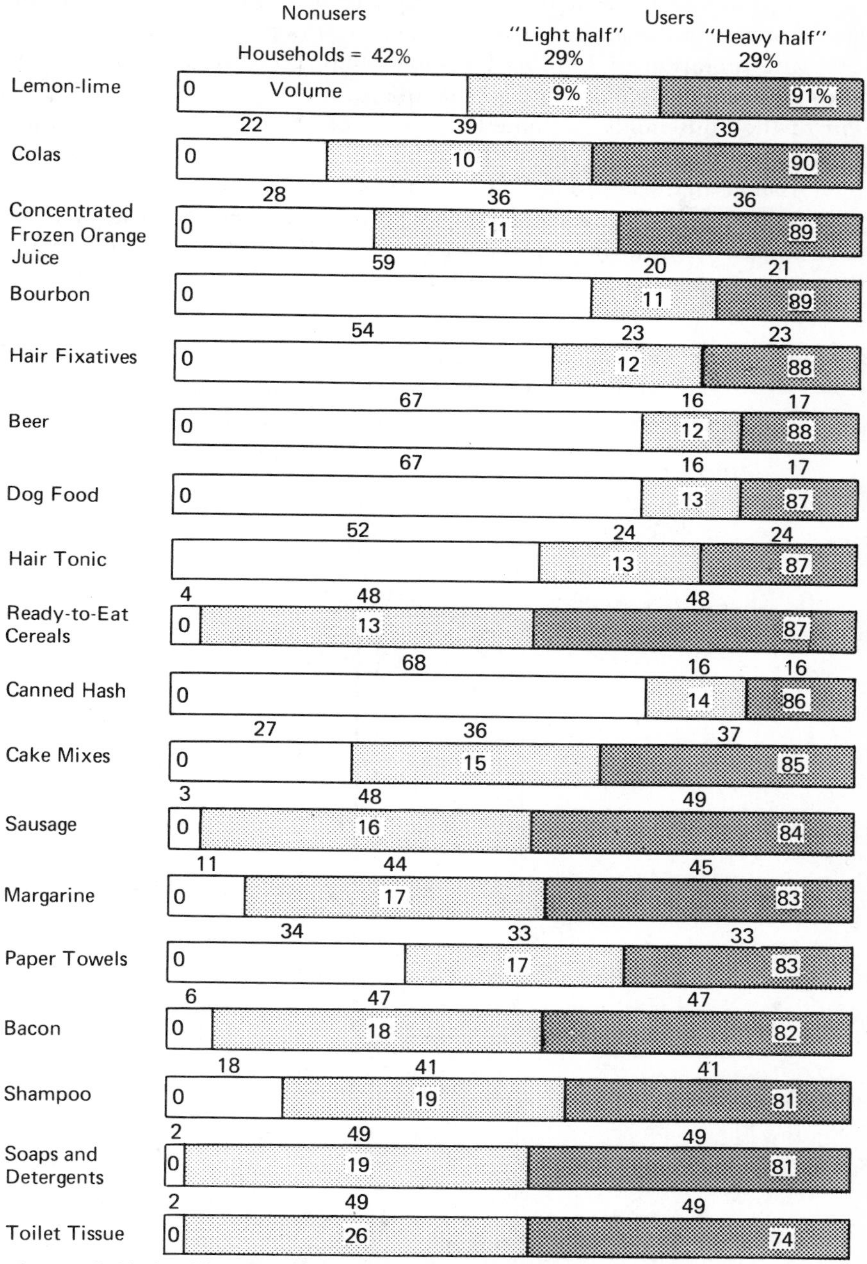

	Nonusers	Users	
	Households = 42%	"Light half" 29%	"Heavy half" 29%
Lemon-lime	0 Volume	9%	91%
Colas	22 / 39 → 0	10	39 / 90
Concentrated Frozen Orange Juice	28 / 36 → 0	11	36 / 89
Bourbon	59 → 0	11	20 / 21 / 89
Hair Fixatives	54 → 0	12	23 / 23 / 88
Beer	67 → 0	12	16 / 17 / 88
Dog Food	67 → 0	13	16 / 17 / 87
Hair Tonic	52 → 0	13	24 / 24 / 87
Ready-to-Eat Cereals	4 / 48 → 0	13	48 / 87
Canned Hash	68 → 0	14	16 / 16 / 86
Cake Mixes	27 / 36 → 0	15	37 / 85
Sausage	3 / 48 → 0	16	49 / 84
Margarine	11 / 44 → 0	17	45 / 83
Paper Towels	34 / 33 → 0	17	33 / 83
Bacon	6 / 47 → 0	18	47 / 82
Shampoo	18 / 41 → 0	19	41 / 81
Soaps and Detergents	2 / 49 → 0	19	49 / 81
Toilet Tissue	2 / 49 → 0	26	49 / 74

Source. P. Kotler, *Marketing Management: Analysis, Planning, and Control* (Englewood Cliffs, N.J: Prentice Hall Inc. 1972), p.176.

eighteen different household consumables. Readily available government data provide similar information for more durable consumer goods.[3]

Interpretation of Exhibit 9-1 shows that 42 percent of the households consume no lemon-lime soft drinks (thus, nonusers), while 29 percent of the households consume 91 percent of all lemon-lime soft drinks (thus, heavy users). The rest of the table can be read in similar fashion.

Assume that the product of concern is breakfast cereal. Immediately the problems with using secondary usage data, as mentioned above, become apparent. Data in Exhibit 9-1 cover ready-to-eat cereals, but what about cereals that require more preparation (e.g., hot cereals)? Nor do

Exhibit 9-2

NONUSER GAP FOR BREAKFAST CEREALS

Assume: 25% of relevant consumers never eat cereal for breakfast

Nonuser Gap

  = 25% (IMP − product line gap − total distribution gap)
  = 25% (100% − 20% − 40.1%)
  = 25% (39.9% of IMP)
  = **9.98% of IMP**

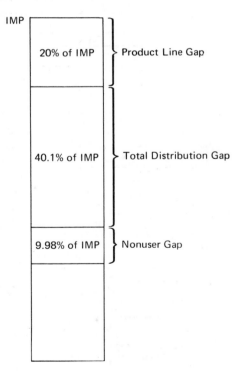

the data differentiate between cereal consumed at breakfast and cereal consumed at other times (e.g., cereal as a snack). Nor does the chart provide usage data for the potential user of concern—the individual. Rather, the usage data are on a household basis. The interested firm does not have enough information from the exhibit accurately to estimate the number of individual nonusers. The data in the exhibit are defined along parameters different from those the firm desires and are not as complete as the firm desires.

At this point, the firm can either make ball park estimates on usage —in light of the information in Exhibit 9-1—or can do or sponsor a study to procure more exacting breakfast cereal usage data.

Assume that the firm has determined that 25 percent of the 220 million potential consumers in the United States do not eat breakfast cereal at all. In this case, the *nonuser gap equals 25 percent of IMP* IF the firm has neither a product line gap nor any distribution gap.

Carrying on the example from earlier chapters, however, assume that the relevant firm has a *product line gap* of *20 percent of IMP* (see Chapter 5) and a *total distribution gap* of *40.1 percent of IMP* (see Chapter 7). This implies that even with complete usage of breakfast cereals by all potential users and a dominant market position by this firm in its relevant markets, this firm's sales volume could reach an absolute maximum of 39.9 percent of IMP (i.e., 100 percent — 20 percent product line gap—40.1 percent total distribution gap = 39.9 percent). That is to say, usage of product line elements not sold by a firm and usage attributable to distribution beyond the firm's own distribution coverage, intensity, and exposure are not part of the firm's usage gap.

In the case above, therefore, the firm's *nonuser gap* = 25 percent × 39.9 percent of IMP = approximately **10 percent of IMP**. Exhibit 9-2 presents a summary of the calculations and a market structure profile portraying the resulting nonuser gap.

SIZE OF LIGHT USER GAP

The label "light user" is attached to all customers who use a product but do not use it on every use occasion.

In order to determine the size of the light user gap, the firm compares the average use per user with the firm's own definition of "full use" as specified when IMP is originally estimated. In the case of breakfast cereal, full use for an individual consumer was defined as using the product seven times per week.

Assume that the firm finds out (through secondary data, its own research, or a sponsored research project) that the average user of breakfast cereal consumes cereal for breakfast three times per week. The resultant *light user gap* is $\frac{4}{7}$ or **57 percent of IMP** if the firm has no product line gap and no distribution gaps and if no nonuser gap exists.

In the actual breakfast cereal case reviewed above, however, the firm has a 20 percent product line gap, a 40.1 percent total distribution gap, and a 10 percent nonuser gap. Since these gaps exist, this firm's maximum sales volume is approximately 30 percent of IMP—if it is assumed that all users are full users and that this firm has a dominant position in its relevant markets.

Exhibit 9-3
LIGHT USER GAP FOR BREAKFAST CEREAL

Assume: Breakfast cereal users consume breakfast cereal 3 times per week on average, full use has been defined as 7 times per week on average.

Light User Gap

$= \frac{4}{7}$ (IMP − product line gap − total distribution gap − nonuser gap)

$= 57\%$ (100% − 20% − 40.1% − 9.98%)

$= 57\%$ (29.92%)

$= $ **17.08% of IMP**

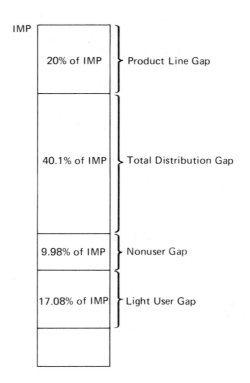

The *light user gap* of 57 percent translates, therefore, into 57% of 30% of IMP = **17.1% of IMP.** Exhibit 9-3 presents a summary of the calculations and a market structure profile portraying the resulting light user gap.

SIZE OF LIGHT USAGE GAP

"Light usage" implies that on a single use occasion when a product is used, it is not used in a "full use" as defined when IMP is estimated.

In the cereal example above, for example, assume that a single full use means a one-ounce serving. Assume also that the firm finds that the average actual serving is eight-tenths of an ounce. This leaves a 20 percent light usage gap, which would equal 20 percent of IMP in the absence of any of the other gaps already covered (product line gap, total distribution gap, nonuser gap, and light user gap). In the case above, however, these other gaps have already accounted for 87.2 percent of IMP. As a result, the *light usage gap* equals only 20% × 12.8% = **2.6% of IMP.** Exhibit 9-4 shows the calculation as well as a market structure profile portraying this light usage gap.

It makes less sense to talk about or to calculate a light usage gap when a single use occasion of a product is not defined in terms of a particular volume (e.g., serving, dosage, etc.). Most household appliances and many other durable goods are products falling into this category. The same is true for some nondurable products such as clothing.[4]

The size of the *total user gap* equals the summation of the three user gaps covered above. In the breakfast cereal example above, the *total usage gap* equals nonuser gap (10 percent of IMP) plus light user gap (17.1 percent of IMP) plus light usage gap (2.6 percent of IMP) = **29.7% of IMP.** Figure 9-1 shows this total usage gap.

USAGE GAP-RELATED GROWTH OPPORTUNITIES

Each different type of usage gap represents a separate and distinct growth opportunity for the firm. These three resulting opportunities (10, 11, and 12 below) are added to the list of nine growth opportunities already covered. The resulting list of growth opportunities is as follows:

(1) Natural changes in the size of IMP.

(2) Discovering new uses or new user segments for existing products to provide new IMP's for the firm's present products.

(3) Developing innovative product differentiations to expand existing IMP's.

Exhibit 9-4
LIGHT USAGE GAP FOR BREAKFAST CEREAL

Assume: The average size of a breakfast cereal serving is $\frac{8}{10}$ of an ounce;

and that a full serving has been defined as one full ounce.

<u>Light Usage Gap</u>

$= \frac{2}{10}$ (IMP − product line gap − total distribution gap − Nonuser gap − light user gap)

$= 20\%$ (100% − 20% − 40.1% − 9.98% − 17.08%)

$= 20\%$ (12.84%)

$= $ **2.57% of IMP**

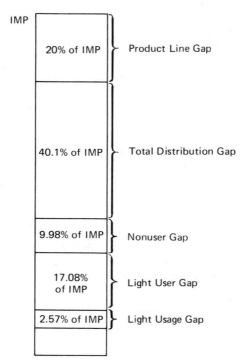

(4) Introducing new product lines to provide new IMP's for the firm.

(5) Filling out existing product lines to close product line gaps.

(6) Creating new product line elements through innovation or significant product differentiation.

(7) Expanding geographic distribution coverage.

(8) Expanding distribution intensity (i.e., the number of outlets for the relevant product in each geographic area where the firm now distributes the product).

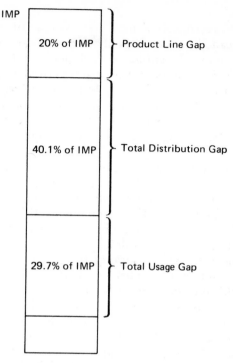

FIGURE 9-1.   Total usage gap.

(9) Expanding distribution exposure (i.e., to improve the exposure of the firm's relevant product line within individual outlets).

(10) Stimulating nonusers to use the product.

(11) Stimulating light users to use more.

(12) Increasing the amount used on each use occasion.

STIMULATING NONUSERS TO USE THE PRODUCT

The introduction of a new innovation or significant new product differentiation to the marketplace represents a new IMP to be exploited by firms selling the relevant new product line or product line element. Trash compactors and twin-blade shaving systems (e.g., Trac II) represented such new IMP's.

The first task of the relevant firm in introducing such products to the "mass market" is to educate the market about what the product does and how it works. This in an informational campaign aimed at the mass market—a market of nonusers—a campaign intended to convert these nonusers into users.

As nonusers are converted into users, competition grows as more firms follow the leader and enter the market with their own variation of the same innovation or differentiation. Each new firm is trying for a share of the growing body of users in this market. In the growth and early maturity phases of the industry life cycle for the relevant product, however, a significant group of nonusers still exists and continues to call for attention on an industrywide basis—i.e., all of the competing firms are interested in continuing to convert more nonusers of the product into users.

Unless the relevant firms continue for some time to aim at the "nonuser segment," the life cycle of the new innovation can peak out far short of ever coming close to converting all potential users into users. In markets where no single competitor is dominant, this phenomenon often occurs because the single firm, without a dominant market share, finds it difficult to justify spending its dollars to convert nonusers into users unless it has some reasonable assurance that these converted consumers will use this firm's relevant brand(s).

In view of this phenomenon, it is not surprising that most advertisements to convert nonusers into users are sponsored by firms dominant in the relevant industry. Clairol ads try to stimulate women to color their hair. Pitney-Bowes ads encourage business firms to install mailing systems. United States Tobacco Company (manufacturer of Copenhagen, Skoal, and Happy Days) ads proclaim the advantages of "smokeless tobacco."

In industries where no firm (or a few firms) dominates, industry trade associations sometimes bear the burden of attempting to convert nonusers to use the product—any brand. Recall from your own experience ads for dairy products, orange juice, glass, etc.

As nonusers are converted into users—whether they become light users or heavy users—the nonuser gap is closed. In the breakfast cereal example above, assume that the number of nonusers is reduced from 25 percent of all potential users to 15 percent of all potential users. As a result, the nonuser gap shrinks from 10 percent of IMP to 6 percent of IMP.

STIMULATING LIGHT USERS TO USE MORE

For most product lines, many consumers who do use the product do not use it on every "use occasion" (as defined in estimating IMP), thus creating for each firm selling the relevant product line a "light user gap."

In defining a light user gap and designing strategies to close such a gap, the firm must carefully distinguish between strategies oriented to stimulate light users to use more for a given purpose (or use) and strategies oriented to stimulate light users to use the product for a *new purpose* (or new use). The latter type of strategies, oriented toward new uses of the product or "extended uses," were covered under growth opportunity (2)—new uses for the product. For each potential new use of this sort, the firm usually should estimate a new and separate IMP and build a separate market structure profile.

Light user gaps can exist for most consumer nondurables, for services, and for some consumer durables. Food products serve as a good example of consumer nondurables that usually have light user gaps. Services such as restaurants ("Take your wife out to eat tonight"), life insurance ("Let's start a modest life insurance program now—with the right to add up to seven new policies later"—New York Life), and long distance telephone ("Let's straighten it out with a long distance call") also face light user gaps. Some durable goods manufacturers also. depict light user gaps for their products (e.g., Clairol's ad for a facial mirror—mirror, mirror—shows separate mirrors on the wall, desk, shelf and door).

As light users are stimulated to use more of the relevant product, the light user gap closes. In the breakfast cereal example above, assume that the average breakfast cereal consumer is stimulated to have breakfast cereal five times per week instead of three. As a result, the light user gap closes from 17 percent of IMP to 8.5 percent of IMP.

INCREASING THE AMOUNT USED ON A SINGLE USE OCCASION

Stimulating the user to use more of a product on a single use occasion represents the twelfth growth opportunity. By doing so, the firm is "closing the light usage gap."

As indicated above, for some products (e.g., consumer appliances), a light usage gap makes no sense and does not appear in the relevant market structure profile. For most products, however, a light usage gap does exist and as such provides yet another opportunity for firms to stimulate their own sales volume growth. "Take your time on your next long-distance telephone call." "Spend more on your next visit to the restaurant." "Buy a larger insurance policy." "Take a larger dish of ice cream." "Have two beers instead of one." All of these represent stimuli oriented to close light usage gaps.

As a firm is successful in bringing about an increase in the amount of the product used on a single use occasion, the light usage gap is closed. Assume in the breakfast cereal case above, for example, that the average size serving increases from the present $8/10$ of one ounce to $9/10$ of one ounce. As a result, the size of the light usage gap is cut in half, from 2.6 percent of IMP to 1.3 percent of IMP.

The prospective benefits of such a small gap closure may seem insignificant but can be quite significant indeed if the benefits of the gap closure are translated directly into the relevant firm's own sales (as opposed to competitive sales). One way in which a firm can ensure itself of receiving a large share of the incremental sales resulting from closing the light usage gap is to close the gap by means of a change in its own packaging strategy. This may mean a larger can of beer, individually packed dosages, or servings of the "full use" size, etc. One marketer of medicinal products, for example, changed the size of its individual packets to hold two tablets of the medicine (the full use dosage) instead of one. As a result, the proportion of users taking two tablets instead of one increased from 70 percent to 85 percent. This translated directly into more sales for this particular firm (not competitors).

Closing the light usage gap can, therefore, often be a more appropriate strategy choice than closing the nonuser or light user gaps—especially in situations where a firm is not the dominant competitor in the relevant product line.

Efforts directed at closing the light usage gap may also constitute the most appropriate strategy choice when the light usage gap accounts for a large share of IMP. As a product line life cycle matures and as the product line gap, the distribution gaps, the nonuser gap, and the light user gap are closed, the light usage gap may become quite significant as a proportion of IMP. In the breakfast cereal example above, for example, the light usage gap could be as large as 20 percent of IMP if the product line gap, distribution gaps, nonuser gap, and light user gaps were completely closed.

CAUTIONS AND COMPLEXITIES IN CONSIDERING USAGE GAP-RELATED GROWTH OPPORTUNITIES

As presented up to this point, the development of usage gap-related growth opportunities/strategies has been presented as being rather straightforward. In actual practice, a number of cautions and complexities also enter the picture.

INCLUDING SOME "EXTENDED USES" IN THE IMP FOR CERTAIN PRODUCTS

In some of its ads, Early Times (bourbon) advertises a variety of new drinks that can be made with Early Times. Ragu Italian cooking sauce ads feature new recipes calling for Ragu. Lysol® Spray Disinfectant

Exhibit 9-5
EXTENDED USES—GET LIGHT USERS TO USE MORE

Summer odors and germs. No job is too big (or too little) for Lysol® Spray.

Spray the intake vent of your air conditioner. It's a little thing, but it's a great way to clean the air it circulates. LYSOL Spray actually neutralizes odors in the air. Gets the whole room nice and fresh.

The summer cottage. A big job. So you get out the LYSOL Brand Spray Disinfectant to kill germs on things like garbage pails and diaper pails. Laundry hampers.

LYSOL Spray kills athlete's foot fungus on shower and bathroom floors. Controls mold, mildew and their odors.

Once over lightly with LYSOL Spray keeps your sheets and bedding smelling fresh and clean, even in muggy weather.

LYSOL Spray. Take it with you wherever you go this summer. Use it in public washrooms, motels, cabanas.

The spray that does it all. It's Lysol.

©1972 Lehn & Fink Products Co.

Courtesy of Lehn & Fink Products Company (A Division of Sterling Drug, Inc.)

ads show Lysol® being used in every different room of the house (see Exhibit 9-5). For each of these products, an almost unlimited number of somewhat different uses are possible. A firm marketing such a product is better off to include all such similar uses in a single IMP and view these ads as attempts to make light users of the respective products' full users.

The motivation for this approach is primarily one of expediency; for many products there are simply too many alternative ways of using the product for a firm explicitly to recognize each potential use. In estimating IMP in such cases, full use for a potential consumer is defined in terms of a certain volume per unit of time. Advertisements can focus upon describing some of the many possible uses of the product and pointing out the advantages of the firm's particular brand(s).

RECOGNIZING MONEY SUBSTITUTES AND CANNIBALISM

In attempting to convert nonusers into users and to convert light users into heavy users, frequently the firm's and the industry's major constraint is the limited income of the potential consumers. Given a limited income, the consumer usually must sacrifice the purchase and use of one product if he or she is to begin using (or to start using more of) another product.

In view of this phenomenon, major barriers to closing usage gaps are the many alternative uses for the consumers' dollars. The firm (and industry) should, therefore, explicitly recognize the indirect competition coming from "money substitutes" for the relevant product lines when designing strategies to increase usage. The firm must make the relevant product more appealing to consumers than alternative products having totally different functions.

Looking at usage gaps and opportunities in this light, a single firm facing large usage gaps for many different products may be competing against itself in some instances. This is not an altogether unhealthy situation, however, since competition within a firm can help make the individual product lines of the firm more competitive in their own industries against outside firms. General Motors, for example, would like its own brands (Chevrolet, Pontiac, Oldsmobile, Buick, and Cadillac) to be the best competitors in the industry. By competing with each other inside GM, these divisions develop effective competitive positions against Ford, Chrysler, AMC, and imports.

SETTING A "HEAVY USE" STANDARD AND SEGMENTING USER GROUPS

One of the obstacles to making an aggressive, yet realistic, estimate of IMP is to determine the number of "use occasions" that could reasonably call for the use of the relevant product. One way to make this estimate is to study the usage habits of the "heavy user segment" of the market and to set up an ideal usage standard for the market as a whole based upon the heavy user's usage habits.

Some firms may feel uncomfortable with such an aggressive definition—especially when dealing with product lines that are in their maturity or saturation phase (where the nonusers and light users remaining are more difficult to convert). In such instances, a firm may be wise to segment the market into usage segments with a separate IMP, a separate market structure profile, and a separate selling program for each of the usage segments. Exhibit 9-1 suggests one possible division into three segments: nonusers, light users, and heavy users.

In more mature industries, such a specialized segmented approach to the market may be the most realistic and effective way to bring about an increase in the firm's own sales for the relevant product line.

REDUCING NONUSER AND LIGHT USER GAPS: A TASK FOR INDUSTRY LEADERS AND/OR TRADE ASSOCIATIONS

One point made earlier in the chapter is worth reinforcing here. Firms with smaller market shares and/or firms entering a market quite late (in terms of stage of product life cycle) and without a significant innovation or product differentiation are not in appropriate positions to take the industry lead in attempting to convert nonusers or stimulate light users.

For firms with large market shares and/or for industry trade associations, however, advertisements and other strategies to stimulate nonusers to use a product [growth opportunity (10)] and to stimulate light users to use more of the relevant product [growth opportunity (11)] may be very appropriate and effective, regardless of what stage of life cycle an industry appears to be in. The industry's leading firm(s) stands to gain the most from a closure of industrywide usage gaps. Part of an industry trade association's responsibility is to promote sales for the industry as a whole.

STRATEGIES WHICH INCREASE UNIT VOLUME SALES BUT SOMETIMES DO NOT INCREASE TOTAL DOLLAR SALES FOR THE FIRM

The focus of the approach in this text is upon bringing about an increase in unit sales volume. Some strategies can increase the usage of the product and the absolute volume of the product sold by the firm but may not increase the total dollar sales and/or total profits for the firm.

This phenomenon is most likely to occur when a market is quite mature and competition is heavy. In such situations some competitors use a bigger product at the same price (e.g., the 120-mm cigarettes), a "buy two and get one free" approach, or simply a lower price to capture or maintain market share.

These same strategies may at the same time stimulate increased usage by making it possible for the customer to consume more of the product for the same price traditionally paid for less of the product. Whether or not such direct or indirect decreases in price per unit volume do actually increase total usage of the product and/or increase or decrease total dollar sales and profits for a firm depends upon the relevant demand curve's characteristics for the firm and the industry.

Price-related strategies such as this can be particularly effective in terms of stimulating increased usage and improved firm sales dollar volume when the industry as a whole is operating on an elastic portion of its demand curve (refer to Chapter 3). In such instances, effective price decreases result in sizable unit volume increases as well as increases in total dollar sales. The same strategy may or may not result in increased profits for the firm.[5]

CONVERTING THE LAST POTENTIAL USER IS TOO EXPENSIVE

The more broadly the firm has defined the group of potential users, the larger is the body of potential users who are to be converted from nonusers into users. The larger the body of potential users, the higher is the probability that some of the potential users, sometimes many of the potential users, simply cannot be converted into users at a reasonable cost to the firms selling the relevant product line.

The first user converted is converted very quickly and inexpensively. By the time the bulk of the group of potential users have become actual users, the time and expense required to convert the last group of potential users frequently makes it prohibitive and inadvisable for a firm to continue to pour resources into a "stimulate the nonusers" strategy.[6] The exact point in time to give up on the remaining nonusers is determined by the returns (in terms of increased sales volume) the firm is likely to realize from the expenditure of the same resources on any of its other growth opportunities/strategies.

The same "principle of diminishing returns" applies for trying to convert the last light users into heavy users and trying to make every single last use a full use (thus completely closing the light usage gap). The firm is usually better off to change emphasis to other strategies once significant usage has been obtained. It is simply too expensive (in light of the firm's other possible alternative strategies) to try to squeeze the last drop out of any or all of the three usage strategies.

SUMMARY

This chapter first considers the definition and measurement of usage gaps and then examines usage gap-related growth opportunities and strategies.

A firm can face three separate but interrelated usage gaps for each IMP the firm recognizes. A *nonuser gap* refers to the proportion of IMP accounted for by customers who could potentially use the product but are not using it. A *light user gap* refers to the proportion of IMP accounted for by those who do use the product but do not use it on every "use occasion." A *light usage gap* refers to the proportion of IMP accounted for by use occasions met with a use of the relevant product—but less than a "full use."

Each usage gap represents a separate and distinct growth opportunity for the firm. The three growth opportunities are to:

- Stimulate nonusers to use the product.
- Stimulate light users to use the product on more use occasions.
- Increase the amount of the product used on each use occasion when the product is used.

Cautions, complexities, and special insights that one should bear in mind when considering usage gap-related growth opportunities and strategies include the following:

- For the sake of expediency, "extended uses" should be included in a single IMP estimate for products with a very broad range of possible uses.
- Money substitutes (as opposed to functional substitutes) should be recognized as possible competition when designing usage gap-related growth strategies.
- In more mature markets, it is often helpful to segment the market into "user segments."
- It is usually most appropriate for dominant competitors and/or trade associations to take the lead in implementing usage gap-related growth strategies.
- Beware of strategies that close usage gaps and increase firm unit sales volume but do not increase the firm's profits.
- Converting the last potential user is too expensive.

REVIEW QUESTIONS

1. Should a firm define the group of potential users and the number of use occasions aggressively or conservatively? Discuss.

2. What is the difference between a light user gap and a light usage gap?

3. Where can a firm get data on usage habits of actual and potential customers?

4. The larger the product line gap and distribution gaps tend to be (as proportions of IMP), the smaller the usage gaps tend to be (as proportions of IMP). Why is this true?

5. As product line gaps and distribution gaps are closed, what is likely to happen to the size of the usage gaps? Why?

6. During what stage of the product line life cycle are usage gap-related growth strategies likely to close most quickly?

7. Why is usage segmentation most appropriate in later stages of the product line life cycle?

8. Why are usage gap-related growth strategies usually not appropriate for less dominant firms in an industry? When and how can such firms effectively use such strategies?

9. Why is attempting to convert the last user too expensive?

NOTES

1. For example, the *United States Statistical Abstract* provides government data on ownership rates for consumer durables. Also, see Exhibit 9-1.

2. Part Three considers such analysis of cost/benefit trade-offs in greater depth.

3. See *United States Statistical Abstract*.

4. It is possible to encourage heavier use of such products, thus attempting to shorten the average useful life and, therefore, increasing IMP (short run). In order to do this, however, an expanded definition of IMP for such products is required.

5. The focus of the analysis in this situation is the elasticity of demand at the relevant points of the firm's demand curve and the industry's demand curve. Refer to Chapter 3 for a discussion.

6. Consumer behaviorists characterize the last group of potential users as "laggards"—which diffusion group they describe as having the slowest "adoption process." For a discussion, see E. M. Rogers, *Diffusion of Innovations* (New York: Free Press, 1962).

10

Competitive Gaps and Firm Sales

The past several chapters have explained away most of the huge gap that usually exists between industry market potential (IMP) and the firm's own sales for a given product line. As explained up to this point, the overall gap is made up of a *product line gap,* a *total distribution gap,* and a *total usage gap.* Once these three gaps and the firm's own sales in this product line have been subtracted from IMP, the proportion of IMP remaining is referred to as the *competitive gap.*

This chapter first considers the derivation and measurement of the competitive gap. Following is a review of competitive gap-related growth opportunities. The chapter concludes with a discussion of some cautions and complexities for one to bear in mind when considering and evaluating competitive gap-related opportunities.

MEASURING THE SIZE OF THE COMPETITIVE GAP

The overall competitive gap is a residual, in that it equals what is left over from IMP after the product line gap, the total distribution gap,

Exhibit 10-1
DETERMINING THE SIZE OF THE COMPETITIVE GAP

Product line gap   = 20% of IMP
Total distribution gap   = 40.1% of IMP
Total usage gap   = 29.7% of IMP
Firm sales   = 4.1% of IMP

                    TOTAL   93.9% of IMP

Therefore,
Competitive gap = 100% − 93.9% = **6.1% of IMP**

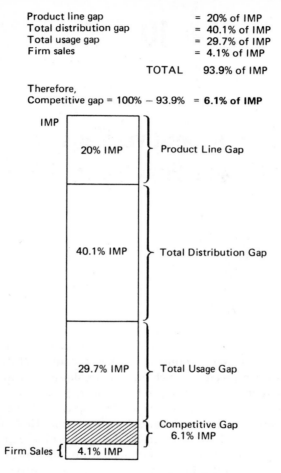

the total usage gap, and the firm's own sales have been subtracted from IMP.

Since the measurements of the product line gap, the total distribution gap, and the total usage gap have already been covered, the major task remaining in order to come up with the size of the competitive gap is to measure the relevant firm's sales for this product line. For a product line with only one use and for which only one IMP and one market structure profile have been developed, this is rather straightforward—the firm simply determines its unit volume sales for the product line over the past operating period. This figure is subtracted from

IMP along with the gaps mentioned above, and the residual equals the competitive gap.

For example, assume: IMP equals 80 billion units; the product line gap equals 20 percent of IMP; the total distribution gap equals 40.1 percent of IMP; the usage gap equals 29.7 percent of IMP; and firm sales for this product line in the last operation period equaled 3.3 billion units (i.e., 4.1 percent of IMP). Then the *competitive gap* equals:

$$100\% - 20\% - 40.1\% - 29.7\% - 4.1\% = \textbf{6.1\% of IMP}$$

Exhibit 10-1 displays this in the form of a market structure profile.

In some cases, however, as considered in previous chapters, it is appropriate for the firm to develop more than a single IMP and single market structure profile for a given product line. This is true when a product can have more than one use (e.g., cereal as a breakfast cereal or as a snack) or when the firm has chosen to segment the market and deal with one or more of the segments individually. In either case, the firm should develop a separate market structure profile for each relevant use or segment. When doing so, in addition to measuring separate product line gaps, separate total distribution gaps, and separate total usage gaps for each profile, the firm may have to do some research on its own firm sales in the relevant product line to determine which unit sales of the product belong with which market structure profile.

In the cereal case cited throughout the text, for example, assume that two IMP's and two market structure profiles are relevant as shown in Exhibit 10-2, where the figures show the firm's sales of cereal as a breakfast food equal to 3.3 billion units and the firm's sales of cereal as a snack equal to one billion units. Note also the different-size IMP's and the different market structure profiles. If these figures are used, the competitive gaps for the firm equal 6.1 percent of IMP for breakfast cereal and 4 percent of IMP for cereal as a snack.

DETERMINING THE SIZE OF THE SUBSTITUTE'S POSITION TO BE PENETRATED

In the chapter considering product line gaps, it was seen that the proportions of current industry sales accounted for by each element of a product line sometimes should not be used as the main determinant of the size of the firm's product line gap. This is particularly true when one of the product line elements is relatively new to the market and represents an innovation or significant product differentiation. In the

Exhibit 10-2
MULTIPLE MARKET STRUCTURE PROFILES FOR
A PRODUCT WITH MULTIPLE USES

Example: Industry Market Potentials for Cereal (A Product with Multiple Uses)

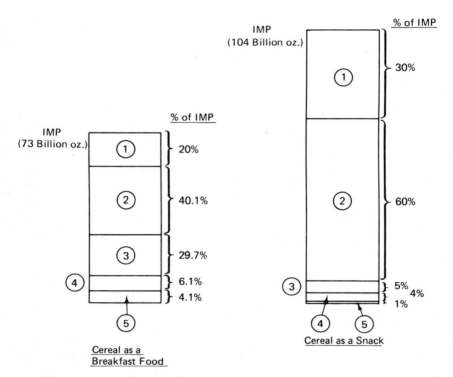

Cereal as a
Breakfast Food

Cereal as a Snack

(1) Product line gap
(2) Total distribution gap
(3) Total usage gap
(4) Competitive gap
(5) Firm sales

example used in that chapter, low-cost electronic calculators were estimated to have captured only 18 percent of the personal calculator market
in 1972. The proportion of IMP assigned to this significant new innovation was, however, 75 percent of IMP so as to reflect the higher market
share that would in all likelihood eventually be captured by the new
innovation. (Refer to Table 5-1.)

A similar adjustment may be called for if a firm feels that product line elements that it does market can penetrate the sales positions of product line elements that it does not market—*even when its own product line elements represent no innovation or significant new product differentiation.*

A firm marketing antacids in liquid form, effervescent form, and in swallowable tablets, for example, may see a form that it does not sell—e.g., chewable tablets—holding a steady or growing share of the antacid market and may not, therefore, feel it realistic to penetrate the share held by chewable tablets. Another firm which markets the chewable tablet form, however, may feel that it is very realistic to penetrate present market positions held by any or all of the other forms of antacids.

In either case above (innovation or no innovation), the firm adjusts the product line gap to make it smaller. In one case, the adjustment reflects an innovative new product line element (electronic calculator) and in the other case, the adjustment reflects the firm's attitude regarding the possibility of using product line element(s) that it does sell (chewable antacid) to penetrate the position(s) of one or more elements that the firm does not sell.

In terms of the market structure profile, the firm desiring to "penetrate the substitute's position," adjusts its full product line gap (FPLG) downward to equal a "real product line gap" (RPLG). The growth opportunity of penetrating the substitute's position(s) *does not show up* in the market structure profile *as part of the product line gap. This growth opportunity* (of penetrating the substitute's position) *shows up instead as part of the competitive gap.*

THE RELEVANT SUBSTITUTE'S POSITION

Three factors determine the size of the "relevant substitute's position(s) to be penetrated": (1) *the full substitute's position,* (2) *a distribution factor,* and (3) *a usage factor.*

The *full substitute's position* is the amount the original product line gap is cut back—i.e., the full product line gap minus the real product line gap. This full substitute's position is *not,* however, an accurate measure of the size of the relevant growth opportunity for the firm. One factor limiting the firm's ability to grow by means of penetrating the substitute's position is the firm's own limited distribution coverage, intensity, and exposure. Just as these distribution limitations preclude the firm from realizing some sales of elements of the product line that the firm does sell, so too they preclude the firm from realizing some sales of its own product line elements as substitutes for product line elements that it does not sell. The extent of the firm's distribution capability is referred to as a *distribution factor*. The distribution factor, in essence, equals the IMP left after dropping the total distribution gap divided by the IMP left before dropping the total distribution gap.[1]

A second factor limiting the firm's ability to grow by means of penetrating the substitute's position is a less than complete use of the product line element(s) whose position is (are) to be penetrated. Just as less than complete use accounts for part of the gap between firm sales and market potential for product line elements that the firm does sell, less than complete use does the same thing for would-be sales of substitute product line elements whose position(s) the firm is attempting to penetrate. The extent of usage of the relevant product line versus what has been defined as full usage equals a *usage factor*. This usage factor equals the IMP left after dropping the total usage gap divided by the IMP left before dropping the total usage gap.[2]

The size of the substitute's position to be penetrated is determined by the product of the three factors reviewed above:

Full substitute position × distribution factor × usage factor [3]

In many cases, the relevant substitute's position and the growth opportunity represented by same can be very significant. This is particularly true when a firm recognizes a large product line gap. In the personal calculator case presented earlier (Table 5-1), for example, a firm producing low-cost electronic calculators but not mechanical low-cost adding machines in 1972 might well have faced a market structure profile such as the one presented in Fig. 10-1. In that case, the firm estimates that low-cost electronic calculators could penetrate a significant portion of the 80 percent of market then (1972) held by a substitute (the mechanical low-cost adding machine).

COMPETITIVE GAP-RELATED
GROWTH OPPORTUNITIES

The final three growth opportunities, as expressed in terms of market structure profiles, relate to the competitive gap and the firm's existing sales (or present position).

To this point, twelve opportunities have been covered. These have included:

(1) Natural changes in the size of IMP.

(2) Discovering new uses or new user segments for existing products to provide new IMP's for the firm's present products.

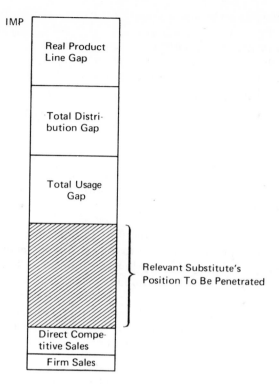

FIGURE 10-1. Relevant substitute's position can be significant.

(3) Developing innovative product differentiation to expand existing IMP's.

(4) Introducing new product lines to provide new IMP's for the firm.

(5) Filling out existing product lines to close product line gaps.

(6) Creating new product line elements through innovation or significant product differentiation.

(7) Expanding geographic distribution coverage.

(8) Expanding distribution intensity (i.e., the number of outlets for the relevant product in each geographic area where the firm now distributes the product).

(9) Expanding distribution exposure (i.e., to improve the exposure of the firm's relevant product line within individual outlets).

(10) Stimulating nonusers to use the product.

(11) Stimulating light users to use more.

(12) Increasing the amount used on each use occasion.

The final three growth opportunities are:

(13) Penetrating the substitute's position(s).
(14) Penetrating direct competitor's position(s).
(15) Defending the firm's present position (i.e., present firm sales).

PENETRATING THE SUBSTITUTE'S POSITION(S)

"Penetrating the substitute's position" is a conscious strategy directed toward closing the "relevant substitute's position(s)" when such a position is recognized in the market structure profile—for example, as in Fig. 10-1.

Such a strategy may reflect an effort to sell a firm's innovative new product line element in preference to an existing element. For example, Bell & Howell is attempting to sell their innovative "cube system" in preference to Kodak's more traditional circular tray system (see Exhibit 10-3).

Alternatively, a strategy to penetrate the substitute's position may be used when a firm is attempting to sell a product line element that

Exhibit 10-3
BELL & HOWELL SLIDE CUBES ATTEMPT TO PENETRATE
SUBSTITUTE'S POSITION (BULKY ROUND TRAYS)

The cube
beats the circle 8 to 1.*

Bulky round trays can't match the compact Bell & Howell® Slide Cube™ cartridge system for storage convenience. That's obvious.

What isn't so obvious is how this can mean bigger sales and profits for you. Because of its compact size your customers will *show and store* their slides in the Slide Cube cartridge. This means additional and continuing volume and traffic for you after you've sold a Slide Cube™ projector.

And, the Slide Cube projector measures just 9"x9"x8." So it requires less shelf and display space than many circular tray models.

The whole line of full-featured, handsome Slide Cube projectors really sells. And, we're going to increase those sales in 1974 with the biggest Slide Cube consumer advertising campaign ever undertaken.

Stock and demonstrate the Slide Cube system and help yourself to bigger volume and profits.

□ BELL & HOWELL

The Bell & Howell Slide Cube Projector. More profits in less space.

*Slide Cube cartridges store slides in about ⅓ the space of 80-slide round trays.

©1974 BELL & HOWELL COMPANY. All Rights Reserved. Bell & Howell and Slide Cube are trademarks of Bell & Howell Company.

it does make in preference to one or more product line elements that it does not make—for example, Kawasaki motorcycles versus small automobiles; Contac cold capsules versus cold tablets and liquids; and Blistex lip ointment versus competitive Chapstick.

PENETRATING DIRECT COMPETITOR'S POSITION(S)

Perhaps the most obvious and popular of all growth strategies is that of "penetrating the direct competitor's position(s)."

What is meant by "direct competitive positions" are market shares (i.e., existing sales) held currently by competitive brands that are the same product line element(s) as the relevant firm's own product line element(s) (as opposed to positions currently held by product line elements that the relevant firm itself does not sell).

In penetrating direct competitive positions, the firm seeks somehow to differentiate its product from similar products of direct competitors. For example, Bristol Myers company contrasts its deodorant, Ultra Ban, with four direct competitors. Ultra Ban "tested *better* in helping stop wetness"—and is differentiated as such from its competitors in Ban advertisements.

A firm's efforts to differentiate its product through promoting some small physical difference or performance difference between its own brand(s) and competitive brands can lead to some confusion in drawing up and interpreting a market structure profile. This problem and its resolution are discussed below under "Cautions and Complexities."

Penetrating direct competitor's positions becomes a very important strategy as a life cycle for a product line begins to mature and firms find themselves all competing for larger shares of a market for which the overall growth rate either is slowing down or has already peaked out. The logic for emphasizing strategies aimed at the competitive gap under such circumstances can be seen clearly in the form of a market structure profile for a mature market. A firm that has been a long-time competitor in such a market is likely to face a profile such as the one depicted in Fig. 10-2. Note that the competitive gap is now the largest of all the gaps.[4]

DEFENDING THE FIRM'S PRESENT POSITION

A major task for a firm that has established itself as a leader in a growing market (e.g., IBM) or a firm that has a dominant share in a more mature market (e.g., Clorox Bleach) is to "defend the firm's present position."

Such a defense involves continual reinforcement of the dominant firm's present customers and a close monitoring of competitors' growth

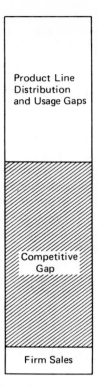

FIGURE 10-2.   Competitive gap (and the related growth oppor-
                         tunity) can become very important in a mature
                         market.

strategies aimed at the relevant firm's dominant position.[5] Innovative
new product line elements or significant new product differentiations can
erode a leader's market position, as can a heavy competitive advertising
campaign and/or more subtle segmentation strategies. Defending a position is *not a passive strategy.*

CAUTIONS AND COMPLEXITIES
IN CONSIDERING COMPETITIVE
GAP-RELATED GROWTH
OPPORTUNITIES

The consideration of competitive gap-related growth opportunities is
somewhat more straightforward and less complex than the consideration
of most growth opportunities viewed in earlier chapters. Several cautions

and complexities should, nevertheless, be borne in mind when these competitive gap-related opportunities are evaluated.

COMPETITIVE GAP OR PART OF PRODUCT LINE GAP?

During the discussion of growth opportunity (14) (penetrating the direct competitor's position), a complication was mentioned which can arise in drawing up a market structure profile when a firm attempts to penetrate a competitor's position by promoting some small physical difference or small performance difference between its own product and competitive brands.

When or under what circumstances does such an actual or "created" difference actually mean that the firm using such a strategy has in effect come up with a new product line element?

For example, Mazola differentiates its cooking oil from Crisco and Wesson oils because of Mazola's basic ingredient—corn oil. Is corn oil a separate product line element? If so, Crisco and Wesson should recognize the market position held by corn oils as a product line gap to be closed [growth opportunity (5)]—not a direct competitive gap. Alternatively, Crisco and Wesson could recognize corn oil's position as a substitute's position to be penetrated [therefore, representing growth opportunity (13)].

The same question could arise when one is building and considering market structure profiles for many other products. Should printing calculators under $250 all be considered as one product line element? Or, should each different combination of features (e.g., memory, 12-digit, % Tax/Discount, printer shutoff, etc.) represent a different product line element?

The primary determinant of whether or not to recognize a particular differentiation as a separate product line element is the attitude of the relevant body of customers. Often, a primary research study of consumer buying attitudes toward and reasons for purchasing particular brands may be necessary in order to determine whether a differentiation is important enough to recognize as a separate product line element. If a major reason why customers buying the brand or brands having a particular differentiation (whether the differentiation is one of size, style, color, flavor, form, quality/price, or any of the other product line dimensions outlined in the chapter defining product line gaps) is specifically because of that differentiation, then a new product line element does indeed exist and should be recognized by each firm in that market.

Sales data availability (for your firm and the industry as a whole) is another important factor to keep in mind when determining which different product line elements to recognize. As a general principle, a firm should try to avoid defining an excessive number of different product line elements, since recognizing a large number of elements not only unduly complicates the market structure profile but also can call for the expenditure of too much time and money on accumulating separate sales data for each different element for the firm itself and for the industry as a whole.

PENETRATING THE SUBSTITUTE'S POSITION(S): AN EXPENSIVE STRATEGY

Very much like strategies designed to close nonuser and light user gaps, a strategy intended to penetrate a substitute's position(s) is usually inappropriate for a firm that is not a leader in the relevant industry. Kawasaki or Honda or Harley-Davidson could appropriately attempt to sell motorcycles against subcompact automobiles, because if the strategy is successful and converts some would-be auto buyers into motorcycle buyers, each of these firms stands to get a good share of that new business, because each has a significant share of the existing motorcycle market. A similar strategy by a relatively small and less well-known manufacturer would most likely generate more new motorcycle sales for the major motorcycle firms than for itself.

An important exception to the generalization above is when a firm with any market share (large, small, or even insignificant) is the first firm (or one of the first firms) to introduce to the market an innovation or significant product differentiation that in all likelihood will penetrate the existing industrywide sales position of a substitute(s). As a caution for smaller firms following such a strategy, such firms better have a basis for protecting their innovation from larger competitors over the longer term. Such protection can take the form of patents, copyrights, or a very advanced technology that will take competitors some time to decipher and translate into operational and competitive product line entries.

USING SEGMENTATION TO PENETRATE COMPETITOR'S POSITION(S)—CALLS FOR A CHANGE IN MARKET STRUCTURE PROFILE

As indicated earlier in the chapter, in a mature market the competitive gap can become the dominant gap in the market structure profile, thereby representing the largest growth opportunity for an individual competing firm. For example, review the profile presented in Fig. 10-2.

An important market strategy in such mature markets is segmentation—by any of the means reviewed in Chapter 4 (covering the meaning and estimation of IMP). As mentioned in that chapter, such a strategy is used to focus upon individual homogeneous groups of potential customers. The firm designs a "customized" market offering for each "segment" upon which the firm desires to concentrate its selling effort.

Recall also, however, that when a firm segments an overall market, each segment relevant for the firm now represents a separate IMP and

Exhibit 10-4
SEGMENTING A MARKET STRUCTURE PROFILE
IN A MATURE MARKET

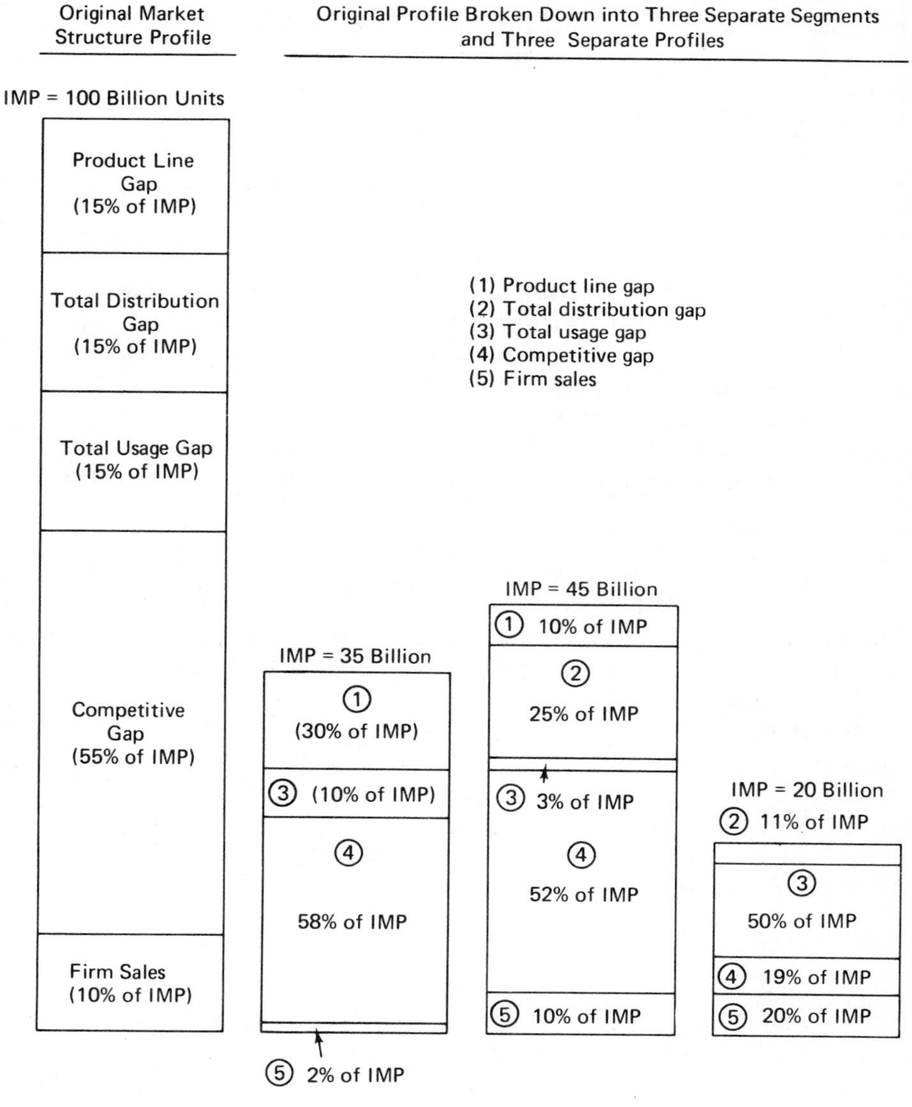

Original Market Structure Profile	Original Profile Broken Down into Three Separate Segments and Three Separate Profiles

IMP = 100 Billion Units

Product Line Gap (15% of IMP)
Total Distribution Gap (15% of IMP)
Total Usage Gap (15% of IMP)
Competitive Gap (55% of IMP)
Firm Sales (10% of IMP)

(1) Product line gap
(2) Total distribution gap
(3) Total usage gap
(4) Competitive gap
(5) Firm sales

IMP = 45 Billion

① 10% of IMP
② 25% of IMP
③ 3% of IMP
④ 52% of IMP
⑤ 10% of IMP

IMP = 35 Billion

① (30% of IMP)
③ (10% of IMP)
④ 58% of IMP

⑤ 2% of IMP

IMP = 20 Billion

② 11% of IMP
③ 50% of IMP
④ 19% of IMP
⑤ 20% of IMP

separate market structure profile. In so viewing each segment, the firm can use the concept of a market structure profile to provide better perspectives for developing its sales strategies for each individual relevant segment. For example, Exhibit 10-4 shows an original profile broken up into three smaller profiles, one for each of three segments recognized.

Having segmented a market as such, a firm may find that in one or more of the relevant segments its major growth gap is no longer the competitive gap, but is, rather, one of the other gaps such as a product line gap (e.g., for a segment wanting a higher quality and high-priced product line element, when the relevant firm sells no such product line element), distribution gap (e.g., a segment patronizing particular types of outlets where the relevant firm has poor distribution intensity), or usage gap (e.g., if usage segmentation is used and the firm desires to focus upon the nonuser segment or a light user segment).

SUMMARY

The chapter first considered the derivation and measurement of the competitive gap and then examined competitive gap-related opportunities and some cautions and complexities the firm should keep in mind when evaluating these opportunities.

The overall competitive gap is a residual, in that it equals what is left over from IMP after the product line gap, the total distribution gap, the total usage gap, and the firm's own sales have been subtracted from IMP.

A substitute's position to be penetrated (relevant substitute's position) can exist when one of the product line elements is relatively new to the market and represents an innovation or significant product differentiation or when a firm feels that product line elements which it does market can penetrate the sales positions of product line elements which it does not market—*even when its own product line elements represent no innovation or significant new product differentiation*. The relevant substitute's position equals the product of a "full substitute's position" times a "distribution factor" times a "usage factor" and is recognized as a specific part of the overall competitive gap.

Growth opportunities related to the competitive gap and present firm sales are

- Penetrating the substitute's position(s).
- Penetrating direct competitor's position(s).
- Defending the firm's present position (i.e., present firm sales).

Several cautions and complexities should be borne in mind when one is evaluating these competitive gap-related opportunities. These include the following:

- It is often difficult to tell when to recognize when a competitive differentiation of a product should be recognized as a new product line element.
- Penetrating the substitute's position is an expensive strategy—usually not appropriate for smaller, less dominant firms in an industry.
- When segmentation is used to penetrate competitive positions, a change in the firm's market structure profiles is appropriate.

REVIEW QUESTIONS

1. Why is the competitive gap referred to as a residual?
2. Under what circumstances might a firm recognize a substitute's position to be penetrated?
3. What is a substitution factor and how is it determined?
4. What is the difference between a "full substitute's position" and a "relevant substitute's position" and which is larger than the other? Why?
5. When a relevant substitute's position is added to a given market structure profile, does the direct competitive gap increase, decrease, or remain the same? Explain.
6. When one competitor introduces a new and innovative product line element in an attempt to penetrate competitive positions, what change(s) takes place in the market structure profiles of: (1) the competitors; (2) the firm with the innovation?
7. Why must "defending one's present position" be an active, rather than a passive, strategy?
8. During what stage of the product line life cycle are strategies related to the competitive gap likely to be most important? Why?
9. Why is "penetrating the substitute's position" an inappropriate strategy for some firms?
10. When a firm is using segmentation, how is the firm helped by breaking a single market structure profile into a number of smaller profiles?

NOTES

1.   It should be noted that the definition of ideal or complete distribution for the element(s) whose position(s) is to be penetrated can vary from the definition of complete distribution for product line elements that the firm produces. When this is the case, the size of the distribution gaps should be adjusted accordingly.

2.   As in the case of distribution, usage rates (and gaps) for the element(s) whose position(s) is to be penetrated may vary from the usage rates for product line elements that the firm produces. When this is the case, the size of the usage gaps should be adjusted accordingly.

3.   When a substitute's position is to be recognized, the size of the distribution gap and usage gap in the market structure profile will change—sometimes slightly (when only a small full substitute's position is recognized) and sometimes quite significantly (when a large full substitute's position is recognized).

4.   For an interesting conceptual framework for and discussion of the development of strategies oriented to penetrate competitive positions, see C. Davis Fogg, "Planning Gains in Market Share," *Journal of Marketing,* Vol. 38 (July, 1974), pp. 30–38.

5.   "Dissonance reduction" and the "reaction threshold theory" are areas of thought that have contributed explanations and suggestions relevant for a firm attempting not only to defend but also to capitalize upon a leadership position in a market. For discussions of these theories, see: W. J. Bilkey, "Consistency Test of Psychic Tension Ratings Involved in Consumer Purchasing Behavior," *Journal of Social Psychology* (February, 1957), pp. 81–91; and S. Oshikawa, "Can Cognitive Dissonance Theory Explain Consumer Behavior?" *Journal of Marketing* (October, 1969), pp. 44–49.

PART THREE

Market Structure Profile Analysis as an Aid for Making Growth Planning Decisions

Part Three reviews some of the many ways in which market structure profiles can provide visual and quantitative perspectives to help firms make better growth planning decisions. Individual firms generating market structure profiles for their own product lines can come up with many variations and extensions of the uses discussed in this section.

The first chapter of Part Three describes in general how market structure profile analysis can aid in examining the benefit/cost trade-offs associated with each alternative growth opportunity. The following chapter provides specific examples of how market structure profile analysis can be used to estimate the incremental sales likely to result from taking advantage of the various growth opportunities. The final chapter of Part Three provides some additional notes and suggestions for using market structure profile analysis.

11

Using
Market Structure Profile Analysis
to Help Compare
Strategic Growth Opportunities

The comparison of strategic-growth alternatives begins with an estimation of the likely incremental benefits (in terms of new firm sales and profits) to be derived from various alternatives. In some situations, firms rely strictly on judgment and past experience in making such estimates. At other times, firms may acquire secondary data or generate primary data to help make such estimates.

One of the functions of market structure profile analysis is to facilitate the estimation of the likely results (in terms of incremental firm sales and profits) of implementing alternative growth strategies. (The next chapter provides specific examples of such estimations.) The profile does not give management a definitive estimate of the likely result of the strategy, but it certainly can aid the manager in estimating a range of possible outcomes and in assigning explicit (if formal decision theory is used) or implicit probabilities to various possible outcomes or payoffs (i.e., incremental sales and profits) associated with each strategic alternative.

GENERAL RELATIONSHIPS: MARKET STRUCTURE PROFILES, GROWTH OPPORTUNITIES AND NEW FIRM SALES

A market structure profile serves as a focal point for showing the inter-relationships among and between the fifteen growth opportunities discussed in Part Two. Exhibit 11-1 summarizes these growth-opportunity interrelationships.

Exhibit 11-1
SUMMARY OF GROWTH OPPORTUNITIES
EXPRESSED IN TERMS OF
MARKET STRUCTURE PROFILES

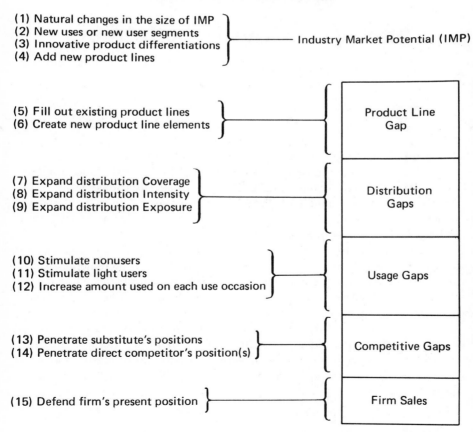

(1) Natural changes in the size of IMP
(2) New uses or new user segments
(3) Innovative product differentiations
(4) Add new product lines

Industry Market Potential (IMP)

(5) Fill out existing product lines
(6) Create new product line elements

Product Line Gap

(7) Expand distribution Coverage
(8) Expand distribution Intensity
(9) Expand distribution Exposure

Distribution Gaps

(10) Stimulate nonusers
(11) Stimulate light users
(12) Increase amount used on each use occasion

Usage Gaps

(13) Penetrate substitute's positions
(14) Penetrate direct competitor's position(s)

Competitive Gaps

(15) Defend firm's present position

Firm Sales

Examples of each of these growth opportunities include the following:

(1) *Natural changes in the size of industry market potential* (IMP) —Gerber's baby food sales boom during the late 1940's and early 1950's due to increasing number of births.

(2) Develop and promote *new uses* for an existing product—Clorox promotes use of bleach as a household disinfectant.

(3) *Innovative product differentiations*—Introduction of low-priced electronic calculators during early to mid-1970's expands calculator market.

(4) Add a *new* separate and distinct *product line*—Xerox gets into the computer business.

(5) *Fill out an existing product line*—Ford adds a "precision size" car, Granada, to their line of automobiles.

(6) *Create new product line elements*—Miller Brewing Company adds Lite, a "diet" beer.

(7) *Expand* geographic *distribution coverage*—Kimberly Clark expands distribution of Kimbies to the East Coast.

(8) *Expand distribution intensity* within a given geographic area— The proportion of drug stores in the Midwest handling Ultrabrite toothpaste grows from 50 percent to 70 percent.

(9) *Expand distribution exposure* within individual distribution outlets—Average shelf space per outlet for Kellogg Cereals increases from 12 facings to 15 facings.

(10) *Stimulate nonusers* to start using a product—Walt Garrison wants you to start using some Skoal.

(11) *Stimulate light users to use more* of a product—Did you have your Wheaties this morning?

(12) *Increase serving/dosage*—Alka Seltzer packages two tablets in each foil package.

(13) *Penetrate substitutes' position*(s)—Use a felt tip pen instead of a ball point.

(14) *Penetrate direct competitors' position*(s)—Use a Flair instead of a BIC Banana.

(15) *Defend the firm's present position*—IBM introduces a new generation of computers.

Market structure profiles provide the firm with significant insights concerning the incremental sales that each growth strategy is likely to yield. Review for a moment how each of the fifteen growth opportunities leads to incremental firm sales as expressed in the form of market structure profiles (Table 11-1).

Table 11-1
MARKET STRUCTURE PROFILES, GROWTH OPPORTUNITIES,
AND NEW FIRM SALES

Growth opportunities 1–4	Can represent totally *new markets* for the firm's present product line(s). The new market structure profile(s) incorporating these new markets represents the size of the *new sales* growth opportunity. As new IMP's are recognized and focused upon by the firm, *new firm sales* result.
Growth opportunities 5–6	Represent *new product line elements* for the firm within existing lines and, as such, mean *new firm sales*.
Growth opportunities 7–9	Represent *expanded/improved distribution and availability* of the firm's relevant product line. This means *new firm sales*.
Growth opportunities 10–12	Represent *expanded usage* of the product by relevant potential users. This means *new firm sales*.
Growth opportunities 13–15	Represent *improved market share*. This usually means *new firm sales*.

USING MARKET STRUCTURE PROFILES TO HELP ESTIMATE THE INCREMENTAL SALES LIKELY TO RESULT FROM IMPLEMENTING ALTERNATIVE GROWTH STRATEGIES

Figure 11-1 and Table 11-1 review *in a very general way* how incremental sales resulting from various growth strategies can be expressed in terms of market structure profiles.

Exact estimates of the incremental firm sales likely to result from taking advantage of each growth opportunity cannot be made—even by using market structure profiles. The framework provided by market structure profile analysis does, however, provide a number of guideposts to help the executive structure his analysis and come up with more

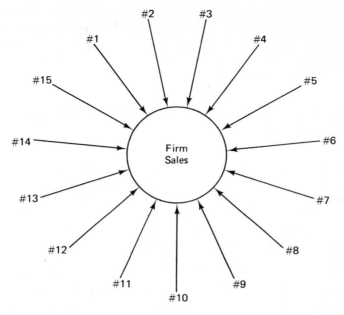

FIGURE 11-1.

accurate estimates of incremental firm sales likely to result from each growth opportunity.

   Three market structure profile measures provide particularly helpful insights for making such estimates. These three measures are *industry market potential* (IMP), *relevant industry sales* (RIS), and *real market share (RMS)*. *Industry market potential* (IMP) has already been discussed in some detail. *Relevant industry sales* (RIS) equals firm sales plus the competitive gap(s). *Real market share* (RMS) equals

$$\frac{\text{Firm sales}}{\text{Firm sales plus the competive gap(s)}} \quad \text{or} \quad \frac{\text{Firm sales}}{\text{Relevant Industry sales}}$$

   These three measures—*IMP, RIS,* and *RMS*—become important bases for estimating the incremental sales to be achieved through the various possible alternative growth opportunities. As viewed in terms of market structure profiles, the firm can realize incremental firm sales as a result of: (1) *increasing the firm's total IMP;* (2) *increasing relevant industry sales* (RIS) (i.e., firm sales plus the competitive gap) while maintaining its present real market share; and/or (3) *improving its real market share* (RMS).

Overlooking alternative number (3) above for the moment, consider how the firm can increase IMP and RIS while at the same time maintaining its current real market share (RMS). Each of the fifteen growth opportunities—as summarized in Figure 11-1—implies an increase in either or both IMP or RIS.

HOW MUCH WILL IMP AND RELEVANT INDUSTRY SALES (RIS) INCREASE?

The **first step** toward estimating incremental firm sales is to determine *how much IMP and relevant industry sales (RIS) will increase* for each growth opportunity. As summarized in Table 11-2, estimating incremental IMP and RIS is quite straightforward for nine of the growth opportunities [(1), (4), (5), and (7)–(12)] but can involve additional research and considerable judgment for the remaining six opportunities [(2), (3), (6), and (13)–(15)].

In interpreting Table 11-2, keep in mind that over time as the firm fills out a product line, as the firm expands its distribution, and as the relevant product line life cycles mature (i.e., usage gaps close quite naturally), the key proportion referred to in the table, RIS ÷ IMP, increases. Except where mentioned otherwise in the table, comments therein refer to the effects of each growth opportunity upon RIS at a given point in time, rather than over the long term.

Table 11-2

ESTIMATING THE INCREMENTAL
INDUSTRY MARKET POTENTIAL (IMP) AND
RELEVANT INDUSTRY SALES (RIS) LIKELY TO
RESULT FROM EACH GROWTH OPPORTUNITY [(1)–(15)]

Growth Opportunity	Estimating Incremental IMP and Relevant Industry Sales (RIS)
(1) Natural growth of IMP	Accurate estimate of increased size of IMP is usually possible by using secondary data and projections (see Chapter 4). Proportion RIS ÷ IMP is likely to be the same before and after IMP grows.
(2) New uses or new user segments	Accurate estimates of new IMP(s) are possible by using secondary data or generating primary data. Proportion of RIS ÷ IMP is likely to be substantially smaller for the new IMP(s) than for the old IMP(s) (at least at first) because of larger usage gaps and/or larger distribution gaps.

Table 11-2 *(Continued)*

Growth Opportunity	*Estimating Incremental IMP and Relevant Industry Sales (RIS)*
(3) Innovation or significant new product differentiation	Estimating whether and how much IMP will increase as a result of the significant improvement in price/preference of the relevant new product innovation (or differentiation) versus previously existing elements is dependent upon executive judgment and the interpretation of any primary or secondary data that might be used to help make such an estimate. [The proportion RIS $\div$ IMP is likely to increase also as a result of the innovation, if the relevant firm has been the innovator. See opportunity (6) below.]
(4) Adding new product line(s)	Accurately estimating IMP for new product line is straightforward (see Chapter 4). RIS $\div$ IMP proportion depends upon firm's own intention as to extent of product line and completeness of distribution and upon size of current usage gaps.
(5) Filling out existing product line(s)	The proportion RIS $\div$ (IMP — product line gap) remains the same after adding a new product line element as before. Since proportion of IMP assigned to each product line element was determined in developing the original market structure profile (see Chapter 5), making incremental RIS estimate is straightforward. (RIS increases.)
(6) Creating new product line elements	This is similar to growth opportunity (3) in that it represents the addition of an innovative new element to an existing product line. This contrasts with growth opportunity (3), however, in that no new IMP is projected to result from the new innovation or differentiation. The task here is, therefore, to estimate to what extent the sales of existing elements will be penetrated by the new element. If the firm in question is offering the new element, this firm's RIS $\div$ (IMP — product line gap) proportion will increase. Judgment and interpretation of relevant secondary and/or primary data are used to estimate just how much this proportion will increase.
(7)–(9) Closing distribution gaps	The proportion RIS $\div$ (IMP — product line gap — distribution gaps) remains the same after closing distribution gaps as before. Since the proportion of IMP assigned to each geographic region and for varying extents of distribution intensity and exposure were determined in developing the original market structure profile (see Chapters 7 and 8), making incremental RIS estimates is straightforward. (RIS increases.)

Table 11-2 *(Continued)*

Growth Opportunity	Estimating Incremental IMP and Relevant Industry Sales (RIS)
(10)–(12) Closing usage gaps	Incremental RIS equals whatever the closed part of the usage gap equals as a proportion of IMP. Since the definition of full usage was determined in developing the original IMP estimate (and market structure profile itself—see Chapter 9), making the incremental RIS estimates is quite straightforward over the longer run. Over the short run, however, an adjustment in the incremental RIS estimate may be necessary for the following reason. As new users are converted, over the short run at least, their usage rate (i.e., on what proportion of the use occasions the new users will use the product and what volume of the product they will use each time those new users do use the product) may be less than the usage rate for the current average user. This means that over the short run, the total usage gap will not close in direct proportion to the proportion of nonusers being converted into users. Over the longer run, however, the average usage rate for the converted nonusers is more likely to approach the average usage rate for current users.
(13) Penetrating substitute's position(s)	RIS increases by the amount of the full substitute's position recognized times the distribution and usage factors. Review Chapter 10 for definitions and examples of these factors.
(14) Penetrating direct competitive position(s)	Both IMP and RIS can be affected by this strategy—but quite indirectly—see comments later in this chapter.
(15) Defending present position	Neither IMP nor RIS are directly affected. Strategy is, however, related indirectly to improvements in IMP and RIS—see comments later in the chapter.

WHAT WILL HAPPEN TO THE FIRM'S REAL MARKET SHARE (RMS)?

The **second step** toward estimating incremental firm sales is to determine the likely effect of each of the fifteen alternative growth opportunities upon the relevant firm's real market share (RMS). Note that, although each growth opportunity certainly can result in increased firm sales, an increase in firm sales does not always imply an increase in real market share.

In considering the concept of "real market share," keep in mind that competitive sales of product line elements that the relevant firm does not sell are not included in the "competitive gap." Also, competitive sales of product line elements that the firm does produce are included in the competitive gap only to the extent of the relevant firm's own distribution coverage, intensity, and exposure. Because the product line gap element and the distribution gap element are omitted from overall competitive sales, the firm's resulting *real market share* (RMS) is larger than traditional market share measures would show.

Table 11-3 specifically examines the likely effects of each of the fifteen alternative growth opportunities upon the firm's real market share. Estimating the exact real market share resulting from taking advantage of each growth opportunity is subject to the judgmental factors discussed in the table. The firm's primary concern should be to estimate whether, in light of factors such as those mentioned in the table, its real market share is likely to increase, remain about the same, or decrease.

The changes in industry market potential (IMP), relevant industry sales (RIS), and real market share (RMS) for the relevant firm ultimately

Table 11-3
ESTIMATING THE LIKELY EFFECT OF EACH OF THE FIFTEEN (15) ALTERNATIVE GROWTH OPPORTUNITIES UPON THE FIRM'S REAL MARKET SHARE (RMS)

Growth Opportunity	Likely Effects Upon Real Market Share (RMS)
(1) Natural growth of IMP	The relevant firm can expect the same real market share as before unless a competitor focuses specifically upon the growth segment of IMP (in which case the relevant firm's real market share may decline). Relevant firm may increase its own real market share by focusing upon growth segment of IMP.
(2) New uses or new user segments	If the relevant firm is the leader in promoting the new use or to a new user segment, the firm can expect at least as large a real market share (and usually a larger share) in the new profile(s) as in the existing one(s) for this product line. If a competitor firm takes the lead, the relevant firm can expect a smaller real market share in the new profile(s) than in its existing one(s) for this product line.

Table 11-3 *(Continued)*

Growth Opportunity	Likely Effects Upon Real Market Share (RMS)
(3) Innovation or significant product differentiation	If the relevant firm is the one that has introduced the innovation, this firm can expect a larger real market share than it has at present as long as the firm can protect its innovation—e.g., with a patent—or in some other way maintain superiority in the price/performance of its new element versus other firms' competitive entries. The likely increase in RIS further enhances this firm's situation. If the relevant firm is a follower with the innovation or does not come out with this entry at all (even after competitors have successfully introduced the new element), the relevant firm's real market share may stay the same but RIS and, therefore, firm sales as well, will be declining.
(4) Adding new product line(s)	Since the firm has no sales at all in this product line at present, an increase or decrease in real market share is not possible. Given a particular competitive situation in the market, the firm should eventually be able to build for itself a real market share equivalent to the share it holds today in markets where the competitive situation is similar.
(5) Filling out existing product line(s)	In most instances, it is realistic for the firm to assume that its real market share will remain the same as the firm fills out the relevant product line. At least two forces, however, may be at work to cause a change in the firm's real market share as the firm fills out its product lines and should be considered (i.e., researched) closely by the firm before it fills out a product line. Cannibalism can be one problem—i.e., sales of the new product line element may eat into the same firm's sales of another product line element. In such an instance, while RIS increases, firm sales may not increase proportionally as much—resulting in a declining real market share for the firm. On the other hand, if the various product line elements complement each other (in terms of color or style, for example), firm sales may increase more than RIS on a proportional basis as the firm fills out its product line—thus resulting in an increased real market share. [*Note:* No distribution or usage assumptions need be made concerning the new product line element(s), since whatever distribution and usage exists for these elements will be reflected naturally in the RIS.]

Table 11-3 (*Continued*)

Growth Opportunity	Likely Effects Upon Real Market Share (RMS)
(6) Creating new product line elements	Same as for growth opportunity (3).
(7)–(9) Closing distribution gaps	As a firm expands its distribution coverage, over the short run its real market share will usually decline. Over the longer run the firm can expect its overall real market share to increase, decrease, or remain the same—depending upon the competitive conditions in the new geographic areas covered and upon the resources the firm allocates to penetrating competitors' positions in the new market. Expanding distribution intensity and/or exposure will usually result in a larger real market share (despite the larger RIS) for a firm which starts with very low intensity and exposure (low in terms of the firm's own definition of complete distribution —see Chapters 7 and 8). For a firm already close to having "complete distribution intensity and exposure," however, a further expansion of distribution intensity and/or exposure will lead to an increase in firm sales less than proportional to the increase in RIS, therefore resulting in a declining real market share.
(10)–(12) Closing usage gaps	The firm(s) leading the way with strategies oriented to close usage gaps will be expanding RIS for all firms in the relevant industry. This firm will also usually expand its own real market share. Often, however, especially at later stages of a product line life cycle, the incremental benefits for the leading firm(s) (in terms of increased RIS and real market share) will be outweighed by the incremental cost (e.g., in promotion dollars) required to bring about those benefits. In earlier stages of a life cycle, such an investment may be very worthwhile—especially for the larger and more dominant firms in the relevant industry.
(13)–(14) Closing competitive gaps	These opportunities/strategies are oriented directly toward improving the firm's real market share by bringing about an increase in firm sales, whether or not RIS is increasing. (RIS may indeed increase at the same time because of the simultaneous closure of other gaps in the market structure profile.)

Table 11-3 *(Continued)*

Growth Opportunity	Likely Effects Upon Real Market Share (RMS)
(15) Defending present market share	As the name of the opportunity implies, the goal here is to maintain present real market share. This is an important strategy for larger, more dominant firms in an industry—regardless of the stage of life cycle for the relevant industry. Strategy is also important for any firm for which RIS is increasing—for whatever reason.

determine the incremental sales likely to result from each growth opportunity/strategy. The more IMP, RIS, and RMS increase, the more new firm sales are likely. Table 11-4 summarizes the changes in IMP, RIS, and RMS discussed in Tables 11-2 and 11-3 for each of the fifteen growth opportunities.

Once the firm has estimated the specific effects of each growth opportunity upon IMP, RIS, and RMS (as summarized in Tables 11-2, 11-3, and 11-4), the firm is in a much better position than before (without using market structure profile analysis) to estimate incremental firm sales within a fairly small range.

The following chapter provides specific examples of how market structure profile analysis can be used to help estimate incremental firm sales likely to result from taking advantage of various growth opportunities.

SUMMARY

One of the functions of market structure profile analysis is to facilitate the estimation of the likely results (in terms of incremental firm sales and profits) of implementing alternative growth strategies. The profile does not give management a definitive estimate of the likely result of the strategy, but it certainly can aid the manager's judgment in estimating a range of possible outcomes and assigning explicit or implicit probabilities to various possible outcomes or payoffs (i.e., incremental sales and profits) associated with each strategic alternative.

This chapter examines how market structure profile analysis can aid in examining the benefit/cost trade-offs associated with various growth opportunities. The following chapter provides specific examples of how market structure profile analysis can be used to estimate the

Table 11-4

GENERALIZATION CONCERNING THE LIKELY EFFECTS OF EACH GROWTH OPPORTUNITY UPON INDUSTRY MARKET POTENTIAL (IMP), RELEVANT INDUSTRY SALES (RIS), AND REAL MARKET SHARE (RMS)

Growth Opportunity	For Existing Profile(s)				For New Profile(s) Created — Compared With Existing Profile		
	IMP	RIS	RIS/IMP	RMS	IMP	RIS/IMP	RMS
(1)	↑	↑	Same	Same	None		
(2)	Same	Same	Same	Same	Yes	Smaller	Larger (if leader) Smaller (if follower)
(3)	↑	↑ (if leader) ↓ (if follower)	↑ (if leader) ↓ (if follower)	↑	None		
(4)	Same	Same	Same	Same	Yes	Depends (see Table 11-2)	Depends (see Table 11-3)
(5)	Same	↑	↑	Same	None		
(6)	Can ↑	↑ (if leader) ↓ (if follower)	↑ (if leader) ↓ (if follower)	↑	None		
(7)–(9)	Same	↑	↑	Depends (see Table 11-3)	None		
(10)–(12)	Same	↑	↑	↑ (if leader) ↓ (if follower)	None		
(13)	Same	↑	↑	Same	None		
(14)	Same	Same	Same	↑	None		
(15)	Same	Same	Same	Same	None		

195

incremental sales likely to result from taking advantage of various growth opportunities.

Market structure profiles serve as a focal point for showing the interrelationships among and between the fifteen growth opportunities discussed earlier in the book and can provide the firm with significant insights concerning the incremental sales that each growth strategy is likely to yield.

Three market structure profile measures provide particularly helpful insights for making such estimates. These three measures are *industry market potential* (IMP), *relevant industry sales* (RIS) and *real market share* (RMS). *Industry market potential* (IMP) has already been discussed in some detail. *Relevant industry sales* (RIS) equals firm sales plus the competitive gap(s). Real market share (RMS) equals

$$\frac{\text{Firm sales}}{\text{Firm sales plus the competitive gap(s)}} \quad \text{or} \quad \frac{\text{Firm sales}}{\text{Relevant industry sales}}$$

As viewed in terms of market structure profiles, the firm can realize incremental firm sales as a result of: (1) *increasing the firm's total IMP;* (2) *increasing relevant industry sales* (RIS) (i.e., firm sales plus the competitive gap) while maintaining its present real market share; and/or (3) *improving its real market share* (RMS).

The **first step** toward estimating incremental firm sales is to determine *how much IMP and relevant industry sales (RIS) will increase* for each growth opportunity. As summarized in Table 11-2, estimating incremental IMP and RIS is quite straightforward for nine of the growth opportunities [(1), (4), (5), and (7)–(12)] but can involve additional research and considerable judgment for the remaining six opportunities [(2), (3), (6), and (12)–(15)].

The **second step** toward estimating incremental firm sales is to determine the likely effect of each of the fifteen alternative growth opportunities upon the relevant firm's real market share (RMS). Note that, although each growth opportunity certainly can result in increased firm sales, an increase in firm sales does not always imply an increase in real market share. Table 11-3 examines specifically the likely effects of each of the fifteen alternative growth opportunities upon the firm's real market share.

Once the firm has estimated the specific effects of each growth opportunity upon IMP, RIS, and RMS (as summarized in Tables 11-2, 11-3, and 11-4), the firm is in a much better position than before (without using market structure profile analysis) to estimate incremental firm sales within a fairly small range.

The following chapter provides specific examples of how market structure profile analysis can be used to help estimate incremental firm sales likely to result from taking advantage of various growth opportunities.

A firm can use the principles of market structure profile analysis as summarized (in Tables 11-2, 11-3, and 11-4) to estimate potential incremental firm sales related to each alternative growth opportunity. The resulting estimates, having been derived through systematic thinking and analysis, provide the relevant firm with very meaningful input for making its growth planning decisions.

REVIEW QUESTIONS

1. If market structure profile analysis does not promise to give managers definitive estimates of the likely results of a growth strategy, of what use is this sort of analysis?

2. What types of situations are favorable for the strategy, "Fill out existing product line"?

3. What type of costs is a firm likely to incur when implementing the strategy, "New uses or new user segments for a product"?

4. What is the difference between relevant industry sales (RIS) and real market share (RMS)?

5. What is the difference between the "real market share" measure and more traditional market share measures?

6. When a firm adds a new innovative product line element, what happens to IMP? To RIS? To RMS? To firm sales? Why?

7. When a firm closes a nonuser gap, what happens to IMP? To RIS? To RMS? To firm sales? Why?

8. What is the difference between the short-run effects and the long-run effects (upon IMP, RIS, RMS, and firm sales) of the strategies whose effects are considered in Tables 11-2 and 11-3?

12

Examples of Using
Market Structure Profile Analysis
to Estimate Incremental Firm Sales

A firm can use the principles of market structure profile analysis as summarized at the end of the last chapter (in Tables 11-2, 11-3, and 11-4) to estimate potential incremental firm sales related to each alternative growth opportunity. The resulting estimates, having been derived through systematic thinking and analysis, provide the relevant firm with very meaningful input for making its growth planning decisions.

The examples below are based upon the market structure profile for breakfast cereal as developed in the various chapters of Part Two. As a starting point, a brief summary and review of the derivation of that profile is presented.

REVIEW OF THE MARKET STRUCTURE PROFILE
FOR BREAKFAST CEREAL FOR FIRM XYZ
(AS ORIGINALLY DERIVED IN PART TWO)

INDUSTRY MARKET POTENTIAL (FROM CHAPTER 4)

Industry market potential (IMP) equals 80.3 billion units—derived as shown in Table 12-1.

198

Table 12-1

Assumption	Cereal as a Breakfast Food
Number of potential consumers	220 million
Number of use occasions	7/week/person
Full serving size	approximately 1 oz
	220m × 365 × 1 oz
IMP =	80.3 billion oz

PRODUCT LINE GAP (FROM CHAPTERS 5 AND 6)

Product line gap equals 20 percent of IMP—derived as shown in Table 12-2.

Table 12-2
FULL PRODUCT LINE GAP FOR CEREAL AS A BREAKFAST FOOD: FIRM XYZ

Product Line Elements	Current Industry Sales (in units—where one unit = 1 oz) Cereal as Breakfast Food	% of Current Industry Sales	Our Firm Sells
a. Regular cereal	9.375 billion units	50%	X
b. Presweetened cereal	3.750 billion units	20%	No
c. Natural cereal	5.625 billion units	30%	X
Total	18.75 billion units	100%	80%

Full product line gap = 100% − 20% = **20% of IMP**

DISTRIBUTION GAP (FROM CHAPTERS 7 AND 8)

Distribution coverage gap and *distribution intensity gap* equal 20.7 percent of IMP and 8.32 percent of IMP, respectively—derived as shown in Table 12-3:

Distribution exposure gap equals 11.1 percent of IMP—derived as shown in Table 12-4.

Table 12-3
DISTRIBUTION COVERAGE AND INTENSITY GAPS FOR BREAKFAST CEREAL: FIRM XYZ

1	2	3	4	5	6	7
Area	% of IMP	Product Line Coverage	Distribution Coverage	Distribution Coverage Gap as % of IMP	Distribution Intensity Gap	Distribution Intensity Gap as % of IMP
Southwest	9.7% ×	80%	=	7.8%		
Greater Los Angeles	5.5% ×	80%	=	4.4%		
Remaining Pacific	10.6% ×	80%	=	8.5%		
New England	6.0% ×	80% ×	+	×	10% =	0.48%
Metropolitan New York	7.6% ×	80% ×	+	×	10% =	0.61%
Middle Atlantic	11.8% ×	80% ×	+	×	10% =	0.94%
East Central	17.0% ×	80% ×	+	×	20% =	2.72%
Metropolitan Chicago	4.0% ×	80% ×	+	×	10% =	0.32%
West Central	12.7% ×	80% ×	+	×	20% =	2.04%
Southeast	15.1% ×	80% ×	+	×	10% =	1.21%
	Product line gap = 20% of IMP		Total distribution coverage gap = 20.7% of IMP		Total distribution intensity gap = 8.32% of IMP	

Table 124
DISTRIBUTION EXPOSURE GAP FOR BREAKFAST CEREAL: FIRM XYZ

1	2	3	4	5	6	7	8
Area *	% of IMP	Product Line Coverage	Distribution Intensity	Distribution Intensity as % of IMP	Distribution Exposure as a % of Ideal Distribution Exposure	Distribution Exposure as % of IMP	Distribution Exposure Gap as % of IMP
New England	6.0%	80% ×	90% =	4.32% ×	75% =	3.24 from 4.32 =	1.08%
Metropolitan New York	7.6%	80% ×	90% =	5.47% ×	75% =	4.10 from 5.47 =	1.37%
Middle Atlantic	11.8%	80% ×	90% =	8.50% ×	75% =	6.38 from 8.50 =	2.12%
East Central	17.0%	80% ×	80% =	10.88% ×	90% =	9.79 from 10.88 =	1.09%
Metropolitan Chicago	4.0%	80% ×	90% =	2.88% ×	90% =	2.59 from 2.88 =	0.29%
West Central	12.7%	80% ×	80% =	8.13% ×	90% =	7.32 from 8.13 =	0.81%
Southeast	15.1%	80% ×	90% =	10.87% ×	60% =	6.52 from 10.87 =	4.35%
					Total distribution exposure gap =		11.1%

* Assume no coverage in Southwest, Greater Los Angeles, Pacific.

USAGE GAP (FROM CHAPTER 9)

Nonuser gap, light user gap, and *light usage gap* equal 10 percent of IMP, 17.1 percent of IMP and 2.6 percent of IMP, respectively— derived as shown in Tables 12-5A, B, and C.

Table 12-5A

NONUSER GAP FOR BREAKFAST CEREAL

Assume: 25 percent of relevant consumers never eat cereal for breakfast.

Nonuser Gap

$= 25\%$ (IMP — product line gap — total distribution gap)
$= 25\%$ (100% — 20% — 40.1%)
$= 25\%$ (39.9% of IMP)
$= \textbf{9.98\% of IMP}$)

Table 12-5B

LIGHT USER GAP FOR BREAKFAST CEREAL

Assume: Breakfast cereal users consume breakfast cereal three times per week on average; full use has been defined as seven times per week on average.

Light User Gap

$= \frac{4}{7}$ (IMP — product line gap — total distribution gap — nonuser gap)
$= 57.1\%$ (100% — 20% — 40.1% — 9.98%)
$= 57.1\%$ (29.9% of IMP)
$= \textbf{17.08\% of IMP}$

Table 12-5C

LIGHT USAGE GAP FOR BREAKFAST CEREAL

Assume: The average size of a breakfast cereal serving is $\frac{8}{10}$ of an ounce; a full serving has been defined as one full ounce.

Light Usage Gap

$= \frac{2}{10}$ (IMP — product line gap — total distribution gap — nonuser gap — light user gap)
$= 20\%$ (100% — 20% — 40.1% — 9.98% — 17.08%)
$= 20\%$ (12.84% of IMP)
$= \textbf{2.57\% of IMP}$

COMPETITIVE GAP AND FIRM SALES (FROM CHAPTER 10)

Firm Sales and the *competitive gap* equal 4.1 percent and 6.1 percent of IMP, respectively—derived as shown in Tables 12-6 and 12-7.

Table 12-6
FIRM SALES OF CEREAL AS A BREAKFAST FOOD

Firm sales of cereal as a breakfast food	= 3.3 billion ounces
As a % of IMP, FS $\dfrac{3.3}{80.3}$	= 4.1% of IMP

Table 12-7
DETERMINING THE SIZE OF THE COMPETITIVE GAP(S) *

Product line gap	= 20% of IMP
Total distribution gap	= 40.1% of IMP
Total usage gap	= 29.7% of IMP
Firm sales	= 4.1% of IMP
Total	$\overline{93.9\%}$ of IMP

Therefore, Competitive gap = 100% − 93.9% = 6.1% of IMP

Note: In order to keep the analysis in this section as straightforward as possible, no substitute's position to be penetrated is recognized in this case.

In sum, therefore, the market structure profile for this firm for cereal as a breakfast food appears as displayed in Fig. 12-1.

ESTIMATING INCREMENTAL FIRM SALES FOR EACH ALTERNATIVE GROWTH OPPORTUNITY

Consider how the firm with the market structure profile described in Tables 12-1 through 12-7 and in Fig. 12-1 can estimate incremental firm sales for each alternative growth opportunity.

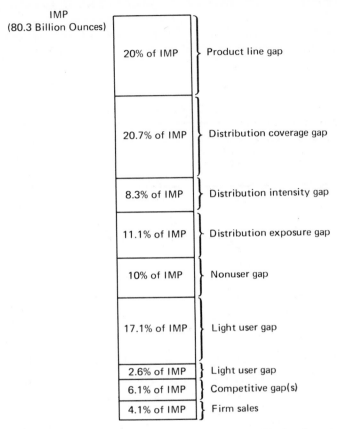

FIGURE 12-1.   Resulting market structure profile for firm A for
cereal as a breakfast food.

(1) NATURAL GROWTH OF IMP—EXAMPLE OF ESTIMATING INCREMENTAL FIRM SALES

Assume that the number of potential consumers will rise from 220 million today to 225 million between now and the operating period of concern. Recall the effects of such a growth opportunity upon firm sales as described in Tables 11-2, 11-3, and 11-4; the firm can reasonably expect the ratio FS/IMP to remain the same after the natural increase as before. For the case in point, therefore, estimated incremental firm sales are derived as follows:

% increase in IMP	= $\dfrac{5 \text{ million}}{220 \text{ million}}$ = 2.22%

Current firm sales = 3.3 billion ounces

Incremental firm sales will equal
2.22% (3.3 billion ounces) = 0.073 billion ounces (i.e.,
73 million ounces)

As discussed in Chapter 4 and summarized in Table 11-3, the firm's incremental sales may be more or less than this 2.22 percent—for example, if the firm itself or a competing firm focuses efforts upon the group of new potential customers.

(2) NEW USES OR NEW USER SEGMENTS—ESTIMATING INCREMENTAL FIRM SALES

Assume that the firm explicitly recognizes a new use or new user segment for the relevant product line. For example, in the case in question, the firm could recognize the use of cereal as a snack. Having done so, the firm would then generate a separate IMP and separate market structure profile for cereal as a snack. The firm might come up with an IMP and market structure profile such as the ones in Fig. 12-2.

In its research, the firm may first find that a significant proportion of its current sales of the relevant product line are already accounted for by the newly recognized use. In the example (Fig. 12-2), the firm found 1.1 billion ounces of its current cereal sales consumed as a snack (i.e., in addition to the 3.3 billion ounces of cereal consumed at breakfast).

The mere recognition of a possible new use or new user segment for a product does not result in incremental firm sales. It does, however, open up a new growth horizon for the firm. In the cereal as a snack example, the firm finds itself with a 20 percent real market share at present (i.e., Firm sales ÷ relevant industry sales, or 1% ÷ 5%). By taking the lead in developing and implementing a program oriented toward this new use of the product, the firm should be able to maintain or increase that real market share while at the same time realizing substantial growth in the firm's relevant industry sales.

The projection of potential incremental sales related to the recognition and exploitation of the new use depends upon what subsequent growth opportunities related to the new IMP and new profile are pursued. Given the particular new profile in Fig. 12-2, for example, narrowing the total distribution gap appears to offer a great deal of promise (in terms of ultimately leading to new firm sales). The projection of incremental sales using such a strategy is covered below [under growth opportunities (7) to (9)].

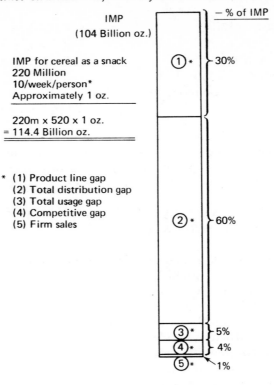

IMP
(104 Billion oz.)

IMP for cereal as a snack
220 Million
10/week/person*
Approximately 1 oz.

220m x 520 x 1 oz.
= 114.4 Billion oz.

* (1) Product line gap
(2) Total distribution gap
(3) Total usage gap
(4) Competitive gap
(5) Firm sales

— % of IMP

① * 30%

② * 60%

③ * 5%
④ * 4%
⑤ * 1%

Cereal as a snack

FIGURE 12-2.   IMP and market structure profile for a new use
of the product.

(3) *INNOVATION OR SIGNIFICANT NEW PRODUCT DIFFERENTIATION—ESTIMATING INCREMENTAL FIRM SALES*

As indicated in Tables 11-2, 11-3, and 11-4, an innovative new element addition to an existing product line offers the firm a great opportunity for improving firm sales. Such a strategy can increase IMP, can improve the firm's RIS and its RIS/IMP ratio, and can enlarge the firm's real market share.

In the breakfast cereal case, for example, consider the time before "natural cereals" were introduced to the market and the period after these cereals were introduced and assume that:

(1) The number of potential customers equaled 180 million before and 220 million after.

(2) Current cereal sales were split 50/50 between regular cereals and presweetened cereals and that the relevant firm sold only regular cereal before; and that after, the sales split was as shown in Table 12-2.

(3) The firm's ratio of total distribution gap ÷ (IMP − product line gap) equaled the same before as after adding the new "natural cereals."

(4) The firm's ratio of usage gap for the firm ÷ (IMP − product line gap − total distribution gap) equaled the same before as after adding the new natural cereals.

Reflecting these assumptions, the two contrasting market structure profiles displayed in Fig. 12-3 result.

Incremental firm sales as a result of leading the way with the new cereal equal:

$$4.1\%(80.3 \text{ billion oz}) - 2.0\%(65.7 \text{ billion oz})$$
$$= 3.29 \text{ billion oz} - 1.3 \text{ billion oz}$$
$$= \textbf{1.98 billion oz}$$

(which equals a **60% increase** over current firm sales).

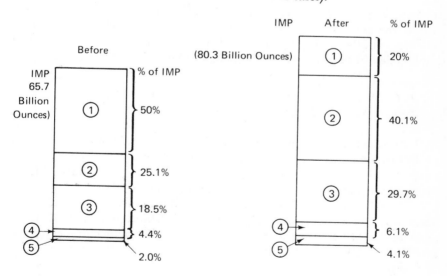

(1) Product line gap (4) Competitive gap
(2) Total distribution gap (5) Firm sales
(3) Total usage gap

FIGURE 12-3. Market structure profile for firm XYZ before and after introducing an innovative new product line element.

Note that (as summarized in Tables 11-2, 11-3, and 11-4) the new firm sales result from increased IMP (from 65.7 billion to 80.3 billion), improved RIS and RIS/IMP ratio (from 6.4 percent of IMP to 10.2 percent of IMP), and from improved real market share (from $2.0/6.4 = 31.2$ percent to $4.1/10.2 = 40.2$ percent).[1]

(4) ADDING NEW PRODUCT LINES—ESTIMATING INCREMENTAL FIRM SALES

Adding a new product line implies adding a totally new type of firm sales rather than incremental sales of an existing product line. The specific estimate of the firm's sales for the product line depends upon and is determined by the factors mentioned in Tables 11-2 and 11-3.

We reiterate the points made in those two tables. In terms of estimating IMP and RIS, accurately estimating IMP for a new product line is straightforward (see Chapter 4). RIS $\div$ IMP proportion depends upon the firm's own intention as to extent of product line and completeness of distribution and upon size of current usage gaps. In terms of estimating the firm's real market share (and ultimately, new firm sales), since the firm has no sales at all in this product line at present, an increase or decrease in real market share is not possible. Given a particular competitive situation in the market, the firm should eventually be able to build for itself a real market share equivalent to the share it holds today in markets where the competitive situation is similar.

(5) FILLING OUT EXISTING PRODUCT LINE(S)— ESTIMATING INCREMENTAL FIRM SALES

Assume that the firm would add a full complement of regular cereals to its current product line, thus closing the 20 percent product line gap portrayed in Table 12-2. The new market structure profile faced by the firm after filling out the product line appears in Fig. 12-4.

The size of the new gaps are determined as indicated in Tables 11-2 and 11-3. The proportions of: (1) Total distribution gap $\div$ (IMP − product line gap), (2) Total usage gap $\div$ (IMP − product line gap), and (3) RIS $\div$ (IMP − product line gap) remain the same after the product line gap is closed as before. In the example, the relevant firm's real market share is also assumed to remain the same (i.e., 40.2 percent) after the product line gap is closed as before. This may or may not be a valid assumption—depending upon points discussed in Table 11-3 and in Chapters 5 and 6. If not valid, adjustment (upward or downward) of projected real market share should be made accordingly.

In the example used (Fig. 12-4), projected incremental sales = 5.1

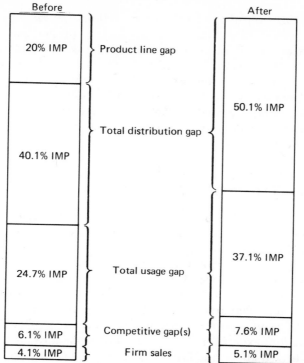

FIGURE 12-4.   Market structure profile before and after filling out the product line.

percent of IMP minus 4.1 percent of IMP = 1 percent of IMP or approximately **800 million oz** (a *volume increase of approximately 24 percent* for the firm).

(6) CREATING NEW PRODUCT LINE ELEMENT(S)— ESTIMATING INCREMENTAL FIRM SALES

This growth opportunity is quite similar to growth opportunity (3) in that it can improve the firm's RIS and its RIS/IMP ratio and can enlarge the firm's real market share. In contrast to growth opportunity (3), no increase in IMP is projected for this opportunity.

Using the same example as above for estimating incremental sales for growth opportunity (3), make the same assumptions except for assumption 1, which should now read:

(1) The number of potential customers equals 180 million both before and after the new "natural cereal" is introduced.

The estimation of incremental sales follows the same procedure as for growth opportunity (3) above and resulting proportions of IMP in the new market structure profile will be the same as those summarized in Fig. 12-3. Incremental sales will be determined, however, on the smaller IMP (65.7 billion ounces). In this example, therefore, estimated incremental sales will equal 4.1 percent (65.7 billion ounces) minus 2.0 percent (65.7 billion ounces) = 2.69 billion ounces minus 1.31 billion ounces = **1.38 billion ounces** (a *volume increase of approximately 42 percent* for the firm).

(7) EXPANDING DISTRIBUTION COVERAGE— ESTIMATING INCREMENTAL FIRM SALES

An estimate of incremental sales resulting from closing a distribution coverage gap must reflect certain assumptions regarding the distribution intensity and exposure achieved in the newly covered geographic area(s). Assume, for example, that the firm for which the distribution profile is summarized in Tables 12-3 and 12-4 expands into the Southwest (7.8 percent of IMP, if a 20 percent product line gap is assumed—see Table 12-3) and Greater Los Angeles (4.4 percent of IMP if a 20 percent line gap is assumed—again, see Table 12-3). What incremental sales can the firm expect for this product line from such an expansion?

As indicated above, the firm must include in its analysis an estimate of the completeness of distribution intensity and exposure the firm anticipates achieving in the new geographic area(s) by the time of the operating period(s) for which the incremental sales estimate is being made. Assume, in this case, that the firm anticipates 60 percent intensity in each new area and 50 percent exposure in each new area by the time of the relevant operating period(s).

Given this projected distribution coverage, intensity, and exposure, an estimate of incremental sales can be made as follows:[2]

• *Projected Decline in Total Distribution Gap*

Area	% of IMP with 20% Product Line Gap	Projected. Distribution Intensity	Projected Distribution Exposure	Projected Decline in Total Distribution Gap
Southwest	7.8% ×	60% ×	50% =	2.34% of IMP
Greater Los Angeles	4.4% ×	60% ×	50% =	1.32% of IMP
Projected decline in total distribution gap			=	3.66% of IMP

- *New Total Distribution Gap*
  = old gap − 3.66%
  = 40.1% of IMP − 3.66% of IMP = **36.44% of IMP**

- *New Total Usage Gap* (If it is assumed that usage characteristics are the same in new geographic areas as in old area)
  Ratio of: old gap ÷ (IMP − product line gap − total distribution gap)
  = 29.7% of IMP ÷ (100% of IMP − 20% of IMP − 40.1% of IMP)
  = 29.7% ÷ 39.9% = 74.4%
  New Total Usage Gap
  = 74.4%(IMP − product line gap −new total distribution gap
  = 74.4%(100% of IMP − 20% of IMP − 36.44% of IMP)
  = 74.4%(43.56% of IMP)
  = **32.4% of IMP**

- Incremental new RIS as result of expanding distribution coverage as indicated above:
  = New RIS − Old RIS
  New RIS = IMP − PLG − new total distribution gap
  − new total usage gap
  = 100% − 20% − 36.44% − 32.4% = 11.16% of IMP
  Old RIS = 10.2% of IMP
  Incremental RIS = 11.16% of IMP − 10.2 % of IMP
  = **0.96% of IMP**

- *Incremental New Firm Sales*

  - The incremental RIS (i.e., 0.96% of IMP) resulting from the expanded distribution equals the maximum incremental new firm sales possible. It is highly unlikely, however, that the firm will obtain an effective 100 percent real market share of the incremental RIS.

  - More likely, as suggested in Table 11-3 and Chapter 7, the firm's real market share of the incremental RIS will be less than, or at most equal to, its real market share achieved in its existing markets. Therefore:

  - Firm's *old real market share* before expanding distribution
    = old firm sales ÷ old RIS
    = 4.1% of IMP ÷ 10.2% of IMP
    = **40.2% (of old RIS)**

- If firm is successful in achieving the same real market share in the new markets, then the firm's *incremental sales* will equal:

$$= 40.2\%(\text{incremental RIS})$$
$$= 40.2\%(0.96\% \text{ IMP})$$
$$= 0.386\% \text{ of IMP}$$
$$= 0.386\%(80.3 \text{ billion oz}) = \text{approximately } \mathbf{310}$$

    million oz (i.e., a *sales volume increase of approximately*

$$\frac{.310}{3.29} = \text{approximately 9.4\% for the firm)}$$

- If firm achieves less than 40.2% real market share in its new market, its incremental sales will be less than 310. For example, a *20% real market share* in the new market *would yield incremental sales of*

$$20\%(0.96\% \text{ of IMP} = 0.192\% \text{ of IMP}$$
$$= 0.192\%(80.3 \text{ billion oz})$$
$$= \text{approximately } \mathbf{154 \text{ million}}$$
$$\mathbf{oz}$$

(8) EXPANDING DISTRIBUTION INTENSITY— ESTIMATING INCREMENTAL FIRM SALES

A firm expands distribution intensity by gaining new distribution outlets in any given geographic area. As considered above, the type and number of distribution outlets desired by the firm for "complete distribution" of that product line are specifically defined by the firm as the first step in determining the size of the distribution intensity gap. A certain proportion of IMP is assigned to each outlet falling within the "complete distribution" definition. The summation of the IMP in outlets where the firm does not yet have distribution equals the distribution intensity gap for that particular geographic region.

Similar to estimates of incremental sales resulting from closing distribution coverage gaps, estimates of sales resulting from closing distribution intensity gaps must also reflect certain assumptions regarding the distribution exposure achieved in the new outlets. Assume, for example, that the firm for which the distribution profile is summarized in Tables 12-3 and 12-4 expands its intensity in the East Central from the current 80 percent intensity to 95 percent intensity. What incremental sales can the firm expect for this product line from such an expansion?

As indicated above, the firm must include in its analysis an estimate of the completeness of distribution exposure the firm anticipates achieving in the new outlets by the time of the operating period(s) for which the incremental sales estimate is being made. Assume, in this case, that the firm anticipates 70 percent exposure in each new outlet by the time of the relevant operating period(s).

Given this projected new distribution intensity and exposure in the East Central, an estimate of incremental sales likely to result can be made as follows:[3]

* *Projected Decline in Total Distribution Gap*

Area	% of IMP (with 20% Product Line Gap)	Projected Distribution Intensity as a % of IMP	Present Distribution Intensity as a % of IMP
East Central	13.6% ×	95% = 12.92%	13.6% × 80% = 10.88%

	Improved Intensity as a % of IMP	Projected Distribution Exposure In New Outlets	Improved Distribution Intensity & Exposure as a % of IMP
	12.92 − 10.88 = **2.04% IMP**	70%	70% (2.04% of IMP) = 1.43% of IMP

Projected decline in total distribution gap = **1.43% IMP**

* *New Total Distribution Gap*
  = old gap − 1.43%
  = 40.1% of IMP − 1.43% of IMP = **38.67% of IMP**
* *New Total Usage Gap*
  Ratio of old gap ÷ (IMP − product line gap − total distribution gap)
  = 29.7% ÷ 39.9% = 74.4%
  New Total Usage Gap
  = 74.4% (IMP − PLG − new total distribution gap)
  = 74.4% (100% of IMP − 20% of IMP − 38.67% of IMP)
  = 74.4% (41.33% of IMP) = **30.75% of IMP**
* *Incremental New RIS* as a result of expanding distribution intensity as indicated above:
  = New RIS − Old RIS

New RIS = IMP − PLG − new total distribution gap − new total usage gap

= 100% of IMP − 20% of IMP − 38.67% of IMP − 30.75% of IMP

= 10.58% of IMP

Old RIS = 10.2% of IMP

Incremental RIS = 10.58% of IMP − 10.2% of IMP

= **0.38% of IMP**

- *Incremental New Firm Sales*
  - Comments made above for estimating incremental sales resulting from expanded distribution coverage also apply here.
  - Firm's old real market Share = $\dfrac{4.1\%}{10.2\%}$ = 40.2% (of old RIS)
  - If firm is successful in achieving the same real market share for its new outlets, then *incremental sales*

    = 40.2% (incremental new RIS)

    = 40.2% (0.38% of IMP)

    = 0.153% of IMP = 0.153 (80.3 billion oz) = **123 million oz**

    (i.e., a *sales volume increase* of $\dfrac{0.123}{3.29}$ = *approximately 4% for the firm*)

  - As suggested in Table 11-3 and Chapters 7 and 8, the firm's real market share may be either larger or smaller than the 40.2 percent in its existing markets—depending primarily upon the firm's completeness of distribution intensity at the present time in the relevant market(s). For the case in point, the firm's intensity in the East Central area is already quite good. As a result, incremental sales may well be less than the projected 123 million ounces.

(9) EXPANDING DISTRIBUTION EXPOSURE— ESTIMATING INCREMENTAL FIRM SALES

Expanding distribution exposure for a product line means improving in-store factors such as shelf space, facings, location, displays, inventory, etc., in individual outlets. As indicated earlier in the book, the firm must develop a meaningful exposure measurement index for rating exposure in individual outlets. The firm then defines complete exposure as a certain rating on that index and proceeds to generate an exposure rating for outlets of various types and/or in various locations (refer to Chapters 7 and 8 for examples).

Assume that the firm for which the distribution profile is summarized above in Tables 12-3 and 12-4 expands its distribution exposure in the Southeast from 60 percent to 90 percent. What incremental sales can the firm expect for this product line from such an expansion? An estimate of the incremental sales likely to result can be made as follows: [4]

• *Projected Decline in Distribution Gap*

Area	Distribution Intensity as a % of IMP (with 20% Product Line Gap & 10% Intensity Gap —from Table 12-4, Col. 5)	Projected Distribution Exposure as a % of IMP	Present Distribution Exposure as a % of IMP	Improved Distribution Exposure as a % of IMP
Southeast	10.87% of IMP	90% × 10.87% of IMP = 9.78% of IMP	60% × 10.87 = 6.52% of IMP	9.78% of IMP minus 6.52% of IMP = **3.26% of IMP**

Projected decline in total distribution gap = **3.26% of IMP**

• *New Total Distribution Gap* (TDG)
  = old gap − 3.26% of IMP
  = 40.2% − 3.26% = **36.93% of IMP**
• *New Total Usage Gap* (TUG)
  Ratio of old gap = 74.4% [see opportunity (8)]
  New total usage gap
  = 74.4%(IMP − PLG − new total distribution gap)
  = 74.4%(100% of IMP − 20% of IMP − 36.93% of IMP)
  = 74.4%(43.07) = **32.04% of IMP**
• *Incremental New RIS* as a result of expanding distribution exposure as indicated above:
  = new RIS − old RIS
  New RIS = IMP − PLG − new TDG − new TUG
      = 100% of IMP − 20% of IMP − 36.93% of IMP
      − 32.04% of IMP
      = **11.03% of IMP**
  Old RIS = **10.2% of IMP**
  Incremental RIS = 11.03% of IMP − 10.2% of IMP
          = **0.83% IMP**

- *Incremental New Firm Sales*
  - Comments made above for estimating incremental sales resulting from expanded distribution coverage also apply here.
- Firm's *old real market share* $= \dfrac{4.1\%}{10.2\%} = $ **40.2%** (of old RIS)
- If the firm is successful in achieving the same real market share to the extent of its expanded distribution exposure, then incremental sales

  $$= 40.2\%(\text{incremental new RIS})$$
  $$= 40.2\%(0.83\% \text{ of IMP})$$
  $$= 0.333 \text{ IMP} = 0.333\%(80.3 \text{ billion oz})$$
  $$= \textbf{268 million oz} \text{ (i.e., a } \textit{sales volume increase}$$

  of $\dfrac{0.268}{3.29}$= approximately **8.1%** for the firm)

- As suggested in Table 11-4 and Chapters 7 and 8, the firm's real market share may be either larger or smaller than the 40.2 percent in its existing markets—depending primarily upon the firm's completeness of distribution exposure in the relevant market(s). For the case in point, the firm's exposure in the Southeast is quite weak at present (60 percent). As a result, incremental sales should be at least the projected 268 million ounces.

(10) STIMULATING NONUSERS—ESTIMATING INCREMENTAL FIRM SALES

In order to estimate the incremental sales that are likely to result from stimulating a certain number of nonusers to begin using the product, certain assumptions must also be included concerning the likely usage rates of the new users. (I.e., on what proportion of the use occasions will the new users use the product and what volume of the product will be used by them each time these new users do use the product?) The example below assumes that the new users will have the same usage rate as existing users. As suggested in Table 11-2 and Chapter 9, this assumption may sometimes have to be modified—at least for estimates covering only the short run (e.g., the next operating period only).

In the breakfast cereal example described in Table 12-5A, assume that the number of nonusers is reduced from 25 percent of all potential users to 15 percent of all potential users. The likely incremental sales resulting may be estimated as follows: [5]

- *Present Total Usage Gap Size* = approximately **29.7% of IMP** (see Fig. 12-1)

- *Present Nonuser Gap Size*
  $= 25\%$(IMP $-$ product line gap $-$ total distribution gap)
  $= 25\%(100\% - 20\% - 40.1\%)$
  $= 25\%(39.9\%$ of IMP)
  $= $ **9.98% of IMP**
- *Projected New Nonuser Gap Size*
  $= 15\%(100\% - 20\% - 40.1\%)$
  $= 15\%(39.9\%)$
  $= $ **5.99% of IMP**
- *New Light User Gap*
  $= \frac{4}{7}$(IMP $-$ product line gap $-$ total distribution gap $-$new nonuser gap)
  $= 57.1\%(100\% - 20\% - 40.1\% - 5.99\%)$
  $= 57.1\%(33.9\%$ of IMP)
  $= $ **19.38% of IMP**
- *New Light Usage Gap*
  $= \frac{8}{10}$ (IMP $-$ product line gap $-$ total distributor gap $-$ new nonuser gap $-$ new light user gap)
  $= 20\%(100\% - 20\% - 40.1\% - 5.99\% - 19.38\%)$
  $= 20\%(14.53\%$ of IMP)
  $= $ **2.91% of IMP**
- *Projected New Total Usage Gap*
  $= $ new nonuser gap $+$ new light user gap $+$ new light usage gap
  $= 5.99\%$ of IMP $+ 19.38\%$ of IMP $+ 2.91\%$ of IMP
  $= $ **28.28% of IMP**

- *Incremental RIS*
  $= $ new RIS $-$ old RIS
  New RIS $= $ IMP $-$ PLG $-$ TDG $-$ new total usage gap
  $\qquad = 100\%$ of IMP $- 20\%$ of IMP $- 40.1\%$ of IMP $-$ 28.28% of IMP)
  $\qquad = $ **11.62% of IMP**
  Old RIS $= $ **10.2% of IMP**
  Incremental RIS $= 11.62\%$ of IMP $- 10.2\%$ of IMP
  $\qquad\qquad = $ **1.42% of IMP**

- *Incremental New Firm Sales*
  Firm's old real market share (RMS)
  $$\frac{4.1\%}{10.2\%} = \textbf{40.2\% of old RIS}$$

Firm's new RMS of the new RIS may be more or less than its old real market share, depending upon whether the firm itself leads the way in "converting new users" (see discussions in

Table 11-3 and Chapter 9). Assume that the firm does lead the way. In this case, the firm may get a 50 percent RMS of the new RIS.

Estimated Incremental Sales, therefore,
$$= 50\% \times 1.42 \text{ of IMP}$$
$$= 0.71\% \text{ of IMP} = 0.71\%(80.3 \text{ billion oz}) = \textbf{570 million oz}$$
(i.e., *sales volume increase of*
$$\frac{0.570}{3.29} = approximately \ 17.3\% \text{ for the firm)}$$

(11) STIMULATING LIGHT USERS—ESTIMATING INCREMENTAL FIRM SALES

In estimating the incremental sales that are likely to result from stimulating light users to use the relevant product on more use occasions, an assumption must be made concerning the volume of the product that will be used by these light users for each of these "extra" uses of the product (by these light users). The example below assumes that the light user will use an amount per new or "extra" use equal to the average for all users—i.e., $\frac{8}{10}$ oz of cereal per serving.

In the breakfast cereal example described in Table 12-5B, assume that the average breakfast cereal consumer is stimulated to have cereal for breakfast five times per week rather than three times per week. The likely incremental sales resulting may be estimated as follows: [6]

- *Present Total Usage Gap* = approximately **29.7% of IMP** (see Fig. 12-1)

- *Present Nonuser Gap* = **9.98 of IMP** (Table 12-5A)

- *Present Light User Gap* (if it assumed that full use is 7 times/week and average use is 3 times/week)
  $$= \frac{4}{7}(\text{IMP} - \text{product line gap} - \text{total distribution gap} - \text{new}$$
  $$\text{nonuser gap)}$$
  $$= 57.1\%(100\% - 20\% - 40.1\% - 9.98\%)$$
  $$= 57.1\%(29.92\%)$$
  $$= \textbf{17.08\% of IMP}$$

- *Projected New Light User Gap* (if it is assumed that average use increases from 3 to 5 times per week)
  $$= \frac{2}{7}(29.92\% \text{ of IMP})$$
  $$= 28.6\%(29.92\% \text{ of IMP}) = \textbf{8.55\% of IMP}$$

- *New Light Usage Gap* (if it is assumed that full use is 1 oz and average use is $\frac{8}{10}$ oz)

  $= \frac{2}{10}$(IMP − PLG − TDG − nonuser gap − new light user gap)

  $= 20\%(100\% - 20\% - 40.1\% - 9.98\% - 8.55\%)$

  $= 20\%(21.37\%$ of IMP$) = $ **4.27% of IMP**
- *Projected New Total Usage Gap*

  = nonuser gap + new light user gap + new light usage gap

  = 9.98% of IMP + 8.55% of IMP + 4.27% of IMP

  = **22.8% of IMP**
- *Incremental RIS*

  = new RIS − old RIS

  New RIS = IMP − PLG − TDG − new total usage gap

  $\qquad = 100\% - 20\% - 40.1\% - 22.8\%$

  $\qquad = $ **17.1% of IMP**

  Old RIS $\ = $ **10.2% of IMP**

  Incremental RIS = 17.1% of IMP − 10.2% of IMP

  $\qquad\qquad\quad = $ **6.9% of IMP**
- *Incremental New Firm Sales*

  Firm's old real market share (RMS)

  $$= \frac{4.1\%}{10.2\%} = 40.2\% \text{ of old RIS}$$

  Firm's new RMS of the new RIS may be more or less than its RMS of the existing RIS depending upon whether the firm itself leads the way in stimulating light users to use more (see discussions in Table 11-3 and Chapter 7).

  If the firm does lead the way, the firm may get a 50 percent RMS of the new RIS.

  Estimated Incremental Firm Sales under this assumption

  $= 50\% \times 6.9\%$ of IMP

  $= 3.45\%$ of IMP $= 3.45\%(50.3$ billion oz$) = $ **2.77 billion oz** (i.e., a *sales increase of*

  $\dfrac{2.77}{3.29} = $ *approximately 84.2% for the firm*)

(12) EXPANDING USAGE VOLUME PER USE OCCASION— ESTIMATING INCREMENTAL FIRM SALES

In the breakfast cereal example, a full use per use occasion is described as a 1-oz serving. Actual average use was shown to equal only $\frac{8}{10}$ oz per serving (see Table 12.5C). If it is assumed that the average actual serving size was increased from $\frac{8}{10}$ oz to $\frac{9}{10}$ oz, what incremental sales would be likely for the firm in question?

- *Projected New Light Usage Gap* (if it is assumed that full use equals 1 oz and average actual use will equal $\frac{9}{10}$ oz)
  $= \frac{1}{10}(\text{IMP} - \text{PLG} - \text{TDG} - \text{nonuser gap} - \text{light user gap})$
  $= \frac{1}{10}\%(100\% \text{ of IMP} - 20\% \text{ of IMP} - 40.1\% \text{ of IMP} - 9.98\%$
      of IMP $- 17.08\%$ of IMP)
  $= 10\%(12.84) = $ **1.28% IMP**
- *Old Light Usage Gap* (from Exhibit 12-5c)
  $= \frac{2}{10}(\text{IMP} - \text{product line gap} - \text{total distribution gap} - \text{non-}$
      user gap $-$ light user gap)
  $= 20\%(100\% - 20\% - 40.1\% - 9.98\% - 17.08\%)$
  $= 20\%(12.84\% \text{ of IMP})$
  $= $ **2.57% of IMP**
- *Incremental RIS*
  $= $ old light usage gap $-$ new light usage gap
  $= 2.57\%$ of IMP $- 1.28\%$ of IMP
  $= $ **1.29% of IMP**
- *Incremental Firm Sales*
  Firm's old real market share (RMS)
  $$= \frac{4.1\%}{10.2\%} - 40.2\% \text{ of old RIS}$$
  Firm's new RMS of the new RIS may be more or less than its RMS of the existing RIS depending upon whether the firm itself attempts to bring about heavier usage rate (i.e., larger serving—e.g., by means of packaging—as discussed in Chapter 9) for its own brand(s).
  If it is assumed that the firm is actively pursuing this strategy, the firm may get a 50 percent RMS of the new RIS. In this case, incremental firm sales would equal:
  $= 50\%(1.29\% \text{ of IMP})$
  $= 0.645\%$ of IMP $= 0.654\%(80.3$ billion oz$) = $ **517 million oz** (i.e., a *sales volume increase* of
  $$\frac{0.517}{3.29} = approximately\ 15.7\% \text{ for the firm})$$

(13) PENETRATING SUBSTITUTE'S POSITION(S)— ESTIMATING INCREMENTAL FIRM SALES

As originally discussed in the chapters on product line gaps and then later in the chapter on competitive gaps, the proportion of current industry sales accounted for by each element of a product line *sometimes* should not be used as the main determinant of the size of a firm's product line gap. This is particularly true when one of the product line elements is relatively new to the market and represents an innovation or significant product differentiation. The example of low-cost electronic calculators was used to clarify this point (refer to Chapter 10 and Fig. 10-2).

A similar adjustment may be called for if a firm feels that product line elements that it does market can penetrate the sales positions of product line elements that it does not market—*even when its own product line elements represent no innovation or significant new product differentiation.* The example of multiple alternative forms of antacids was used to clarify this point (refer to Chapter 10).

In either case above, the firm adjusts the product line gap to make it smaller. In one case, the adjustment reflects an innovative new product line element and in the other case, the adjustment reflects the firm's attitude regarding the possibility of using product line element(s) that it does sell to penetrate the position(s) of one or more elements that the firm does not sell.

In terms of the market structure profile, the firm desiring to "penetrate the substitute's position" adjusts its full product line gap (FPLG) downward to equal a *real product line gap (RPLG).* The growth opportunity of penetrating the substitute's position(s) *does not show up* in the market structure profile *as part of the product line gap. This growth opportunity* (of penetrating the substitute's position) *shows up instead as part of the competitive gap.*

As indicated in Chapter 10, the three factors that determine the size of the "substitute's position to be penetrated" are (1) the full substitute's position, (2) a distribution factor, and (3) a usage factor.

Set aside the breakfast cereal example for a moment (because of the likely insignificance of a substitute's position to penetrate) and consider the electronic calculator example. Assume that the profile shown in Fig. 10-2 is the relevant profile, that the relevant substitute's position equals 30 percent of IMP, that direct competitive sales equal 8 percent of IMP, and that the firm's sales equal 2 percent of IMP; therefore, the ratio of firm sales over firm sales plus direct competitive sales (i.e., FS/FS + DCS) equals 25 percent.

What incremental sales could a firm expect to achieve by following a "penetrate the substitute's position" strategy in this case? If an industrywide effort to penetrate the substitute's position (e.g., recall when electronic calculators were introduced in the early 1970's) were going on, and the relevant firm were taking part in that effort, the firm could expect a share of the industrywide incremental new sales realized equal to its present ratio of FS/FS + DCS (i.e., 25 percent).

Assume, for example, that over the relevant time horizon the relevant substitute's position was closed (i.e., penetrated) from 30 percent of IMP to 20 percent of IMP. The total incremental sales for the firm and its direct competitor(s) would equal 10 percent of IMP. If the firm achieved 25 percent of these new sales, the *firm's incremental sales* would equal 2.5 percent of IMP—more than doubling its current sales.

If the firm leads the industry in attempting to penetrate the substitute's position(s), the firm could expect more than 25 percent of the projected incremental industry sales. If the firm was not at all active compared with its direct competitor(s) in attempting to penetrate the substitute's position(s), then the firm could expect less than 25 percent of the projected industry incremental sales.

(14) PENETRATING DIRECT COMPETITIVE POSITION(S)— ESTIMATING INCREMENTAL FIRM SALES

Strategies designed to "penetrate direct competitive positions" are oriented specifically to improve a firm's current real market share (RMS). The incremental sales resulting from such a strategy depend directly upon how much the firm's RMS is increased. How much RMS is improved depends heavily upon the amount of resources (i.e., costs) allocated to the strategy; the more resources committed to the strategy, the more RMS and, in turn, the more firm sales are likely to increase.

Table 11-3 implied that any time the firm's real market share (RMS) is improved, the direct competitive position(s) has been penetrated. Part or all of the benefits (in terms of incremental sales) of many different growth opportunities are measured, therefore, in terms of the penetration of the direct competitive position(s) (and the resulting improvement in RMS).

Strategies designed exclusively to penetrate direct position(s) are rare; some other growth opportunity is usually involved as well, either directly or indirectly. For example, although advertising is an important tool in attempting to penetrate direct competition positions, the same advertising can also lead to a change in a firm's definition of completeness of distribution gaps and increase its RIS. The same advertising can also help close usage gaps—and, therefore, increase the firm's RIS.

New product innovations and differentiations [growth opportunities (3) and (6)] are also important tools in attempting to penetrate direct competitive positions. Strategies focusing upon growth opportunity (2) (new uses or new user segments) can also be viewed as attempts to penetrate direct competitive positions.

To estimate the overall likely effects of a strategy that results in the penetration of direct competitive position(s), the firm should specifically recognize the simultaneous effects upon the relevant market structure profile of all of the growth opportunities involved.

(15) DEFENDING THE FIRM'S PRESENT POSITION (REAL MARKET SHARE)—ESTIMATING INCREMENTAL FIRM SALES

Just as "penetrating direct competitive position(s)" usually interrelates with the results from other growth opportunities, so too does growth opportunity (15)—"defending the firm's present position." What is implied in this strategy is an attempt by the firm to maintain its current real market share (RMS) while at the same time taking advantage of any improvement in relevant industry sales (RIS).

Table 11-2 shows that growth opportunities (1), (3) and (5) to (13) can all result in increased RIS. Under each of these situations, therefore, the firm has an opportunity to realize new sales if it maintains its current RMS. Because of these close interrelationships, the estimation of incremental sales is accomplished by considering the overall changes in the market structure profile and focusing upon improvements in RIS. Incremental firm sales resulting from defending the firm's present position equal RMS times incremental RIS.

SUMMARY

A firm can use the principles of market structure profile analysis as summarized at the end of Chapter 11 (in Tables 11-2, 11-3, and 11-4) to estimate potential incremental firm sales related to each alternative growth opportunity. The resulting estimates, having been derived through systematic thinking and analysis, aid the manager in estimating a range of possible outcomes or payoffs (i.e., in terms of incremental sales and profits) and in assigning explicit or implicit probabilities to the likelihood of realizing alternative payoffs.

This chapter uses the market structure profile developed for breakfast cereal (in the chapters of Part Two) and considers how a firm with such a profile can specifically estimate incremental firm sales for each of the 15 alternative growth opportunities considered in the text.

The particular estimation methods presented are used in order to help clarify for the reader the logic involved in making incremental sales estimates with the aid of market structure profile analysis. This logic becomes particularly important when one is estimating the results of simultaneously taking advantage of several growth opportunities related to a single product line.

REVIEW QUESTIONS

1. In considering the results of a natural growth of IMP opportunity, how can a firm gain a larger proportion of the incremental IMP than it has of current IMP?

2. If a firm explicitly recognizes a new use of a product and takes the lead in promoting this new use, will the firm's RMS for this profile increase or decrease? Why?

3. From what three sources can new sales be expected for a firm that is taking advantage of growth opportunity (3)? Explain.

4. What is the difference between growth opportunities (3) and (6) in terms of the sources from which a firm can expect new firm sales?

5. Because of the possibilities of cannibalism and/or the complementarity of products, adjustments may be necessary in estimating incremental firm sales likely to result from a "filling out the product line" strategy. What particular adjustments may be necessary? Why?

6. In estimating the incremental sales likely to result from closing a distribution coverage gap, why must assumptions concerning distribution intensity and exposure in the newly covered areas also be made?

7. If a firm's distribution intensity is already quite good in an area, can the firm expect its overall RMS to increase or decrease as a result of closing its intensity gap in that area? Explain.

8. In estimating the incremental sales likely to result from closing a nonuser gap, why must assumptions concerning usage rates for the converted users also be made?

9. Will a firm's RMS increase or decrease from implementing a strategy to stimulate light users? How about for a strategy to expand usage volume per use occasion? Explain.

10. Will a firm's RMS increase or decrease if a "penetrate the substitute's position" is being pursued by direct competitors? Explain.

11. How can a firm penetrate direct competitive positions?

12. Under what circumstances is a "defend the firm's present position" most appropriate—and how can a firm estimate likely incremental firm sales when taking advantage of these circumstances?

NOTES

1. Alternatively, the ultimate effects of this strategy could be estimated in terms of penetrating a substitute's position, as discussed in Chapter 10 (competitive gaps). Either method of estimation may be used; incremental firm sales will be the same.

2.   Note that more direct methods for coming up with the same estimate can be used. The particular method shown here is used to help clarify for the reader the logic of the incremental sales estimate. Understanding this logic becomes particularly important when one is attempting to estimate incremental sales while simultaneously taking advantage of several growth opportunities related to a single product line.

3.   Ibidem.

4.   Ibidem.

5.   Ibidem.

6.   Ibidem.

13

Additional Notes and Suggestions for Using Market Structure Profile Analysis

Chapters 11 and 12 considered how market structure profile analysis can facilitate the estimation of the likely results (in terms of incremental sales and profits) of implementing alternative growth strategies. Market structure profiles can be used in a variety of other ways as well, some of which are discussed in this chapter.

MARKET STRUCTURE PROFILE LIFE CYCLES

Life cycles are typically defined for industrywide sales (the industry life cycle), for an individual firm's full product line sales (a firm's product line life cycle), and/or for the sales for a firm's individual models (model life cycles). The interrelationship among and between these different life cycle concepts are shown in Fig. 13-1 for two different products: computers and razor blades.

The projection of these life cycles focuses primarily upon *sales data* for the industry, product, and/or model. Projecting and monitoring changes over time in the complete market structure profile for a product

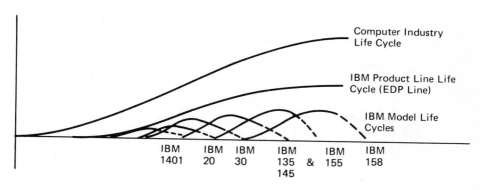

(a) Computers

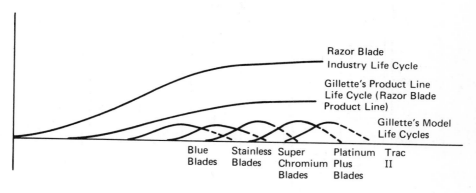

(b) Razor Blades

FIGURE 13-1.   Interrelationships among various life cycle concepts.

line, on the other hand, provides an opportunity to be much more analytical and thorough in planning and explaining the future sales growth of the relevant product line.

Consider, for example, the *market structure profile life cycle* presented in Fig. 13-2. In projecting and monitoring that profile life cycle, the firm must very specifically and continually consider all fifteen growth opportunities enumerated above—as they relate to possible changes in the market structure profile over time.

In doing so, the firm projects much more than simply whether and, if so, how much industry sales and firm sales will grow each year.[1] Projecting a complete market structure profile life cycle gives the firm a framework for analytically determining and explaining *why* firm sales are projected to grow (or decline) and by how much each year over the

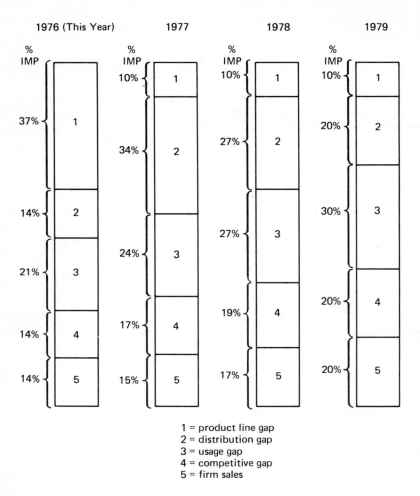

| | 1976 (This Year) | 1977 | 1978 | 1979 |

FIGURE 13-2.   Example of a market structure profile life cycle.

planning period. As such, the framework of the market structure profile life cycle facilitates for the firm the regular analytical consideration of the whole spectrum of growth opportunities.

The product line gap can increase or decrease over time—depending upon the competitive market situation and the firm's projected role in and reactions to the entry of new product line elements. Over what period of time and to what extent does the firm plan to close its distribution coverage gap? Its intensity gap? Its exposure gap? Over what period of time and to what extent will the nonuser gap, light user gap, and light usage gaps be closed? All of these additional factors can add significant insights for the firm attempting to explain past failures and successes and to plan for better sales volume growth in the future.

LIKELY CHANGES IN A MSP LIFE CYCLE OVER TIME

Projecting market structure profile life cycles is equally as useful and appropriate for a firm's older product lines, for new product lines recently added, and for product lines being considered as future possible additions. For example, a market structure profile life cycle for one of the firm's older product lines might appear as in Fig. 13-3(a). A profile life cycle for a new innovation just introduced by the firm might appear as in Fig. 13-3(b). Finally, a profile life cycle for a product line that has been sold by competitive firms for some time, but which the relevant firm is just now going to add, might appear as in Fig. 13-3(c).

Although only the summation of the distribution, usage, and competitive subgaps developed earlier appear in the exhibit, the details of the subgaps themselves would also be included in actual projections of these market structure profile life cycles.

Because of the methodology used to generate market structure profiles, closing one gap causes gaps appearing below the closed gap on the profile to become larger. In view of this phenomenon, a firm can anticipate the likely gap makeup of a profile over the projected life cycle of the relevant product line. By doing so, the firm can plan well ahead of time the mix of growth strategies that will be most appropriate for the firm at any given time in the future for the relevant product line.

For example, in Fig. 13-2 as the firm closes the product line gap (in 1977), the other three gaps become larger. Firm sales also grow. Why would the distribution gap, usage gap, and competitive gap become larger as a firm fills out its product line? The enlarged gaps are related directly to the new product line element(s) added by the firm. These new elements have their own *distribution gaps*—which are added to the gaps of the firm's old product line elements. These new elements also have their own *usage gaps*. Finally, competitors' sales of elements similar to the new elements added by the firm are now included as part of the *competitive gap*. As the firm closes the distribution gap (in 1978), the usage and competitive gaps continue to grow, and so on.

A slight increase in firm sales has been indicated as each strategy is implemented. Well-planned strategies should yield such sales increases. Note also (in Fig. 13-2) that IMP is projected to increase each year for each life cycle shown. This growth offers another significant opportunity for the firm, particularly in situations where discretionary income is growing quickly.[2]

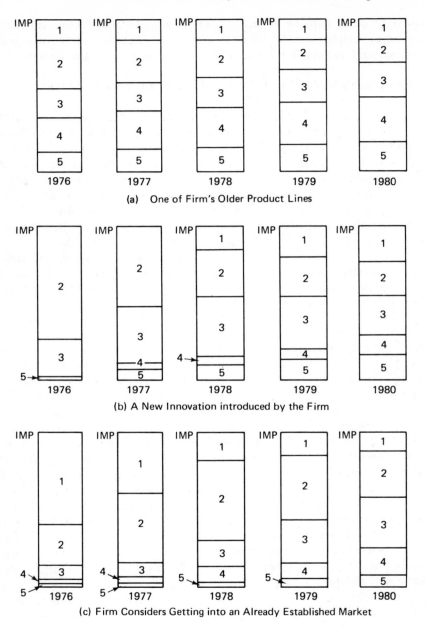

(a)   One of Firm's Older Product Lines

(b) A New Innovation introduced by the Firm

(c) Firm Considers Getting into an Already Established Market

1 = product line gap   4 = competitive gap
2 = total distribution gap   5 = firm sales
3 = total usage gap

FIGURE 13-3.   Market structure profile life cycles.

DEVELOPING MSP LIFE CYCLES

A firm desiring to move toward developing a market structure profile-based system for planning the firm's future growth in individual product lines might begin by having product line managers fill out a form such as the one in Table 13-1 on an annual basis. In filling out this

Table 13-1

Projections	1976	1977	1978	1979	1980
—IMP (unit sales potential)					
—Product line gap (as % of IMP)					
• Full substitute's position					
—Distribution gaps (% of IMP)					
• Coverage					
• Intensity					
• Exposure					
• Total					
—Usage gaps (% of IMP)					
• Nonuser					
• Light user					
• Light usage					
• Total					
—Competitive gaps (% of IMP)					
• Relevant substitute's position					
• Direct competitive positions					
• Total					
—Firm sales (% of IMP)					

form, the managers are forced to consider the whole spectrum of growth opportunities and at the same time to build market structure profiles covering the present year and the entire planning horizon.

In presenting such a form to top management, the product line managers would include comments justifying the derivation of each projection over time and, inherently, a consideration of the development of each growth opportunity over the planning period. The form would be regarded as a complement to, rather than a substitute for, more traditional data projections expected from a product line manager—such as projected figures for dollar sales and expenses, margin after product expenses, return on investment for the product line, etc.

Over time, as product line managers and executives gain experience in generating and interpreting such profiles and profile life cycles, these new tools can become very significant aids in the growth planning process.

BUILDING AND INTERPRETING MARKET STRUCTURE PROFILES AND PROFILE LIFE CYCLES FOR COMPETITORS

With business more complex and competition more severe, an important part of the corporate growth planner's responsibility today is to analyze competitors in order to find out where they are vulnerable and to anticipate their next strategic moves. Market structure profiles and profile life cycles can serve as useful tools for studying competitors.

For many years, corporations have been gathering competitive intelligence. Much information on competitors is of public record or available from market research firms and is, therefore, quite easy to obtain.[3] The problem, however, is to fit that information together with a meaningful configuration. Market structure profiles and profile life cycles provide such configurations and, once generated for a competitor, can provide significant new insights for understanding and predicting competitive actions and reactions in the marketplace.

In Fig. 13-4, what strategy might be anticipated from a competitor faced with Profile Type II? Type III? Type IV? Type V? Type VI? Type VII? Type VIII?

While the firm is gathering information on its own product lines for building its own profiles and profile life cycles, significant economies can be realized by gathering together at the same time similar information on competitors. This is true whether the firm gathers the data itself or contracts out with a research firm to gather such data. Such economies enhance the feasibility of regularly generating, monitoring, and analyzing competitive profiles and profile life cycles.

SPECIAL PERSPECTIVES FOR INTERNATIONAL MARKET PLANNING

As manufacturers expand operations in the international arena by selling products in more and more different countries, the tasks of planning growth and comparing performance become very difficult for the firm's executives and planners. International market structure profile analysis provides executives with the new comparative perspectives on international markets that facilitate and improve international growth planning efforts.

DIVERSE MARKET STRUCTURE PROFILES FOR DIFFERENT COUNTRIES

Market structure profiles vary from country to country for a number of reasons. First, industry market potential (IMP) differs from country

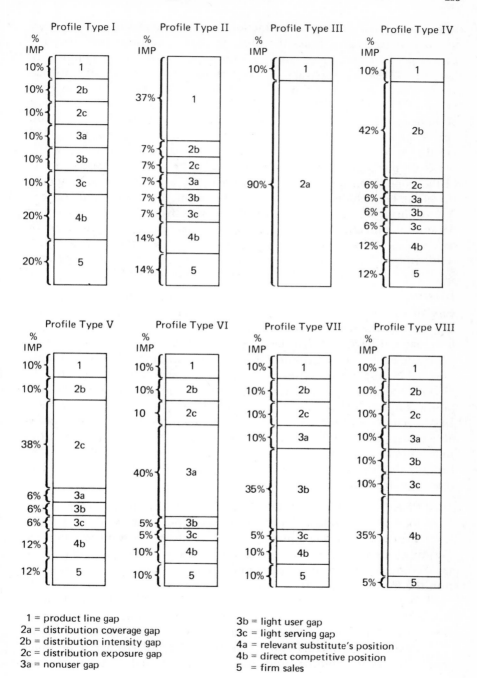

FIGURE 13-4. Some different types of market structure profiles.

to country—most directly as a function of population, since IMP equals number of consumers times the number of use occasions per operating period per consumer. Even among countries with the same population, however, IMP may also vary significantly. Australia and Kenya, for example, both have populations of approximately 13 million. With a gross national product (GNP) per capita of less than $200, however, most of Kenya's population are not yet regular economic participants. Most people in Kenya, therefore, should not be included in estimating IMP for the majority of consumer goods and services.[4] In Australia, where the GNP per capita is over $3000 per capita, however, the vast majority of the population belongs to the economically active sector and should, therefore, be included in estimating IMP for most products and services.

Industry market potential may also vary from country to country because of different habits and customs or because of different climatic conditions. Working either separately or together, these factors may result in a different incidence of "use occasions" per potential consumer for different countries—and, therefore, different IMP's.[5]

DIFFERENT PRODUCT LINE GAPS. A firm's product line gap may vary in size from country to country for a variety of reasons. The firm may not sell the same mix of product line elements in each country. The firm may not have achieved the same levels of distribution for each product line element in each country. Finally and most importantly, consumption habits and customs are likely to vary from country to country. In Germany and most other European countries, for example, effervescent powders (e.g., Enos) are the most popular form of stomach upset remedy. In Mexico, effervescent tablets are dominant. In the United States, chewable tablets and liquids are very important. As a result of such diversities in consumption patterns, a firm offering the same incomplete mix of product line elements worldwide may face dramatically different product line gaps from country to country.

DIFFERENT DISTRIBUTION GAPS. The distribution gap that a firm faces for a given product line varies in size from country to country for several reasons. First, the firm may not distribute the relevant product line (or any element thereof) in all geographic regions of any particular country. Second, within geographic regions where the firm does have distribution the firm's product line (or any element thereof) may not be distributed in an adequate number of outlets. Third, within individual outlets where the firm has distribution, the firm's product line (or any element thereof) may have poor or inadequate shelf space, location, displays, etc.

Finally, legal factors and wholesale and retail customs may differ from country to country and introduce additional distribution gap variance. If all of these factors are considered, it is highly unlikely that a firm will face the same size distribution gap in any two countries.

DIFFERENT USAGE GAPS. The firm's usage gap for a given product line will vary in size from country to country. Differences in the size of usage gap can be caused by variance in the proportions of potential users who do not use the relevant product in different countries (a nonuser component of the usage gap); by variance in the incidence of use of the product by "light users," and by variance in the volume of use or extent of use of the product each time the product is used in each country.

In the case of stomach upset remedies, for example, the proportion of the relevant population (i.e., consumers included when IMP is estimated) taking commercial remedies when stomach upsets occur may vary from country to country, primarily because of local medicinal habits and customs. For similar reasons, the volume or dosage per use may also be different for different countries.

DIFFERENT COMPETITIVE GAPS. A multinational firm marketing a consumer product or service in many different countries of the world is likely to find a different competitive situation in each separate environment. Such differences are caused by the existence of different local competitors in each country and by the varying penetration of multinational competitors into different countries.

As in the case of the other gaps discussed above, it is unlikely that a firm will face exactly the same size competitive gap (as a proportion of IMP) in any two countries.

VARYING PROFILES FOR DIFFERENT COUNTRIES: STRATEGIC INFERENCES

Figure 13-5 presents a range of hypothetical market structure profiles that a firm may face in different countries for a single product line. By defining the size of gaps as proportions of IMP rather than in absolute terms, the market structure profiles for various countries can be compared with one another. Interpreting the particular profiles in Fig. 13-5, we see that the firm's product line gap is most significant (i.e., as a proportion of IMP) in South Africa and Germany. The firm has no distribution whatsoever in the United Kingdom and faces a relatively large distribution gap (48 percent of IMP) in Brazil. Usage gaps are particularly significant in Mexico, the United States, and Germany. Competitive gaps are most important in the United States and Germany. The firm's poorest competitive position is in the United States, where the firm has a 12.5 percent market share (i.e., firm sales divided by firm sales plus

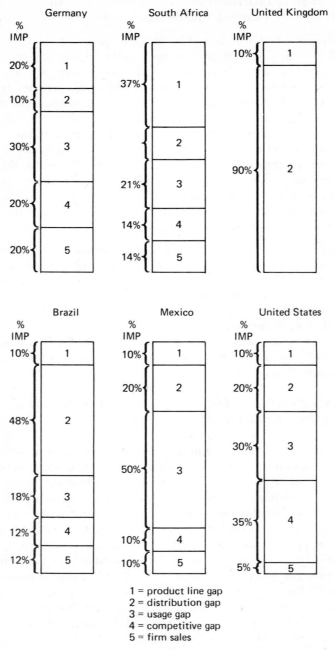

1 = product line gap
2 = distribution gap
3 = usage gap
4 = competitive gap
5 = firm sales

FIGURE 13-5.   Some different types of market structure profiles (hypothetical).

competitive positions). In all other markets except the United Kingdom the firm has a 50 percent market share.

Strategic inferences of the profiles are clear. The keys to further growth of firm sales in *Germany* lie in filling out the firm's product line and in trying to stimulate greater usage. In *South Africa* the emphasis should be upon filling out the firm's product line. In the *United Kingdom*, the firm has yet to introduce its product line (thus the dominance of the distribution gap). In *Brazil* the firm should concentrate upon expanding distribution. In *Mexico*, greater usage of the product should be stimulated—as a leader in the industry (with a 50 percent market share), this firm is in a good position to try to increase usage rates. In the *United States*, usage could be better, but this firm (with its low market share) is not in a good position to try to stimulate usage. The firm's main concern in the United States should be to try to penetrate competitive positions. While implementing the suggested strategies in Germany, South Africa, Brazil, and Mexico, the firm must also strive to maintain its present (dominant) market share in those markets.

USING MARKET STRUCTURE PROFILE GAP MAKEUP AS A BASIS FOR SEGMENTATION

In analyzing various markets, executives and planners are apt to find divergence of demand patterns and behavior that is just as great within individual countries as between countries. This is true in the United States and most other countries. Standard Oil of California, for example, found greater variance within the United States than among five different European countries for gasoline station preferences of consumers.[6] In developing countries the demand situations in large cities, in the areas (often slums) surrounding the large cities, in rural towns and villages, and in the open countryside contrast sharply with one another.[7]

In such market situations—particularly when the market is quite diverse and/or competitive—the market can best be approached on a subset-by-subset basis.[8]

As a case in point, a firm could face, for a single product line, a large product line gap for some market subsets while facing small product line gaps for other subsets. This could happen, for example, if customers in some subsets (e.g., with Profile Type I in Fig. 13-4) favored lower-price product line elements, while customers in other subsets (e.g., with Profile Type II in Fig. 13-4), favored higher-price elements, and the relevant firm (firm XYZ in this case) produced mainly low-priced elements and only one or a few different high-priced elements. This situation could also exist between or among different regional markets (and/or international markets) or in any other situation where product line element preferences can and do exist among different market subsets for the same product line.

In such instances, the market structure profile gap makeup for various subsets of the market offers a meaningful basis for segmenting a market—grouping subjects with similar gap makeup into the same market segment.

For example, if a geographic approach is assumed for the moment, a firm might draw up a market structure profile for each major region of the country or each country of the world where the firm is selling the relevant product line—for example, as in Fig. 13-6.[9] It is possible that each of the many market regions (or countries) might have an entirely different market structure profile, but this is unlikely. Where many different subsets are delineated, it is useful to attempt to categorize together subsets that have similar market structure profiles (i.e., similar in terms of the proportions of IMP assigned to each of the different gaps).

For example, what similarities exist between or among the profiles presented in Fig. 13-6? These profiles represent the actual results of an analysis of six different markets for a particular consumer goods product line of a well-known United States multinational corporation. (As presented here, for the sake of simplicity, each country is treated as a homogeneous market and is not broken down further into several separate segments and profiles.)

In this case (Fig. 13-6), the firm's market situation, as reflected in terms of market structure profiles, seems to be quite similar in Brazil and South Africa. The situations in the United States and the United Kingdom are also comparable in several respects. The Mexican and German profiles stand alone. Quite conceivably, by developing profiles for a number of additional market situations (countries or segments thereof), the firm could come up with a reasonably small number of general market types—each reflecting a particular gap makeup and suggesting a particular strategic mix.

Using market structure profile gap makeup as a basis of segmentation provides a very pragmatic foundation for estimating incremental sales likely to be associated with various growth opportunity alternatives. This form of segmentation is particularly insightful when considering, comparing, and categorizing a firm's various international markets.

A COMMON LANGUAGE AND COMMON FRAMEWORK OF ANALYSIS FOR OTHERWISE DIVERSE PRODUCT LINES AND MARKETS

Corporate executives and planners face the complex task of continually analyzing and interpreting data on many different product lines—product

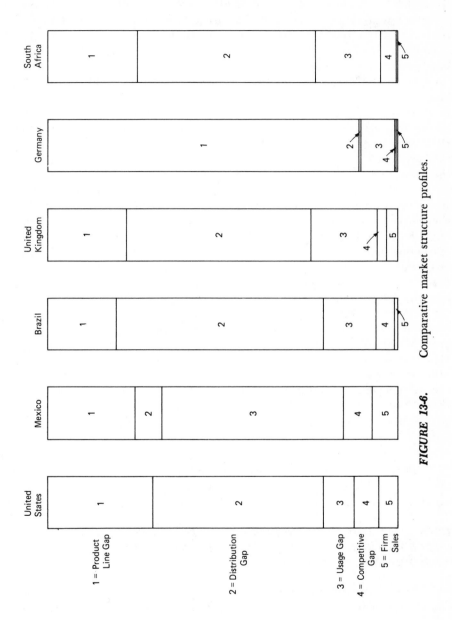

FIGURE 13-6. Comparative market structure profiles.

239

lines that are frequently very difficult to compare in terms of their growth potentials and strategies. If the executive can compare the potentials related to the different product lines, he can allocate in more productive fashion the limited funds that he has available for pursuing new growth opportunities.

Market structure profiles and profile life cycles can be viewed as and used as comparative points of reference for varied and diverse product lines. Market structure profile analysis provides a language and framework that are common to all product lines. In a firm which uses these profiles as a focal point for the analysis of new growth opportunities, product line managers and key planning executives can all talk in the same terms.

From the point of view of the multinational corporation, market structure profile analysis provides a firm's marketing managers around the world with a common vocabulary and a common framework of analysis for making growth planning decisions. The same tool provides marketing executives, planners, and coordinators at the headquarters level with common perspective for setting objectives, developing strategies, and interpreting and comparing performance for individual product lines in geographically diverse markets.

Overall internal marketing communications are improved and decisions concerning the worldwide dispersion of funds for pursuing new growth opportunities are made and explained much more logically. Headquarters executives are also assured to a reasonable degree that significant growth opportunities in individual product lines in individual countries have not been overlooked by local product line managers.

SUMMARY

This chapter discussed some of the many other ways—beyond those presented in Chapters 11 and 12—that market structure profile analysis can aid a firm in making its growth planning decisions.

USING MARKET STRUCTURE PROFILE LIFE CYCLES INSTEAD OF OR IN ADDITION TO INDUSTRY AND PRODUCT LIFE CYCLES

A market structure profile life cycle gives the firm a framework for analytically determining and explaining *why* firm sales are projected to grow (or decline) and by how much each year over the planning period. As such, the framework of the market structure profile life cycle facilitates for the firm the regular analytical consideration of the whole spectrum of growth opportunities. Market structure profile life cycles also act as a common denominator for understanding, comparing, and evaluating the performance of each product line.

Projecting market structure profile life cycles is equally as useful and appropriate for a firm's older product lines, for new product lines recently added, and for product lines being considered as future possible additions.

BUILDING AND ANALYZING PROFILES FOR COMPETITORS

Market structure profiles are a meaningful configuration for analyzing competitors in order to find out where they are vulnerable and to anticipate their next strategic moves. While the firm is gathering information on its own product lines for building its own market structure profiles, significant economies can be realized by gathering together at the same time similar information on competitors which is necessary for drawing up competitive profiles. Such economies enhance the feasibility of regularly generating, monitoring, and analyzing competitive profiles.

SPECIAL PERSPECTIVES FOR INTERNATIONAL MARKET PLANNING

A firm can build separate market structure profiles for each country where the firm sells the product. These profiles offer executives new comparative perspectives for setting growth objectives and monitoring progress in very diverse geographic markets.

USING MARKET STRUCTURE PROFILE GAP MAKEUP AS A BASIS FOR SEGMENTATION

In many market situations—particularly when the market is quite diverse and/or competitive—the market can best be approached on a subset-by-subset basis. In such instances, the market structure profile gap makeup for various subsets of the market offers a meaningful basis for segmenting a market—grouping subsets with similar gap makeup into the same market segment.

Using market structure profile gap makeup as a basis of segmentation provides a very pragmatic foundation for estimating incremental sales and costs likely to be associated with various growth opportunity alternatives. This form of segmentation is particularly insightful when dealing with international markets.

MARKET STRUCTURE PROFILES AS A COMPARATIVE POINT OF REFERENCE FOR DIFFERENT PRODUCT LINES

Market structure profiles can be viewed as and used as a comparative point of reference for varied and diverse product lines. Communications are improved, and the dispersion of funds for pursuing new growth opportunities is decided upon and explained more logically—in a common language and a common framework of analysis.

REVIEW QUESTIONS

1. Compare and contrast industry (and product) life cycles with market structure profile life cycles. How do these complement each other?
2. Explain the changing gap makeup over time in the profiles of:
    (a) Figure 13-3(a)
    (b) Figure 13-3(b)
    (c) Figure 13-3(c)
3. Why is it both economical and useful to generate and analyze market structure profiles for major competitors?
4. Why is market structure profile analysis particularly helpful for comparing a firm's position, setting objectives, and comparing the firm's progress in different foreign markets?
5. How can a firm use market structure profiles as a basis for segmentation?
6. What advantages and disadvantages does segmentation based upon market structure profiles have versus other forms of segmentation? Under what circumstances is this basis for segmentation most appropriate?
7. In your own words, discuss the advantages of market structure profiles as a point of reference for comparing different markets and different product lines.

NOTES

1. The firm's product line life cycle and model life cycles are indicated by the changes in "firm sales" over time. The life cycle of industrywide sales that is most relevant for the firm is indicated by changes over time in the summation of firm sales plus the competitive gaps.
2. Consider, for example, the rapid growth of such income in Japan, Greece, Turkey, and Brazil in the late 1960's and early 1970's. IMP's in such situations grow rapidly as greater proportions of the relevant populations enter the economic mainstream and as already participating sectors become more affluent.

Quite notably, similar increases in IMP in the United States are likely to come much more slowly. For example, over the past fifteen years, discretionary income in the United States has grown more slowly than it has for any of the other 22 OECD (Organization for Economic Development) countries—with the exception of the United Kingdom. See *Economic Growth of OECD Countries,* United States State Department, 1974, 11 pp.

3. For an enlightening discussion of the sophistication now involved in gathering competitive intelligence, see "Business Sharpens Its Spying Techniques," *Business Week* (August 4, 1975), pp. 60–63.

4. Note that, as Kenya becomes more affluent, more Kenyans will enter the economically active sector, and IMP in Kenya for many consumer goods and services will grow proportionally.

5. For examples of the effect of habits and customs upon consumption patterns (thus increasing or decreasing the number of use occasions per potential consumer per operating period), see *A Survey of Europe Today* (London: Readers Digest Association, 1970), p. 66+.

6. For an example of and discussion of similar findings for other products, see: J. D. Sheth, and D. A. Schellinck, "Psychographic and Life Style Differences Between the French and English Canadians." Paper presented at Academy of International Business Annual Conference, San Francisco, December 29, 1974.

7. For a discussion of these contrasts, see J. A. Weber, "Worldwide Strategies for Market Segmentation," *Columbia Journal of World Business* (Winter, 1974), pp. 31–38.

8. Recall the methods of segmentation and the criteria for segmentation discussed earlier in the book. See Chapter 4.

9. When one is drawing up market structure profiles for different market subsets or segments, making all of the profiles the same size facilitates visual comparison. As an aid to quantitative comparison, the different gaps should be expressed as percentages of the relevant IMP. Later on in the estimating of incremental sales, each profile or profile type is weighted as a function of its proportion of overall IMP.

Index